315. 45

WITHDRAWN

STAFF DEVELOPMENT
New Demands, New Realities,
New Perspectives

STAFF DEVELOPMENT
New Demands, New Realities,
New Perspectives

Edited by
ANN LIEBERMAN
Teachers College, Columbia University
and
LYNNE MILLER
University of Massachusetts, Amherst

TEACHERS COLLEGE, COLUMBIA UNIVERSITY
NEW YORK AND LONDON, 1979

Library of Congress Cataloging in Publication Data
Main entry under title:

Staff development.

   Slightly expanded version of Teachers College
record, v. 80, no. 1, Sept. 1978.
   Includes bibliographical references and index.
   1. School personnel management. 2. Teachers—
In-service training. I. Lieberman, Ann.
II. Miller, Lynne, 1945-
LB2831.5.S76   1979 371.1'46 78-27453
ISBN 0-8077-2512-9

79 80 81 82 83 84 85 86   1 2 3 4 5 6 7 8

Manufactured in the U.S.A.

Contents

Editors' Introduction

There can be little doubt that our schools are in crisis, that they have lost the public trust.[1] The exact nature of the crisis and how it can be resolved are topics of heated debate both inside and outside the educational profession. This book developed from our own concern about the schools, how we can work to improve them, and how we can make teachers a pivotal force in that improvement. We take the position that if we are to seek solutions to current problems, we must turn our focus clearly on the schools as they now function and exist and on the teachers who work there. Our intention in this volume is to create understandings before we offer possible solutions.

We see the current crisis as being two-fold: a crisis in mission and a crisis in resources. The crisis in mission centers on a confusion of goals. The conservative "back to basics" trend demands a return to the teaching of traditional skills and values in traditional ways within a social milieu where almost all traditions are under assault. At the same time, schools are expected to do more than just teach basics; public expectations mandate programs in career education and vocational training as well as the development of curricula designed to produce moral and productive workers and citizens. The message is clearly mixed: "Go back—go forward; do more—do less."

The task of schooling becomes further complicated when we consider what many people view as a new breed of student. Whether labelled as passive and silent, hard working and practical, or sullen and hostile, students of the 70s are different from the students of the past decade—largely because the times are different. For one thing, a larger proportion of students stay in school longer (or at least on the school rolls longer), there being no place for the productive energies of adolescents in the labor force or in the home. Students once excluded from public schools because of mental or physical handicaps are now sitting in regular classrooms as the result of state and federal legislation. As the larger culture changes, as its once stable institutions come into question and decline, the schools are being asked to take on added responsibilities for the care

---

1 See "The Tenth Annual Gallup Poll of the Public's Attitude Toward the Public Schools," *Phi Delta Kappan* 60, no. 1 (September 1978): 33-45.

and development of the young. Schools are being asked to do more; and they are asked to do more with less.

The crisis in resources is hard felt by educators and lay people alike. Budget restrictions are now a way of life for local school boards; a national tax revolt may well bring a Proposition 13 into every state and further limit funds available for schools and public services. State departments and a federal bureaucracy geared to expansion and growth in the 1960s are now being asked to contract and to consolidate their efforts. Schools are being closed; teachers are being fired. A new verb, "to be riffed" (derived from reduction in force), has entered our language.

In addition to being asked to do more with less, schools—and more specifically teachers in schools—are being asked to do better. They are being held accountable for outcomes, even though they have had no role in setting goals. For teachers, the reality of their profession is bleak. Morale is low, and, unlike earlier times, there is no place to go. With decreased job mobility, most teachers currently in-service will stay where they are for some time to come.

The teachers we are talking about are not new to their profession. They have, many of them, been through the "school wars." They have lived and taught through every major innovation and social experiment that has been brought into the schools in the last decade and a half. They are innovation-weary and expert-wary. They are in the ironic, yet predictable, position of being blamed for the failures of the educational improvement efforts of the recent past even as they themselves have been among the most active opponents to some of the imports of the "decade of reform." Given the enormous energies spent and frustrations met, we are impressed that teachers "hang in there" at all.

We believe very strongly that it is with these teachers, those presently in-service, that there is the hope and the possibility for an improved educational future. Further, we believe that this future depends on the formulation of new kinds of staff development activities and programs. Based on an understanding of the realities of schools and of teaching, as well as an appreciation of the increasing demands that are being placed on schools and teachers, new and varied perspectives must be developed to guide school improvement efforts that focus on the teacher. That is the intention of this volume. In it we bring together a group of people who have as their central concern the improvement of schools with a major focus on the teacher. The contributors are teachers, researchers, staff developers, project workers, and unionists. All have struggled in their own ways to relate the daily work of teaching to conceptions, theory, and research on staff development.

We choose the term *staff development* instead of in-service or teacher education/training because it suggests a different approach to improvement, one that considers the effects of the whole school (the staff) on the individual (the teacher) and the necessity of long-term growth possibility (development). We reject the idea of giving courses and workshops to individual teachers in isolation from their peers and the school. We further reject the notion that teachers can be "taught" or "trained" to be better teachers by the mastery of mechanical behaviors outside of a context of theory and practice. We accept and explore further the fact that development means working with at least a portion of a staff over a period of time with the necessary supportive conditions.

While the essays included in this volume cover a wide and varied field of vision, we have found that some themes recur throughout. These themes are *legitimation, interdependence, development,* and *teacher identification. Legitimation* is concerned with the establishment of legitimate authority built on collaboration. This rejects top-down planning and calls into question the usefulness of outside experts; it advocates instead the recognition and use of local clinical expertise and talents. *Interdependence* provides a perspective for considering all aspects of staff development: the personal, the organizational, and the political. Not one of these acts in isolation, and no one is more important than the others. All three perspectives are, in fact, levels of influence and must be considered conjointly in any staff development efforts. By *development* we mean a rejection of notions of training and an acceptance of notions of growth—often in a nonlinear and nonrational way. Personal and professional development become the major aim of staff development; the term "professional learning" seems an apt description of what the authors in this volume advocate. Finally, by *teacher identification* we mean a sensitivity to the teacher's point of view and an acknowledgement of the teacher's pivotal role in the planning and implementation of staff development activities—and indeed in all school improvement efforts. Such an identification with teachers leaves us wary of the traditional sources of teacher education and encourages a formulation of new ways to conceptualize and deliver services when they are needed by school staffs.

The book is divided into two sections. The first, New Demands, New Realities, New Perspectives, includes eight essays that develop the themes discussed above and offer some useful frameworks for viewing teaching, schools, and improvement efforts. They focus on developing ways of conceptualizing the problems of staff development. They are not intended to provide a blueprint for solutions, but rather to suggest directions for future study, reflection, and action. The second section, Staff Development at Work, looks at five actual approaches to staff development in practice. In each instance, the authors explain the research, theory, or assumptions on which their work is based and then describe the workings of their programs and projects. Again, these essays are not included as foolproof models to be replicated; rather they present some helpful possibilities and open new terrain for others to explore and develop.

We think that all the essays in this collection are provocative and worthy of your attention. We hope that this book will provide new ways to look at old concerns, promote dialogue among people interested in staff development and school improvement, and provide the impetus for future work in research, theory building, and practice.

ANN LIEBERMAN and LYNNE MILLER
September 1978

STAFF DEVELOPMENT
New Demands, New Realities, New Perspectives

NEW DEMANDS, NEW REALITIES, NEW PERSPECTIVES

Overview

This section includes eight essays that develop conceptualizations about and frameworks for the consideration, design, implementation, and evaluation of staff development and school improvement activities.

Judith Schiffer's essay, "A Framework for Staff Development," opens with an historical overview and contemporary social analysis of the conflict among the three authorities in school decision making: the public (the citizen), the bureaucratic (the administration), and the collegial (the teacher). The author builds a framework for looking at staff development as a response to these three authority prerogatives and argues that the present authority-in-ascent is the collegial. By emphasizing that staff development efforts must consider personal, organizational, and political issues as they relate to authority relations, Professor Schiffer introduces some of the major themes that other authors in this section develop.

Maxine Green's chapter, "Teaching: The Question of Personal Reality," focuses clearly on the individual issues each teacher faces as he/she attempts to make meaning from a perceived personal reality. Professor Green links personal history and biography to choices of action and argues from a phenomenological stance that it is through the activity or *project* of teaching that one achieves his/her personal reality as a teacher. She ends by calling for an integrated commitment to action, which involves the communal as well as the personal context and which will enable teachers to transcend and to transform present realities as they endeavor to create new ones.

Gene Hall and Susan Loucks also emphasize the personal domain in their chapter, "Teacher Concerns as a Basis for Facilitating and Personalizing Staff Development." They discuss the implications for staff development that may be drawn from an empirically tested model, the Concerns Based Adoption Model (CBAM). CBAM measures the developmental level of teacher concerns as they emerge when teachers deal with innovative ideas over time. The authors focus on specific stages of concerns as a way of assessing appropriate interventions that staff developers may make in their work.

Ann Lieberman and Lynne Miller shift attention to social/organizational concerns in their chapter, "The Social Realities of Teaching." Depending on field study approaches, the authors try to synthesize social understandings of what it is like to be a teacher in a school setting by linking conceptions about teaching with actual words and perceptions of teachers themselves. The authors then relate this knowledge about the profession and the daily realities of teaching to current research about improvement efforts and draw implications for staff development and the necessary supportive conditions for effective change.

Milbrey McLaughlin and David Marsh in "Staff Development and School Change" also take a social/organizational approach as they dig deeply into the Rand Change Agent Study and through a secondary analysis describe four broad factors underlying their understanding of staff development. Those factors include institutional motivation, implementation strategies, institutional leadership, and teacher characteristics. Researchers McLaughlin and Marsh argue that staff development is most effective when viewed as part of program building activities within a school, and they end by suggesting specific roles and tasks that organizations might take to develop effective staff development practices.

Richard Williams' chapter, "A Political Perspective on Staff Development," offers a pragmatic-political perspective that provides a balance to some of the other authors. Professor Williams points to the difficulty — if not seeming impossibility — of actually implementing the suggestions about staff development that the other authors make. By looking "at common phenomenon in an uncommon way," he focuses on the organizational self-interest of the various parties involved in staff development. His discussion touches on the involvement of colleges, consultants, the federal government, the state government, school districts, and teacher unions in staff development and indicates how the self-interest of each of these groups imposes on the others. He ends by calling for implementation strategies that include a consideration of private political interests of the groups who enter into staff development activities.

Continuing in the pragmatic-political vein, Maurice Leiter and Myrna Cooper describe "How Teacher Unionists View In-Service Education." Arguing that, "One cannot impose staff development; one must generate and motivate it," the authors challenge the teacher education profession and its structures. They discuss the growth of the union contract in its social context, as well as the union's role in the development of the increased professionalization of teachers. Their analysis of the gap between talk and action, thinkers and doers, further extends Professor Williams' description of organizational self-interest. They end by calling for teacher initiative and authority in the training of themselves.

The final essay in this section by Gary Griffin embraces the complexities of the issues developed by the other authors. In "Guidelines for the Evaluation of Staff Development Programs" Professor Griffin links three essentials: the goals of staff development, the individual and contextual goals, and the structural properties inherent in programs in developing an understanding of the ideological and procedural relations involved in evaluation. His final guidelines call for evaluations that are on-going, informed by multiple data sources, dependent on qualitative and quantitative data, explicit and public, considerate of participants' time and energy, focused on all levels of the organization, and presented in understandable forms. The guidelines, as they are developed here, provide for the leap from knowledge to action.

A Framework for Staff Development

JUDITH SCHIFFER

Teachers College, Columbia University

During the sixties and seventies, new national needs and priorities led to widespread attempts to effect school change. Large sums of money were allocated by the federal government and private foundations for curriculum research and development and for change projects aimed at diffusing innovations throughout the land.

Although hopes for school renewal often centered on aspects of schooling other than teacher training, such as improvements in curriculum, materials, and programs, it soon became apparent that teachers were the bottom line in any change that might take place. If teachers were unwilling or unable to implement an innovation, even the most "teacher proof" package was doomed to failure.

In the past, when there was a high degree of teacher turnover, it was possible to bring teachers into the school whose values and experience were consonant with change goals and who, it was hoped, could effect the desired change with a minimum of training. But as Mann has pointed out, school faculties have become relatively stable;[1] thus, change has to be accomplished by working with the existing staff. This fact, coupled with a concern for making school change, has led to a new emphasis on staff development.

Studies, unfortunately, point to the conclusion that despite determination, effort, and money poured into staff-development projects, they have not been very effective. Generally, failure to produce change in any particular setting is the result of many interacting factors. However, my analysis leads me to conclude that models of staff development are inadequate, having one or more of the following shortcomings: (1) They are

1 Dale Mann, "The Politics of Training Teachers in Schools," *Teachers College Record* 77 (February 1976): 323.

biased toward fulfilling organizational goals through the use of rational change strategies; thus, they fail to adequately take into account the behavioral regularities and values that exist in the school and overlook the need to make attitudinal and normative changes; or (2) they are biased toward making personal change and do not make sufficient provision for organizational accommodation to these changes; and/or (3) they are based on unrealistic assumptions about authority prerogatives; thus, they do not adequately deal with the political question of *who* makes *what* decisions and *how*.

The purpose of this article is to discuss these three shortcomings and to provide a framework for designing staff-development models that do not have them.

The organizational and personal change biases will be discussed only briefly because these aspects are dealt with by other authors in this issue. The bulk of the article concerns the problem of educational authority, an issue that is becoming increasingly crucial to staff development.

THE ORGANIZATIONAL GOALS BIAS

A pivotal question is, "Should the in-service staff-development program be based upon the felt needs of teachers, or upon organizational goals framed by the school board or administrators?"

In-service education has generally been conducted on the premise that the teacher should be free to select the professional improvement activities that he or she deems most rewarding. Therefore, a common practice has been to encourage continuing education by offering teachers released time and/or salary increments for a variety of extra-local activities, such as attendance at conferences and workshops, taking university courses, and travel. In addition, courses that are usually unrelated to a design for school improvement are given at local sites; teachers pick and choose among offerings on the basis of their own interests and felt needs.

This individualistic approach has been encouraged by the National Education Association (NEA) and other teachers' associations on the grounds that teachers are "professionals" with careers that are, in part, independent of the particular setting in which they work. By following their own inclinations for professional and personal growth they can open up their own futures.

There is a point of view, however, that sees the individualistic approach as potentially dysfunctional for a school. In order to provide continuity of experience for children, as well as a meaningful instructional program, what each teacher does individually should be related to an overall educational plan. A school should have what Joyce termed "a mission"[2] and staff members should be expected to strive for increasingly greater commitment to the mission and to acquire the competencies needed to fulfill it. According to this view, organizational goals should be the backbone of the staff-development program.

When there was high teacher turnover in schools, the individualistic approach could coexist with the mission approach. Teachers could find schools relatively compatible with their own values and style; administrators could find teachers whose interests and abilities were reasonably matched with the school's superordinate goals. But today, this flexibility rarely exists. Thus, there is now a greater concern for training teachers in a school to acquire the knowledge, attitudes, and skills required to fulfill its mission. The proliferation of competency-based designs for staff development reflects this concern. In these designs, curriculum and program goals are established in the tradition of the Tyler model—that is, they are based upon a needs assessment. Then, teacher competencies relevant to these goals are determined, and a staff-development program is planned for the purpose of correcting teachers' deficiencies in needed attitudes, knowledge, and skills. In other words, the staff-development program is based on goals determined by some "objective" process, and not upon the felt needs of teachers.

Organizational goals were also the basis of many of the change-oriented staff-development projects of the sixties and early seventies. School change was to be accomplished by introducing into the school an innovation that had been researched and developed outside of it, at a university or R&D center, or by a business firm. Most often, teachers' felt needs were not the basis for the selection of the innovation. Projects were usually initiated by an administrator who applied for a federal or foundation grant, brought in consultants to inspire and train the staff, or simply bought a "complete package" of materials, books, and teacher-training guides. Since the innovation had already been tried out and proven effective in other situations, the critical staff-development task was presumed to be teacher training.

An assumption underlying many staff-development programs that focus on training teachers to fulfill goals they have had little or no part in formulating is that the rational assessment of an idea is the critical factor in attitude and behavior change. Thus, if it can be demonstrated to teachers that an innovation is in line with school needs or that it is clearly superior to methods they are presently using, they will embrace it without

2 Bruce Joyce, *Alternative Models of Elementary Education* (Lexington, Mass.: Blaisdell Publishing, 1969), pp. 55-56.

reservation and assiduously set themselves to the task of acquiring the competencies needed to implement it. This "rational assumption" underestimates the degree to which individuals' values, self-interest, previous experiences, expectations, aspirations, needs, and personality traits influence their acceptance or rejection of an idea, as well as their ability to use it.

Research on adult socialization suggests that adults' values and commitments are quite stable and not very malleable.[3] These have been shaped by cumulative experiences, and are highly resistant to change. Therefore, it is likely that past history is the best predictor of future behavior, unless some fairly powerful interventions take place.

Studies of teachers' values and teaching behavior indicate that there are real differences in value orientations and that these are reflected in teachers' classroom behavior, the social norms they establish in the classroom, and their preferences for certain methods and approaches to teaching. For example, in a study conducted by Bussis and Chittenden,[4] it was found that while there was considerable overlap and variability, distinct differences exist between "traditional" and "open" teacher groups. Teachers in each group had different expectations for children, saw their roles differently, and held different attitudes toward freedom, choice, equality, self-control, and the importance of self-expression and imagination.

Imparting new information and knowledge to teachers with traditional value orientations would rarely be sufficient to enable them to conduct open classrooms. Deep-seated attitudes and expectations can be influenced by new ideas, but real and lasting behavioral change requires a more intensive resocialization experience — one that is powerful enough to bridge the gap between old response patterns and new requirements. Staff-development experiences for teachers that can facilitate attitude and behavior change include: values clarification (that is, the opportunity to discuss educational philosophy with colleagues, and to rethink assumptions about child development, learning, and the role of the school in society); consciousness-raising about the discrepancy between their "ideal" values as expressed in words and their "real" values as expressed in behavior; group process experiences that focus on changing in-

3 See Orville G. Brim and Stanton Wheeler, *Socialization after Childhood: Two Essays* (New York: John Wiley, 1967); and Kenneth A. Feldman and Theodore M. Newcomb, eds., *The Impact of College on Students* (San Francisco: Jossey-Bass, 1969), for research on adult values and behavior change.

4 Anne M. Bussis and Edward A. Chittenden, "An Analysis of an Approach to Open Education," Monograph (Princeton, N.J.: Educational Testing Service, August 1970).

terpersonal norms; the opportunity to try out new teaching behaviors on a small scale and to discuss resultant problems with others; and activities that enable the staff to modify aspects of an innovation so that they are more consonant with existing attitudes and behavior.

Lieberman and Shiman,[5] in their study of change in elementary settings, found that it did not, indeed, follow the rational model relied upon by staff developers who have an organizational goals bias. They found that change usually began when teachers experienced disequilibrium after being exposed to alternatives to their present methods, which they suspected might be much more effective in meeting their goals. Some teachers tried out one or more of these methods on a small scale. Their initial experiments created further disequilibrium; they found that aspects of the innovation were in conflict with some old patterns of action, or with existing regularities in the school. They discussed these problems with colleagues, and found that new issues emerged from these discussions. Ideals were viewed in the context of the realities of teaching and of the school culture. There was much conflict, anxiety, and doubt. In time, behavioral and organizational patterns became modified to fit the innovation, and the innovation was modified to fit the realities inherent in the particular setting. During this process, teachers realized they lacked clarity about the innovation and set out to gain new knowledge and skills. Changes in school arrangements — time schedules, materials, space, procedures, and social norms — were tried out and some were adopted. Original plans were abandoned and replaced by others as new meanings and new needs emerged. The entire process was incremental and evolutionary.

The above sounds quite unsystematic and almost too benign as a model for change. Indeed, Lieberman and Shiman refer to it as a "nonmodel." Obviously, staff developers would prefer to take a more goal-oriented tack and be more linear in their designs for school renewal. But if the rational strategies really do not work in most situations, then a less orderly approach may lead to more school improvement in the long run. This is also true for a collaborative approach to goal setting, and for similar reasons. Collaboration may be a less efficient process than having goals set forth by a bright administrator, but as research indicates, participation of the staff is likely to lead to greater commitment to these

5 Ann Lieberman and David A. Shiman, "The Stages of Change in Elementary School Settings," in *The Power to Change: Issues for the Innovative Educator*, ed. Carmen M. Culver and Gary J. Hoban (New York: McGraw-Hill, 1973).

goals, more motivation to implement them, and greater satisfaction if they are achieved.[6]

In summary, organizational goals are central to an effective staff-development design. However, these goals should be consonant with the existing regularities in the school and its environment and the values and expectations of those who are to implement them (and, as we shall discuss later, those who will be affected by them). This is more likely to occur if goals emerge from the staff or if they are determined collaboratively. Furthermore, the staff-development plan should include resocialization experiences that focus on individual and group values and processes, as well as those that build new knowledge and skills. This is especially important if an innovation is initiated "from above" or if new goals are framed by the school board or by administrators, with little or no staff participation.

THE PERSONAL-CHANGE BIAS

Making personal change is, of course, a basic aim of any staff-development plan. However, there are diverse viewpoints about the reasons for and the focus of such efforts. As has already been indicated, some staff-development models aim to change persons so that they will be able to fulfill organization goals. But the predominant approach is to focus on making personal change without reference to an overall educational plan.

A common assumption is that a school will benefit from the personal and professional actualization of its staff, and that diversity in values, behavior, and teaching style will enhance a school. The traditional individualistic approach to in-service education reflects this belief.

Another approach to staff development is based on the premise that there exists a set of generic competencies that all teachers should have plus specific competencies that an individual teacher may want or need. On the assumption that what makes a good school is a highly competent teaching staff, models of staff development such as microteaching, interaction analysis, and advisory approaches have been devised to strengthen individual teachers' competencies.

If school renewal is the goal of staff development, then models that focus only on improving the individual teacher's classroom performance are incomplete. What happens in an individual teacher's classroom has at

6   Ronald Corwin, *Education in Crisis: A Sociological Analysis of Schools and Universities in Transition* (New York: John Wiley, 1974).

best only an indirect impact on the overall instructional program and the general school climate.

Because the teacher is not only an individual practitioner but is also part of a school staff, strategies have been developed that aim to improve aspects of organizational health: communication adequacy, the ability of the staff to solve problems collaboratively, cohesiveness, and morale. Examples of these strategies are organizational development, T-groups, and sensitivity training. Chin and Benne refer to these as "normative-reeducative strategies" and point out that they are based on the recognition that change requires an alteration of normative orientations of old patterns and commitment to new ones.[7] However, studies of these strategies indicate that they are effective only if organizational patterns and procedures change to accomodate the changes occurring in people.[8] For example, if a staff has learned techniques that make communication more productive and has gained skills in collaborative problem solving, unless time is made available for such activity people will revert back to their old behavior, and the staff-development experience will have been an exercise in futility.

Several case studies document the inadequacy of models of staff development that emphasize personal change and neglect organizational change. Gracey's study of a group of teachers who introduced informal, child-centered methods into their teaching[9] underscores the point that teacher commitment and competency alone are not all that is required for successful implementation of an innovation. These teachers were blocked by parents' and administrators' lack of support, students' demands for grades, the norms existing in the rest of the school that order and quiet prevail in classrooms, and the large number of students in each class. Gross and Giacquinta's study identifies other organizational variables that interfered with the success of an innovation: time schedules, assignment of pupils, grouping practices, the type of report card used, and the unavailability of required instructional materials and equipment.[10]

7 Robert Chin and Kenneth D. Benne, "General Strategies for Effecting Changes in Human Systems," in *The Planning of Change*, ed. Warren G. Bennis, Kenneth D. Benne, and Robert Chin (New York: Holt, Rinehart & Winston, 1961), p. 34.

8 See David G. Bowers, "OD Techniques and Their Results in 23 Organizations: The Michigan ICL Study," *Journal of Applied Behavioral Science* 9 (1973): 21-41; and Sam D. Seiber, "Images of the Practitioner and Strategies of Educational Change," *Sociology of Education* 45 (Fall 1972): 362-85.

9 Harry L. Gracey, *Curriculum or Craftsmanship: Elementary School Teachers in a Bureaucratic System* (Chicago: University of Chicago Press, 1970).

10 Neal Gross, Joseph B. Giacquinta, and Marilyn Bernstein, *Implementing Organizational Innovations: A Sociological Analysis of Planned Educational Change* (New York: Basic Books, 1971).

To summarize, staff-development designs must provide for personal change. However, this in itself will not necessarily result in school renewal; the latter requires that organizational adjustments be coordinated with personal change. Lack of attention to important organizational factors leads to frustration on the part of persons who are changing, a tendency for them to revert back to old behaviors, and, ultimately, failure to implement innovations.

THE PROBLEM OF EDUCATIONAL AUTHORITY

The staff-development literature virtually ignores the matter of educational authority, despite the fact that it is becoming increasingly apparent that this issue is crucial to contemporary staff development. A basic question that ought to be clarified if staff-development models are to be realistic and workable is, "*Who* makes *what* decisions, and under *what circumstances?*" This is important today because changes have occurred that make old assumptions about authority prerogatives anachronistic.

THREE PRINCIPLES OF AUTHORITY

Clark has provided a framework for exploring the relationship among the three most influential sources of authority on the local school system level—the school board, administrators, and teachers.[11] He states that related to these sources of authority are principles of authority, general beliefs about who should exercise power and how. He defines three principles:

The Principle of Public Trust: The principle that public control should be vested in a board of laymen. This board is legally empowered to direct the organization and is held responsible for its welfare; it is to have final authority over the work of the employed staff. This principle relates to a belief that the school should be directed by community interests rather than by professional personnel or government departments.

The Principle of Bureaucratic Authority: The legal provision that authority is vested in a lay board does not insure that laymen will determine policy. This principle states that authority is delegated to or assumed by professional officials.

The Principle of Colleague Authority: The principle that much, if not all, authority should be in the hands of the school faculty. The school

11 Burton Clark, *Educating the Expert Society* (San Francisco: Chandler Publishing, 1962), pp. 152-62.

should be a self-governing community in which teachers have major control of policy and practice.

The principle of public trust was established in colonial times, but it has been a myth for at least a century, during which time the principle of bureaucratic authority became firmly entrenched. In the contemporary era, the meaning of the principle of public trust has shifted, as federal and state governments have become more dominant in educational policy making, and parents clamor for direct as well as representative participation in school decision making. And both the public trust and bureaucratic principles are being challenged by the organized teaching profession, which is beginning to advocate the principle of colleague authority.

Despite these changes, staff-development plans more often than not are predicated upon outmoded assumptions about decision-making prerogatives. These assumptions are reflected in the hierarchical organizational chart found in administration textbooks and in central offices around the nation. It suggests that there is a chain of command that makes it possible to move policy down the line in a linear, rational, and efficient manner: The community elects the school board and presumably thereafter bows to its policy judgments; the board then hires a superintendent and staff to put its policies into effect; the superintendent delegates building decision making to the principals, who develop their schools within the guidelines established by the central administration; and, finally, the teacher, who has had no role in policy setting, implements the plans in the classroom. According to this model, everyone in the hierarchy has clearly delineated roles and responsibilities and a spirit of rationality is presumed to prevail.

Reports of staff-development projects on this model indicate that they frequently fail. The reason for this is that the model is inaccurate. Today, although the formal and legal structure for decision making is hierarchical, the de facto state of affairs might more accurately be diagramed as:

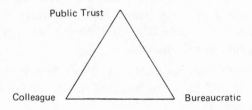

The points of the triangle frequently represent points of conflict. Each of the three sources of authority is claiming a voice in policy decision making and is struggling to establish or retain its own prerogatives. Furthermore, as will be discussed later, new sources of authority have entered the picture, altering the meaning of the three "principles."

One reason for the continued acceptance of the anachronistic model of authority is that it is based on a historical ethos. As Borrowman has noted, "Frequently a point of view, arrived at through trying social experiences, lives on when the cultural patterns which made it valid have completely changed,"[12] and it leads to confusion and unworkable solutions to problems. With a view toward modernizing our assumptions, the three principles of authority will now be traced historically from colonial to contemporary times. Hopefully, a historical perspective will make clearer what is no longer true or useful for staff development.

THE THREE PRINCIPLES OF AUTHORITY IN HISTORICAL PERSPECTIVE

Schools were created and later mandated by the New England Puritans as the exigencies of colonial life made it increasingly difficult for the family and church to take full responsibility for training the young for a Christian life. Since the school was seen as an extension of the primary agencies of socialization, it was assumed that schools would be controlled, inspected, and supervised by the civil authority, and this assumption was reflected in the earliest education laws. The principle of public trust was implemented at first by local lay groups and ministers, and later, as school districts became larger and spread out geographically, through elected school boards.

The principle of public trust began to weaken between the Revolution and the Civil War, as cities and school districts grew in size and states assumed greater control over local policy. Educators argued for the common school, for centralized control of educational systems and standardized curricula and instructional practices, and against democratic localism. These developments had the effect of transferring control to schoolpeople and bureaucrats, and out of the hands of local citizens.

The teacher's task changed as school populations became diverse, and as new patterns of thought emerged out of the Enlightenment. New knowledge about human learning and development suggested new approaches to pedagogy. In contrast to the colonial schoolmaster who was

12   Merle Borrowman, *The Liberal and Technical in Teacher Education: An Historical Survey of American Thought* (New York: Bureau of Publications, Teachers College, Columbia University, 1965), p. vi.

required only to be a pious, moral, and loyal citizen and to possess an education equivalent to what he was required to teach, the nineteenth-century schoolteacher was provided with occupational training. Specialized programs and normal schools were established for teacher education, and the teacher institute provided practicing teachers with opportunities to "correct their deficiencies." Examinations for certification became widespread.

Teachers were also beginning to identify themselves as an occupational group; they formed teachers' associations, most notably the NEA in 1857. However, in the classroom and school, they saw their decison-making authority diminish as "head teachers" took on more responsibility for the direction of curricular and instructional practices, and materials for instruction became standardized on a school, system, city, and statewide basis.

The principalship and city superintendency were institutionalized, and bureaucracy became the predominant structure of the school organization. Although legally the principle of public trust still held, in practice it was superseded by the principle of bureaucratic authority as administrative staffs grew in size and power, and school boards delegated more of their policy-setting prerogatives to the superintendent of schools.

During the first quarter of this century, the municipal reform movement succeeded in depoliticizing schooling, and further shifted educational authority from lay to professional hands. In addition, the business values that dominated the larger society were reflected in the nation's schools by a concern for efficiency, economy, and standardization. This emphasis on "scientific management" coupled with advances in curriculum making and instructional technology led to special graduate programs for administrators. This expert cadre of "professional executives" became designated as the group best equipped to make judgments about school policy.

Administration became a "profession" distinct from teaching; administrators were the planners, and teachers the implementors who were expected to adhere to their superordinates' specifications, often as rigidly as an industrial worker was expected to follow management's orders. However, despite teachers' circumscribed role in the classroom and school, they continued to strive for benefits that would countervail these restrictions and to improve their status. Teachers' associations fought for tenure to protect academic and personal freedom and job security, for better teacher education, certification requirements, and in-service training.

During the progressive era, managerial ideologies shifted from scien-

tific management to "democratic administration." Participation in decision making by the entire staff was considered important for morale and
to inspire commitment to school goals. Teachers were consulted on matters such as textbook selection, student placement, and report-card construction; however, they generally were not considered legitimate sources
of policymaking authority. But due to the successful professionalization
efforts of the NEA and other teachers' organizations, better teacher
preparation, and higher standards of entry into teaching, teachers' role
conceptions grew increasingly "professional." These were among the events
that laid the foundation for a demand that would come later—that is, that
teachers, being the real experts in school affairs, should have a major
role—if not *the* major role—in policymaking.

THE THREE PRINCIPLES OF AUTHORITY IN THE CONTEMPORARY ERA

In the past several decades the principle of public trust has been further
weakened as state education departments have acted to standardize curricula, regulate finances, accredit teacher education programs, and cer-
tify teachers. The nationalizing trend in educational decision making has
had a similar effect. National standardized testing, educational business
firms operating in a national market, and private foundations' funding
of specific innovations greatly influence what takes place in local school
districts across the land. Policy has also been made by the federal government through legislation, the funding of research, local program
development through grants-in-aid, and by the courts, which have
created national educational policies. Finally, efforts by the organized
teaching profession to set national standards for teacher education programs and certification have contributed to the upward drift in educational policy setting.

The upward drift has resulted in a strengthening of the superintendent's
power, and with it the principle of bureaucratic authority. Relative to
the lay school board, the superintendent and his staff have the time and
the expertise to deal with the implications of state and federal guidelines
and mandates, and to write grants. Thus, as Kerr and others have pointed
out, the major role of the school board in many districts has become that
of legitimating the superintendent's actions to the community.[13]

Two other contemporary trends have diminished the school board's

13 Norman D. Kerr, "The School Board as an Agency of Legitimation," in *Governing Education: A Reader on Politics, Power, and Public School Policy*, ed. Alan Rosenthal (New York:
Anchor Books, 1969).

policymaking power. These are: (1) Parents are demanding a more direct voice in decisions about their schools; and (2) teachers are gaining more control over professional matters and local school policy. Parent Power and Teacher Power have also challenged the principle of bureaucratic authority.

Parent Power   Three factors leading to the reemergence of parents as authority sources are: (1) the importance of education in a changing market; (2) parents' resentment of schools' failing their children; and (3) federal programs that have emphasized evaluation and accountability.[14]

Community participation and control was initiated by black parents who felt powerless and unrepresented by urban boards of education. However, urban minority group parents have not been the only ones to demand participation. As the costs of education accelerated, as confidence in public institutions declined, and as parents became concerned about their children's futures in a competitive job market, middle-class parents also became more aggressive about intervening in school affairs.

The demand for parent participation is a demand that schools be responsive to community needs and concerns. A growing body of case reports offers documentation that when school people attempt to make changes that are discordant with such needs and concerns, parents can and often will sabotage these changes.

An exemplary case is reported by Roland Barth.[15] He describes an attempt to bring "order and quality education" to a large, mostly black, inner-city public school system by enlisting the resources of a foundation, a university, and the school district in the development of a school renewal project. Although there was no master plan for the first year, the board hired Barth, then a well-known advocate of the open classroom, to be the instructional principal of the two experimental schools where change was to be initiated, and Barth hired six teachers who shared his educational philosophy.

Barth and the six teachers were white, had been educated in elite schools, and their professional experience was limited to white, upper-class schools. They did not anticipate that the open classroom approach that had proven successful in their previous teaching situations would be antithetical to the needs, values, and expectations of parents in this community, nor that parents would militantly oppose it.

14   National Education Association, *Schools for the 70s and Beyond: A Call to Action*, A Staff Report, Center for the Study of Instruction (Washington, D.C.: National Education Association, 1971), p. 30.

15   Roland Barth, *Open Education and the American School* (New York: Schocken Books, 1973), chap. 3.

The tenets and practices of the open classroom were seen by these parents as being in direct conflict with their aspirations for their children. They believed that the rewards of white middle-class America would become accessible to their children only if they were socialized in the mold of discipline, hard work, and striving, which they assumed led to high income and status in the (presumed) meritocracy. Parents put pressure on the teachers to conduct the business of schooling in conventional ways, and on administrators to put a stop to what they considered neglectful, if not insulting, pedagogy. The administrators that supervised these teachers were extremely sensitive to parental opposition; they became increasingly unsupportive of the teachers' efforts, finally withholding necessary resources and harassing them. At first, the teachers responded by making "concessions of form while keeping the substance of their efforts intact." Eventually, when it was no longer possible to do this, all six teachers quit the district.

The message here is that the assumption commonly made by staff developers that decisions made by school boards and administrators will be docilely accepted by parents is anachronistic.

Teacher Power By the 1960s organized teachers realized that their tactics of lobbying, personal diplomacy, and individual negotiation were relatively ineffectual compared with those used by private employees — namely, strikes and collective bargaining. This was a period of economic prosperity; nationwide economic expansion gave teachers career alternatives, thus increasing their willingness to take the risk of job loss. The striking victories by the United Federation of Teachers (UFT) and the American Federation of Teachers (AFT) through union tactics demonstrated to the nation's teachers the efficacy of militant action, and led to an altered stance by the NEA, which had previously taken a "professional" approach.

During the sixties, teacher power was used primarily to increase teachers' welfare benefits. However, as schools and teachers came under attack by the community, militancy was used reactively. It became a defensive weapon used by teachers vulnerable to community criticism, demands for accountability, and the threat of job loss. Events in New York City, where teachers joined management in the fight against decentralization and community control, are examples of teacher power used for political rather than "educational" purposes.

During the more economically tight and politically conservative seventies, when teachers' jobs became less secure and taxpayers more reluctant to support greater school expenditures, organized teachers directed their efforts toward two objectives: (1) to gain more control over professional matters; and (2) to have a greater voice in local school policy making.

Political action has been the major means of effectuating the first goal, collective bargaining the route to the second.

In the professional sphere, two power struggles are raging: one over the control of the profession, the other over the control of teacher education. Since 1959, the NEA has made tremendous strides in its efforts to place control over the accreditation of teacher education programs, program approval, certification, and licensure in the hands of the organized teaching profession. The design of teacher-education programs and authority over the design and implementation of in-service education are also likely to fall increasingly under teachers' domination. Justification for this is based on the claim that if teachers are to be held accountable, they must have authority. Success in gaining control over professional matters means increased collective strength for teachers vis-à-vis colleges of education, school boards, administrators, and, of course, the public.

Bargaining between teacher organizations and school boards is now an accepted practice buttressed by legislation and court rulings. By 1970 half of the nation's elementary and secondary school teachers were working under a negotiated contract, and twenty-two states had enacted legislation mandating local teacher unit-school board negotiations.

"Wages, salary, hours, and other conditions of employment" are the categories that are negotiable under teacher-school board collective bargaining. Welfare issues such as salaries and class size had top priorities in the early struggles. Today, policy issues are coming into the forefront. Since everything that happens in schools affects teachers' working conditions, NEA and AFT have interpreted the term *conditions of employment* to include "anything two parties can agree on." NEA's *Guidelines for Professional Negotiations* states: "Negotiations should include all matters which affect the quality of the educational system."[16] Contracts increasingly have provisions related to curriculum, the instructional program, textbooks, and other matters clearly falling under the rubric of "policy." The courts, in fact, have supported an expanding legal interpretation of the phrase *conditions of employment*.

Negotiations between teachers and school boards have had far-reaching impact on the balance of power among the three sources of authority. Collective bargaining has increased the demands made on school boards and at the same time eroded their power. Boards must address themselves to the details of school administration because they are stipulated

16   Cited in Robert Bendiner, *The Politics of Schools—A Crisis in Self-Government* (New York: Macmillan, 1970), pp. 104-05.

in the contract. Since teachers place what used to be considered non-negotiable items on the bargaining table, boards often bargain away some of their own prerogatives as well as those of administrators. Items related to recruitment, selection, assignment, and transfer of personnel; the evaluation of teachers and administrators; tenure; academic standards; school building and district organization, class size, discipline, and the number of faculty meetings to be scheduled per year often find their way into the contract.

Obviously, these specifications limit the authority and power of administrators, as well as their flexibility in making curricular and programmatic improvements. It is generally conceded that the principal is the key person for making change in the individual school. But, clearly, collective bargaining has caused the principal's authority to spiral downward.

One effect of negotiations has been that the principal is more likely to feel a conflict between his managerial and educational leadership roles. Principals do not sit at the bargaining table. They are, therefore, in a position of having to implement and enforce policies and procedures they have had no part in devising, and with which they may disagree. Because principals are expected to enforce management's prerogatives, they frequently find themselves in an adversary relationship with the teaching staff, a role quite different from the "facilitating supervisor" role they have traditionally held. That principals are quite concerned about all of this can be quickly ascertained by even a cursory perusal of the last several years' issues of the *National Elementary Principal* and the National Association of Secondary Schools *Bulletin*. They are rife with articles about: (1) principals' eroding power and changed role; (2) the need for principals to learn conflict-management skills; (3) the importance of strengthening principals' professional organizations; (4) plans to lobby for laws that will enable principals to negotiate directly with the board for their own benefits and rights; and (5) the constraints the negotiated contract places on principals' access to their staffs when limits are set for faculty meetings and staff-development activities.

Negotiations between school boards and teachers have strengthened the power of teacher collectivity. Thus, for the first time, the principle of colleague authority—that is, that much if not all authority should reside with the school faculty—is being articulated. Obviously, teachers have neither the time nor the resources to operationalize this principle, and much of the rhetoric surrounding it may be politically motivated, but it is being advocated. Charles Cogen, a past president of AFT, said in 1969 that it was time that school boards realized the obsolescence of the "right to manage concept."[17] Albert Shanker has even suggested that the principalship be eliminated and that the principal's function be subsumed by teacher committees.[18]

Even the generally conservative NEA, which has tended to take a collaborative stance on authority, is unequivocal in its intention to place the control of in-service teacher centers under union/teacher domination. There are several models of teacher centers; most involve some sort of shared governance and participation involving administrators, teachers, and colleges of education. The model that NEA advocates is that the teacher center be "the teachers' own turf and . . . run and operated by the teachers themselves."[19] What takes place in the center will be based upon teachers' own identified needs and problems; administrators, school boards, and professional teacher educators would have little or no role.

The combined effect of teacher professionalization and teacher power has led to professional role conceptions that have implications for staff development. One may argue that teaching is not a profession because it is not built on a codified body of theory and esoteric technical skills, or because the public has not been willing to confer professional status on teachers. Nonetheless, according to pronouncements by NEA and AFT, teachers consider their expertise equal or superior to that of administrators and school boards in the areas of curriculum and instruction, and sometimes claim that the principle of colleague authority is justifiable, and perhaps even workable. Whether or not this principle will supplant the principle of bureaucratic authority, the point to be made is that teachers no longer consider themselves mere "implementors" of other people's decisions, on the bottom rung of the organizational ladder.

To summarize, on the local school level, authority roles and relationships are in a state of flux. School boards have fewer policymaking prerogatives than they had even a decade ago. Administrators' power is being challenged by teachers, and their decisions are being questioned by parents. The organized teaching profession has become strong enough to voice a demand for the principle of colleague authority, and collective bargaining has provided the means for teachers to take an increasingly larger role in setting school policy. Old assumptions about authority

---

17 Charles Cogen, "What Teachers Really Want from Boards," *American School Board Journal* 156 (February 1969): 10.

18 Albert Shanker, "Why Teachers Are Angry," *American School Board Journal* 162 (January 1975): 23–26.

19 National Education Association, "What a Teacher Center Might Look Like," mimeographed (Washington, D.C.: Instruction and Professional Development, Fall 1974), pp. 1–2.

prerogatives should be discarded, and staff-development designs should be built on a realistic assessment of the political realities in the particular school setting.

SUMMARY

Since school renewal must now be accomplished by working with existing staff members, staff development has become a top priority in schools.

Attempts to effect change through staff development have not been notably successful. Some staff-development programs have succeeded with teachers who felt the need for training, but failed with those who did not. Other programs succeeded in motivating a staff to accept an innovation and acquire the skills to implement it, but still did not succeed in getting the innovation implemented in the school or district. Still others succeeded in getting an innovation implemented only to have it disintegrate in response to community backlash.

The thesis of this article is that these unfortunate outcomes resulted, in part, from the use of one-sided or inadequate models of staff development and/or the acceptance of anachronistic assumptions about authority prerogatives.

Some staff-development models are overcommitted to training teachers to fulfill organizational goals they have had little or no part in formulating. These models generally rest upon rational assumptions about the change process, and tend to ignore the diversity and stability of values held by individual staff members, as well as the entrenched norms and behavioral regularities that exist in the school. In addition, such models are often based on politically naive assumptions. Shifts in authority prerogatives and relationships mean that administrators have less sanctioning power and teachers have more power to resist superordinate directives. In addition, teachers' professional role conceptions, their expectation that they be accorded "professional autonomy," their new demand for colleague authority—and teacher power that buttresses this demand— means that teachers have to be persuaded, not ordered, to implement innovations.

Therefore, although organizational goals must guide a staff-development plan, how these goals are determined, and how the goals interface with the staff's needs and educational values, is an issue that must be dealt with. Strategies likely to lead to school improvement are participatory goal setting and activities that provide for a "process of mutual adaptation"[20] between the staff and the organizational goals.

---

20   This is a term used by McLaughlin in describing successful staff-development projects. See

Another set of one-sided staff-development models is overcommitted to making personal change. School renewal, in part, is a function of the opportunities available to teachers for professional development in response to new goals. But it is also a function of the organization's ability to change in line with the changes taking place in people. Therefore, models of staff development that focus almost exclusively on upgrading teachers' competencies, improving group interactions and problem-solving skills, or changing teaching behavior are insufficient. Individual and group behaviors are not the only relevant subsystems. In addition to people, some other subsystems that must be attended to are: goals, climate, technology, supports, rewards, procedures, arrangements of time and space, and structures for decision making.

Finally, staff-development plans should be based on an assessment of political realities in the school and its environment. A critical factor is that of educational authority: *Who* makes *what* decisions and *how?* This issue is becoming increasingly important in an era characterized by aggressive claims by diverse groups for a voice in policymaking. In short, models of staff development should have three foci: *Personal, Organizational,* and *Political.*

Milbrey Wallin McLaughlin, "Implementation as Mutual Adaptation: Change in Classroom Organization," *Teachers College Record* 77 (February 1976): 339-51.

Teaching: The Question of Personal Reality

MAXINE GREENE
Teachers College, Columbia University

The realities of teaching are multiple. Three points of view, three tones of voice begin to suggest the range. The first is John Dewey's:

> The principle that development of experience comes about through interaction means that education is essentially a social process. This quality is realized in the degree in which individuals form a community group. It is absurd to exclude the teacher from membership in the group. As the most mature member of the group he has a peculiar responsibility for the conduct of the interactions and intercommunications which are the very life of the group as a community.[1]

The second is B. Othanel Smith's:

> Our most general notion is that teaching is everywhere the same, that it is a natural social phenomenon and is fundamentally the same from one culture to another. . . . In our view, teaching is a system of action involving an agent, a situation, an end-in-view, and two sets of factors in the situation—one set over which the agent has no control (for example, size of classroom and physical characteristics of pupils) and one set which the agent can modify with respect to the end-in-view (for example, assignments and ways of asking questions).[2]

The third is Martin Buber's. He, too, was writing about the teaching situation—always, he thought, a situation "that has never been before and will never come again."

---

1 John Dewey, *Experience and Education* (New York: Collier Books, 1963), p. 58.

2 B. Othanel Smith, "Toward a Theory of Teaching," in *Theory and Research in Teaching,* ed. Arno A. Bellack (New York: Bureau of Publications, Teachers College, 1963), p. 4.

It demands of you a reaction which cannot be prepared beforehand. It demands nothing of what is past. It demands presence, responsibility; it demands you.[3]

To talk about the personal reality of teachers is to consider their lived lives and their pursuits of meaning in contexts that include a concern for the social dimensions of teaching, for the strategic, *and* for the existentially unique. It is, if possible, to avoid the kinds of either/ors or dichotomies that arise when the social is viewed as antithetical to the individual, or when the cognitive and conceptual are treated as if they were at odds with the affective, the authentic, the humane.

What we understand to be "reality" is interpreted or reflected-on experience. We live in continuing transactions with the natural and human world around us. Perceived shapes, colors, lights, sounds, present themselves to our embodied consciousness. Only as we begin moving into the life of language, thematizing, symbolizing, making sense, do we begin to single out certain profiles, certain aspects of the flux of things to attend to and to name.[4] Once we begin doing that, we begin orienting ourselves to what we think of as the "real." The patterns or schemata we use in the process of sense-making are those made available to us by "our predecessors and contemporaries."[5] We are, after all, functions of a culture; most of those teaching in the public schools speak the same language. The realities we construct — schools, for example, time clocks, running tracks, political parties, dining room tables, public squares — mean what they mean because we have internalized common ways of thinking about them and talking about them. But, at the same time, each of us looks upon the common world from a particular standpoint, a particular location in space and time. Each of us has a distinctive biography, a singular life history. Each of us, to use George Herbert Mead's words, is both an "I" and a "me." The "I" gives us our "sense of freedom, of initiative." It is, Mead said, "the response of the organism to the attitudes of others; the 'me' is the organized set of attitudes of others which one . . . assumes. The attitudes of the others constitute the organized 'me', and then one reacts toward that as an 'I.' "[6] The "me," therefore, is social; it refers to the shared social reality we respond to as we live. There is always,

---

3   Martin Buber, *Between Man and Man* (Boston: Beacon Press, 1957), p. 114.

4   See Maurice Merleau-Ponty, *The Primacy of Perception* (Evanston, Ill.: Northwestern University Press, 1964), pp. 12–42.

5   Alfred Schutz, "Common-Sense and Scientific Interpretation," in Collected Papers I, *The Problem of Social Reality* (The Hague: Martinus Nijhoff, 1967), pp. 15f.

6   George H. Mead, *Mind, Self and Society* (Chicago: University of Chicago Press, 1934), p. 175.

however, the perspective and the agency of the "I"; and this means that there is always the possibility of self-consciousness, of choosing, and of unpredictability. It is with these that I wish to associate the idea of personal reality.

When we look back, most of us realize that we somehow knew about teachers and classrooms very early in our lives, long before we went to school. The specific teachers and classrooms with which we later came in contact, therefore, appeared within a horizon of "pre-acquaintance-ship."[7] We were already familiar with the difference between larger and smaller people, with the spaces and surfaces prohibited to us—and the spaces and surfaces we were expected to explore. We were accustomed to hands that helped and hands that restrained, voices that disapproved and voices that tried to point things out, to help us understand, to help us see. If there were bookshelves in our homes, and sheets of paper, and memo pads, these simply belonged to the world of daily life. They were part of the background or the scenery, taken for granted as what they appeared to be. It was only when we actually became pupils in actual classrooms that we began to identify unique instances of teaching behavior, to select out something called "teaching" against what we had taken for granted. It was then that we began perceiving books and paper in terms of a specified kind of use. It was then that we began noticing chalkboards, charts, attendance sheets, grade books, as indicators, somehow, of a new kind of social world. We did not, of course, see all this in identical ways. We constituted them, as we constituted our classrooms, in the light of the particular problems we faced in becoming pupils (or "third graders," or "bluebirds") among other children in a regularized, oddly public place away from home. The nature of our "interest" and what Alfred Schutz described as "the system of relevances involved"[8] originated in our own biographical situations and in the circumstances that prevailed in our lives at the time we first went to school.

As we grew older along with others and experienced diverse teachers and teaching situations, we built up a structure of meanings. Many of these meanings derived from the ways in which our choices and purposes were supported or frustrated by other people's choices and purposes in the shifting social worlds of the classrooms we came to know. Some derived from our developing commonsense understanding of the workings of those worlds. Then, at least for some of us, there were the meanings that emerged from our reflections on our commonsense understandings, reflec-

7 Schutz, "Concept and Theory Formation," in *the Problem of Social Reality,* p. 59.
8 Ibid., p. 60.

tions made possible by an ability to "do" psychology or one of the social sciences, by a developed skill in tracing certain political currents in the schools, or by an achieved capacity to think in terms of teaching strategies.

There came a time, finally, when we began thinking about teaching as a way of spending our working lives. Like all other human beings, we could not but "future," in some sense, think about what might be. As Jean-Paul Sartre has written, our behavior is not only determined by our relation "to the real and present factors which condition it," but by "a certain object, still to come, which it is trying to bring into being." And Sartre went on to say, "This is what we call *the project*."[9] We may be moved to choose our project because of certain lacks in a social situation in which we are involved: We may want to repair those lacks and make that situation what it might be, rather than what it is. Or our choice of project may be connected with our notion of what we want to make of ourselves, of the kinds of identity we want to create. In either case, we are trying to become what we are not yet by acting on perceived deficiency, or on perceived possibility.

Dewey wrote that "the self is not ready-made, but something in continuous formation through choice of action . . . ."[10] He said that if an individual, say, was interested in keeping at his or her work even if his or her life were endangered, that would be because the individual found his or her self "*in* that work." People who give up in the face of danger or threat or discomfort are people who, in choosing their own security or comfort, are declaring their preference to be people of that sort; they are creating prudent, comfortable selves. Dewey stressed the fact that "self and interest are two names for the same fact; the kind and amount of interest actively taken in a thing reveals and measures the quality of selfhood which exists."[11] To think of the self in this fashion or to define personal reality in this fashion is very different from placing one's credence in "self-actualization" or in any approach focused on an unfolding or realization of an original, authentic self. Dewey believed, as does Sartre, that what we become, what we make of ourselves, depends upon what we do in our lives. And what we do cannot be simply routine and mechanical; it must be conscious, interested, committed. If it is not, if we content ourselves with being behaving organisms rather than reflective persons engaged in ongoing *action*, the quality of our selfhood becomes thin and

9 Jean-Paul Sartre, *Search for a Method* (New York: Alfred A. Knopf, 1963), p. 91.

10 John Dewey, *Democracy and Education* (New York: Macmillan, 1916), p. 408.

11 Ibid.

pallid. We begin to resemble those T. S. Eliot called "hollow men,"[12] or those Thoreau described as living their lives in "quiet desperation."[13]

We who choose ourselves to become teachers obviously have an "interest" when we do so. As has been suggested, that interest arises out of our biographical situation, as much as it does out of a sense of what we are trying to bring into being. There are those who select out the nurturant dimension of teaching and focus on creating themselves as caring persons, motherly or fatherly persons, interested very often in open-ended growth. There are those who attend most particularly to the social dimension of the educational process: the transmission or communication of a way of life; the fostering of the democratic ideal; the shaping of community. There are those who find themselves so challenged, so enlightened by engagement with an academic discipline that they turn toward teaching as a way of introducing others to the domain of history or physics or sociology or literary studies, in the hope that their perspectives also will be expanded, even as they become initiates in the community of scholars— or (perhaps) sophisticated technicians, bibliophiles, mediators for another generation of the young. And there are always persons who turn toward teaching because they see themselves as people committed to arousing others to critical thinking or to "conscientization"[14] or even to bringing about social change. And there are a few who want especially to stimulate awareness and understanding of the arts, and a few who want to train apprentices for one of the fields of scientific inquiry. I am speaking of the interests that appear to motivate persons when they decide to enter into teaching, interests that may be refined or eroded or totally transformed in the course of teacher training, but that remain present in the individual's historical situation, no matter what happens in his or her everyday.

What happens, of course, when we have our initial experiences with teaching in public schools, is that we become sharply aware of limits, of structures and arrangements that cannot easily be surpassed. No matter how practical, how grounded our educational courses were, they suddenly appear to be totally irrelevant in the concrete situation where we find ourselves. This is because general principles never fully apply to new and special situations, especially if those principles are thought of as prescrip-

---

12   T.S. Eliot, "The Hollow Men," in *The Complete Poems and Plays* (New York: Harcourt, Brace, 1952), pp. 56-59.

13   Henry David Thoreau, *Walden* (New York: Washington Square Press, 1963), p. 69.

14   Paulo Freire, *Pedagogy of the Oppressed* (New York: Herder and Herder, 1970), p. 157.

tions or rules. Dewey spoke of principles as modes or methods of analyzing situations, tools to be used "in judging suggested courses of action."[15] They provide standpoints, ways of interpreting or making sense of what is happening; they are not practical, as rules are practical; they do not tell us specifically what to do. Yet, when we first enter into the classrooms for which we are responsible, or when we confront groups of students who are resistant or undisciplined or inept, we long for rules or for someone to tell us "what to do at 9 o'clock." We forget that, for a rule to be universally applicable, all situations must be fundamentally alike; and, as most of us know, classroom situations are always new and never twice alike. Even so, we yearn oftentimes for what might be called a "technology of teaching," for standard operating procedures that can be relied upon to "work." Devoid of these, we project our frustration back upon whatever teacher education we experienced; or (in cases of extremity) we project our frustration outward to the young people in our classes, the creatures who seem to be rejecting what we offer them — an alienated and alienating crowd who do not seem to care about learning how to learn.

Obviously, this does not always happen. But there are few teachers who avoid the anxiety of beginning, few who can see beyond the limits or succeed in breaking through. It is difficult to gain the capacity "of going beyond created structures" (to use the words of Maurice Merleau-Ponty) "in order to create others."[16] And yet, as Merleau-Ponty saw it, this capacity — like the power to choose and vary points of view — is what defines the human being. There are obstacles that inhere in the organization of the public schools, particularly if they are bureaucratically run and visibly hierarchical. There are obstacles raised by the pressures of parents and school boards, perhaps especially in suburban or middle-class communities. There are obstacles to be found in the emphasis on "competencies," in "accountability" arrangements, in the technological language so often spoken, in the ubiquity of testing and measurement.

The problem is that, confronted with structural and political pressures, many teachers (even effectual ones) cope by becoming merely efficient, by functioning compliantly — like Kafkaesque clerks. There are many who protect themselves by remaining basically uninvolved; there are many who are so bored, so lacking in expectancy, they no longer care. I doubt that many teachers deliberately choose to act as accomplices in a

---

15 John Dewey, *Theory of the Moral Life* (New York, Holt, Rinehart & Winston, 1960), p. 137.

16 Maurice Merleau-Ponty, *The Structure of Behavior* (Boston: Beacon Press, 1967), p. 175.

system they themselves understand to be inequitable; but feelings of powerlessness, coupled with indifference, may permit the so-called "hidden curriculum" to be communicated uncritically to students. Alienated teachers, out of touch with their own existential reality, may contribute to the distancing and even to the manipulating that presumably take place in many schools. This is because, estranged from themselves as they are, they may well treat whatever they imagine to be selfhood as a kind of commodity, a possession they carry within, impervious to organizational demand and impervious to control. Such people are not personally *present* to others or in the situations of their lives. They can, even without intending it, treat others as objects or things. This is because human beings who lack an awareness of their own personal reality (which is futuring, questing) cannot exist in a "we-relation" with other human beings. They cannot know what it means to live through a "vivid present in common" with another, to share another's "flux of experience in inner time."[17] Unable to come in touch with their own inner time, they cannot experience what Schutz called "the mutual tuning-in relationship, the experience of the 'We', which is at the foundation of all possible communication."[18] It appears to me that without the ability to enter a "mutual tuning-in relationship," the teacher is in some manner incapacitated; since teaching is, in so many of its dimensions, a mode of encounter, of communication. This is one of the several reasons why I am arguing the importance of a recovery of personal reality.

Dewey, it will be recalled, said that the self is "something that is in continuous formation through choice of action." This suggests that teachers lacking a sense of self are the kinds of people who sit back and affirm that they are defined, indeed identified by their roles. Dewey stressed *"continuous* formation" and meant that persons are forever in process, forever growing and reconstructing their experiences. They are forever in pursuit of themselves. To deny that is to deny possibility, to deny the power to risk and to choose. As Sartre has said, we cannot be obliged to be *what* we are; we must continue making ourselves what we might be. A teacher who has become his/her role resembles the café waiter Sartre has described, the man whose "movement is quick and studied, a little too precise, a little too rapid." He moves like a mechanism, as if "imitating the quickness and pitiless rapidity of things." It is as if he is performing a part, as if he is nothing *but* a café waiter (as an inkwell is

17   Alfred Schutz, "Making Music Together," in Collected Papers II, *Studies in Social Theory* (The Hague: Martinus Nijhoff, 1964), p. 173.
18   Ibid.

an inkwell, as a glass is a glass). He cannot transcend his role; he cannot imagine himself as anything *but* a café waiter; and so he is in bad faith. Sartre has given another example as well: "The attentive pupil who wishes to *be* attentive, his eyes riveted on the teacher, his ears open wide, so exhausts himself in playing the attentive role that he ends up by no longer hearing anything."[19] In all these cases, the individual person (teacher, café waiter, or attentive child) is refusing to confront the fact that it was his/her free choice to get up in the morning and go to the school or the café, and that it is he or she who confers meaning and value on the work being done, the role being played. The crucial point is that the individual, conscious of multiple possibilities, must be aware that he/she is choosing to wait on tables, to study, to teach, choosing each day that he/she lives.

The "choice of action" must be interested as well as reflective; if not, the teacher is likely to be bored, as well as without care. I think of characters in literature who are bored in this sense, who drift without commitment through their lives. There is Frederic Moreau, in Gustave Flaubert's *A Sentimental Education*, the young man who can never choose a coherent line of action, who can never feel involved. At the end of the novel, he is sitting with his friend, who has also failed to realize any of his hopes. Typically, they are looking backward rather than forward. "They had both failed, one to realize his dreams of love, the other to fulfil his dreams of power. What was the reason?"[20] They had dreamed; they had wandered; they had taken no responsibility. "Then they blamed chance, circumstances, the times into which they were born."[21] And that is another mode of bad faith, not unknown among teachers: the habit of blaming ineffectuality on the institution, on circumstances, and the times.

Another example, perhaps more fearful, is to be found in Toni Morrison's novel *Sula*. A vibrant, rebellious girl and woman, Sula is capable of watching from a distance when a child drowns, and when her mother burns to death. Also, she drifts around the cities of the country in pointless boredom, finding that all the cities "held the same people, working the same mouths, sweating the same sweat."[22] And then:

> In a way, her strangeness, her naivete, her craving for the other half of her equation was the consequence of an idle imagination. Had she

19 Jean-Paul Sartre, *Being and Nothingness* (New York: Philosophical Library, 1956), p. 60.
20 Gustave Flaubert, *A Sentimental Education* (New York: Penguin Books, 1976), p. 417.
21 Ibid., p. 418.
22 Toni Morrison, *Sula* (New York: Bantam Books, 1975), p. 104.

paints, or clay, or knew the discipline of the dance, or strings; had she anything to engage her tremendous curiosity and her gift for metaphor, she might have exchanged the restlessness and preoccupation with whim for an activity that provided her with all she yearned for. And like any artist with no art form, she became dangerous.[23]

This may be another way of talking about the necessity of a life project, of some purposeful work to do. It is also another way of suggesting the need for a medium or a meaningful activity if a self is to come into being, if a personal reality is to be achieved. A contrary example, one that dramatizes such an achievement, is Ralph Ellison's *Invisible Man*. At the end, when the narrator (having lived underground) is about to emerge and move back into the social world, he says:

> In going underground, I whipped it all except the mind, the *mind*. And the mind that has conceived a plan of living must never lose sight of the chaos against which that pattern was conceived. That goes for societies as well as individuals. Thus, having tried to give pattern to the chaos which lives within the pattern of your certainties, I must come out, I must emerge.[24]

He had given "pattern to the chaos" by taking the action of telling about it, writing about it, because he was unable to "file and forget." And, in the course of acting according to a "plan of living," he had attained a version of visibility; he had begun to create a self.

I would lay particular emphasis on choice. I believe that teachers willing to take the risk of coming in touch with themselves, of creating themselves, have to exist in a kind of tension; because it is always easier to fall back into indifference, into mere conformity, if not into bad faith. In Albert Camus's *The Plague*, Tarrou sees the sickness that has befallen the town of Oran to signify, among other things, abstractness and indifference. He tells Dr. Rieux that everyone has the plague within him, that "what's natural is the microbe." He goes on to explain:

> All the rest — health, integrity, purity (if you like) — is a product of the human will, of a vigilance that must never falter. The good man, the man who infects hardly anyone, is the man who has the fewest lapses of attention. And it needs tremendous will-power, a never ending tension of the mind, to avoid such lapses. Yes, Rieux, it's a wearying business, being plague-stricken. But it's still more wearying to refuse

23 Ibid., p. 105.
24 Ralph Ellison, *Invisible Man* (New York: Signet Books, 1952), p. 502.

to be it. That's why everybody in the world today looks so tired; everyone is more or less sick of plague.[25]

Self-awareness, self-discovery, self-actualization: These are often made to seem affairs of feeling, mainly, or of intuition. Teachers are asked to heighten their sensitivity, to tap the affective dimension of their lives, to trust, to love. Of course it is important to reach out, to feel, to experience love and concern. But I believe that, if teachers are truly to be present to themselves and to others, they need to exert effort in overcoming the weariness Camus described — a weariness all teachers, at some level, recognize. I believe that, for teachers as well as plague-fighters, "health, integrity, purity," and the rest must be consciously chosen. So must interest and good faith.

I have talked about the original interests that move persons to decide to take up teaching as a career. I have touched on the ways in which the demands of institutional situations make certain teachers set those interests aside. A lover of poetry, for instance, once eager to open the world of poetry to the young, may find it impossible to reconcile that desire (and that love) with the requirements of socialization and control. A person with an interest in physics or chemistry, hoping to inspire young apprentices, may find it too difficult to engage students with actual inquiries and at once maintain order in the classroom. The consequence may be a repression of the original enthusiasm and a resigned decision to have things the way they are "spozed to be."[26] Understandable though this is, the decision is evocative of the one Dewey had in mind when he spoke of people who give up in the face of discomfort or danger: Such teachers are declaring their preference to be teachers who choose to keep order and simply disseminate as many bits of knowledge as they can. This is quite different from the choice to create a situation in which knowledge can be sought and meanings pursued. It is quite different from the choice to institute the kind of dialogue that might move the young to pose their own worthwhile questions, to tell their own stories, to reach out in their being together to learn how to learn. And it may well be that the teachers who make such decisions are alienating themselves still more from what they think of as their personal reality.

For one thing, it is important to move back in inner time and attempt to recapture the ways in which the meanings of teaching

25 Albert Camus, *The Plague* (New York: Alfred A. Knopf, 1948), p. 229.
26 James Herndon, *The Way It Spozed to Be* (New York: Bantam Books, 1969).

(and schooling) were sedimented over the years. It should not be impossible for individual teachers to reflect back upon the ways in which they have constituted what they take to be the realities of their lived worlds. To look back, to remember is to bind the incidents of past experience, to create patterns in the stream of consciousness. We identify ourselves by means of memory; and, at once, we compose the stories of our lives. In Sartre's *Nausea,* Roquentin points out that "everything changes when you tell about life . . . ."[27] There are beginnings and endings; there are significiant moments; banal events are transformed. Hannah Arendt has written of the importance of "enacted stories" and the ways in which stories disclose a "who," an "agent; she has made the point that every individual life between birth and death can eventually be told as a story with beginning and end . . . ."[28]

Looking back, recapturing their stories, teachers can recover their own standpoints on the social world. Reminded of the importance of biographical situation and the ways in which it conditions perspective, they may be able to understand the provisional character of their knowing, of all knowing. They may come to see that, like other living beings, they could only discern profiles, aspects of the world. Making an effort to interpret the texts of their life stories, listening to others' stories in whatever "web of relationships"[29] they find themselves, they may be able to multiply the perspectives through which they look upon the realities of teaching; they may be able to choose themselves anew in the light of an expanded interest, an enriched sense of reality. Those who wished to become nurturant beings may (having entered new "provinces of meaning,"[30] looked from different vantage points) come to see that nurturing too can only be undertaken within social situations, and that the social situation in the school must be seen in relation to other situations lived by the young. Those who chose themselves as keepers of the academic disciplines may come to realize that the perspectives made possible by the disciplines are meaningful when they illuminate the experience of the learner, when they enable him or her to order the materials of his/her own lived world. Those who focused primarily on the social process may come to see that existing individuals, each in his/her own "here" and own "now," act in their intersubjectivity to bring the social reality into being, and that attention must be paid to the person in

27 Jean-Paul Sartre, *Nausea* (New York: New Directions Press, 1959), p. 16.

28 Hannah Arendt, *The Human Condition* (Chicago: University of Chicago Press, 1974), p. 184.

29 Ibid.

30 See Alfred Schutz, "On Multiple Realities," in *The Problem of Social Reality,* pp. 231f.

his/her uniqueness even as it is paid to the community. Seeing more, each one may be more likely to become "a network of relationships"[31] and perhaps be more likely to act in his or her achieved freedom to cut loose from anchorage and choose anew.

The diversification of perspectives has much to do, I think, with the sense of personal reality; but I would add that it is equally important for those engaged in seeking themselves to involve themselves in critique. By that I mean critical reflection upon the social situation, especially the situation they live in common. The dangers of submergence are multiple, as we have seen. Teachers suffer in many ways what they experience as conditioning or manipulation by their superiors or by the "system" itself. To reflect upon the situation, even the bureaucratic situation, is to try to understand some of the forces that frustrate their quests for themselves and their efforts to create themselves as the teachers they want to be. At once, it is to identify the kinds of lacks in that situation that require naming and repair: impersonality, for example; reliance on external criteria of "performance"; inequitable tracking; mindless routines. Coming together to determine what is possible, teachers may discover a determination to transcend.

I am suggesting that a concern for personal reality cannot be divorced from a concern for cooperative action within some sort of community. It is when teachers are together as persons, according to norms and principles they have freely chosen, that interest becomes intensified and commitments are made. And this may open pathways to expanded landscapes, richer ways of being human—unique and in the "we-relation" at one and the same time.

Hannah Arendt has told a story about some former members of the French Resistance who felt that they had "lost their treasure" when the war was over and they returned to ordinary life; and what she wrote seems to apply to teachers and their search for their personal reality.

What was this treasure? As they themselves understood it, it seems to have consisted . . . of two interconnected parts: they had discovered that he who "joined the Resistance, found himself," . . . that he no longer suspected himself of "insincerity," of being "a carping, suspicious actor of life," that he could afford to "go naked." In this nakedness, stripped of all masks—of those which society assigns to its members as well as those which the individual fabricates for himself in his psycho-

31   Maurice Merleau-Ponty, *Phenomenology of Perception* (New York: The Humanities Press, 1967), p. 456.

logical reactions against society—they had been visited . . . by an apparition of freedom, not, to be sure, because they acted against tyranny . . . but because they had become "challengers," and had taken the initiative upon themselves and therefore . . . had begun to create that public space between themselves where freedom could appear.[32]

I want to see teachers become challengers and take the initiative upon themselves. As they do so, as *we* do so, there will emerge a "public space" where personal reality can be at last affirmed.

32   Hannah Arendt, *Between Past and Future* (New York: Viking Press, 1961), p. 4.

Teacher Concerns as a Basis for Facilitating and Personalizing Staff Development

GENE E. HALL, SUSAN LOUCKS

R&D Center for Teacher Education, University of Texas, Austin

The chorus of conversations that follows staff-development workshops aptly defines the typical frustrations in change.

> Teacher: If I have to go to one more training session where they stick 100 of us in an auditorium and lecture about . . .

> Staff Developer: It seems that no matter what kinds of activities we design, we can't win.

> Teacher: I need some good ideas for what to do on Monday, not more theory.

> Staff Developer: I'm working with a school that's in the first year of a major change, and it seems they'll never get it together.

> Teacher: Well, it may be relevant, but it's not what I need!

> Staff Developer: Some teachers seem to give lip service to just about anything; but you never see it working in their classrooms.

> Teacher: I've really learned some things I can use with kids. When's the next session? I want to come back and . . .

The research described herein was conducted under contract with the National Institute of Education. The opinions expressed are those of the authors and do not necessarily reflect the position or policy of the National Institute of Education, and no endorsement by the National Institute of Education should be inferred.

Staff Developer: I've just completed the most fantastic in-service session. The teachers were all enthusiastically involved and can't wait to apply their ideas . . . I wonder what made the session so successful?

The swirl of pros and cons, complaints and praise, moans and musings, will make any listener's head spin. The greatest common denominator seems to be, however, that trainees and trainers alike are awash in a sea of complexities. Even success often appears to result more from a benevolent confluence than from guiding concepts.

Although some guiding concepts do exist, others that could be of real assistance to staff developers in designing and delivering relevant activities need to be developed. Staff developers must be able to meet the individual needs of teachers who face a wide variety of issues and problems. Diagnosing teacher needs and providing relevant staff-development activities is a major goal of the research on the change process that is being conducted at the Research and Development Center for Teacher Education at the University of Texas at Austin. Change aspects are constantly confronted with the technical problems of innovation adoption and the needs of individuals involved in the process. Although staff-development activities may not be targeted toward the adoption of a particular innovation,[1] both staff developers and change agents face the problem of matching interventions with client needs.

This article will describe an aspect of this research that promises to ease the problems of diagnosing group and individual needs during the adoption process. The conceptual structure we will be dealing with is called the Concerns-Based Adoption Model (CBAM), and we will examine one of its primary dimensions: the "concerns" expressed by individuals as they engage in the innovation-adoption process. This model can be truly effective in the planning and delivery of staff-development activities.

SOME BASIC ASSUMPTIONS ABOUT INNOVATION ADOPTION

The development of CBAM was based on extensive experience with educational innovation in school and college settings. The following assumptions were derived from that experience, and they establish the model's perspective on innovation adoption:

1. In educational institutions change is a *process*, not an event. Too

1 Note that for the purposes of discussion in this chapter, the term *innovation* will be used to encompass both process (e.g., team teaching) and product (e.g., a new reading text) changes.

often policymakers, administrators, and even teachers assume that change is the pivotal result of an administrative decision, legislative requirement, new curricular acquisition, or procedural revision. They casually assume that a teacher will put aside an old reading text and immediately apply an individualized program with great sophistication. Somehow the conviction lingers that with the opening of school under the new program the teachers will blend their talents into effective teams. As reflected in CBAM, the reality is that change takes time and is achieved only in stages.

2. The *individual* must be the primary target of interventions designed to facilitate change in the classroom. Other approaches to change (e.g., Organizational Development) view the composite institution as the primary unit of intervention, and place their emphasis upon improving communication and other organizational norms and behaviors. CBAM, however, emphasizes working with individual teachers and administrators in relation to their roles in the innovation process. CBAM rests on the conviction that institutions cannot change until the individuals within them change.

3. Change is a highly *personal* experience. Staff developers, administrators, and other change facilitators often attend closely to the trappings and technology of the innovation and ignore the perceptions and feelings of the people experiencing the change process. In CBAM, it is assumed not only that the change process has a personal dimension to it, but that the personal dimension is often of more critical importance to the success or failure of the change effort than is the technological dimension. Since change is brought about by individuals, their personal satisfactions, frustrations, concerns, motivations, and perceptions generally all play a part in determining the success or failure of a change initiative.

4. The change process is not an undifferentiated continuum. Individuals involved in change go through stages in their perceptions and feelings about the innovation, as well as in their skill and sophistication in using the innovation.

5. Staff development can best be facilitated for the individual by use of a *client-centered diagnostic/prescriptive model.* Too many in-service training activities address the needs of trainers rather than those of the trainees. To deliver relevant and supportive staff development, change facilitators need to diagnose the location of their clients in the change

process and to direct their interventions toward resolution of those diagnosed needs.

6. The staff developers or other change facilitators need to work in an adaptive, yet systemic way. They need to stay in constant touch with the progress of individuals within the larger context of the total organization that is supporting the change. They must constantly be able to assess and reassess the state of the change process and be able to adapt interventions to the latest diagnostic information. At the same time the facilitator must be aware of the "ripple effect" that change may have on other parts of the system.

To accomplish all this, a conceptual model of the change process must provide practical reference points on a constantly changing array of events. The Stages of Concern about the Innovation dimension of the Concerns-Based Adoption Model is proposed as one framework that staff developers can use to aid in diagnosing, planning, delivering, and assessing the effects of staff-development activities.

STAGES OF CONCERN ABOUT THE INNOVATION

The Concerns-Based Adoption Model[2] provides a structure that takes into account each of the assumptions about the innovation-adoption process. Three aspects of change form the basic frame of reference of the model: the concern that users express about the innovation, how the innovation is actually used, and the ways in which the innovation can be adapted to the needs and styles of particular individuals. This article focuses primarily on the first—the concerns of individuals about the innovation.

The power of the concerns dimension lies in the assumption that the process of change is a personal experience for each individual involved in it. Everyone approaching a change, initially implementing an innovation, or developing skill in using an innovation will have certain perceptions, feelings, motivations, frustrations, and satisfactions about the innovation and the change process.

In CBAM, the concept of "concerns" has been developed to describe these perceptions, feelings, and motivations. Research studies have initially verified a set of stages that people appear to move through when they are

---

2 G.E. Hall, R.C. Wallace, Jr., and W.A. Dossett, *A Developmental Conceptualization of the Adoption Process within Educational Institutions* (Austin, Tex.: Research and Development Center for Teacher Education, The University of Texas, 1973).

involved in innovation implementation. These Stages of Concern about the Innovation provide a key diagnostic tool for determining the content and delivery of staff-development activities.

The concept of concerns was first described by Frances Fuller. In her research, Fuller[3] identified a set of concerns preservice teachers expressed as they moved through their teacher education program. These concerns changed from initial concerns *unrelated* to teaching (I'm concerned about getting a ticket to the rock concert next Saturday night), to concerns about *self* in relation to teaching (I wonder if I can do it), to *task* concerns about teaching (I'm having to work all night to prepare my lesson plans for tomorrow), to *impact* concerns (are the kids learning what they need?). All together, Fuller identified six different levels of concern that preservice teachers expressed at different points in their teaching training programs.

As the concept of teacher concerns was being disseminated, it became apparent that the concept had similar application to individual teachers and college professors involved in implementing various educational innovations. Seven Stages of Concern about the Innovation were identified (see figure 1). Apparently a person's stages of concern move through the progression from self, to task, to impact that Fuller had described.

CONCERNS SUPPORTED BY RESEARCH DATA

Subsequent research with the concept of Stages of Concern (SoC) has focused on the development of a reliable and valid measurement procedure for assessing user concerns[4] and on a series of cross-sectional and longitudinal studies that have initially verified the existence of such stages.[5]

The data gathered in these studies flesh out the concept of concerns as it appears in the real world. An individual does not have concerns on only one stage at a time. There is a concerns "profile," with some stages being relatively more intense and other stages having lower intensity. In general, it appears that during implementation of an innovation, stages 0, 1, and 2 concerns will initially be most intense. As implementation begins, stage 3, Management concerns, becomes more intense, with stages

3   F.F. Fuller, "Concerns of Teachers: A Developmental Conceputalization," *American Educational Research Journal* 6, no. 2 (1969): 207-26.

4   G.E. Hall, A.A. George, and W.L. Rutherford, *Measuring Stages of Concern about the Innovation: A Manual for Use of the SoC Questionnaire* (Austin, Tex.: Research and Development Center for Teacher Education, The University of Texas, 1977).

5   G.E. Hall and W.L. Rutherford, "Concerns of Teachers about Implementing Team Teaching," *Educational Leadership* 34, no. 3 (December 1976): 227-33.

FIGURE 1

STAGES OF CONCERN ABOUT THE INNOVATION*

---

6   REFOCUSING: The focus is on exploration of more universal benefits from the innovation, including the possibility of major changes or replacement with a more powerful alternative. Individual has definite ideas about alternatives to the proposed or existing form of the innovation.

5   COLLABORATION: The focus is on coordination and cooperation with others regarding use of the innovation.

4   CONSEQUENCE: Attention focuses on impact of the innovation on student in his/her immediate sphere of influence. The focus is on relevance of the innovation for students, evaluation of student outcomes, including performance and competencies, and changes needed to increase student outcomes.

3   MANAGEMENT: Attention is focused on the processes and tasks of using the innovation and the best use of information and resources. Issues related to efficiency, organizing, managing, scheduling, and time demands are utmost.

2   PERSONAL: Individual is uncertain about the demands of the innovation, his/her inadequacy to meet those demands, and his/her role with the innovation. This includes analysis of his/her role in relation to the reward structure of the organization, decision making, and consideration of potential conflicts with existing structures or personal commitment. Financial or status implications of the program for self and colleagues may also be reflected.

1   INFORMATIONAL: A general awareness of the innovation and interest in learning more detail about it is indicated. The person seems to be unworried about himself/herself in relation to the innovation. She/he is interested in substantive aspects of the innovation in a selfless manner such as general characteristics, effects, and requirements for use.

0   AWARENESS: Little concern about or involvement with the innovation is indicated.

---

*Original concept from G.E. Hall, R.C. Wallace, Jr., & W.A. Dossett, *A Developmental Conceptualization of the Adoption Process within Educational Institutions* (Austin, Tex.: Research and Development Center for Teacher Education, The University of Texas, 1973).

0, 1, and 2 concerns decreasing in intensity. In time, the Impact concerns of stages 4, 5, and 6 become the most intense. As an implementation effort evolves, SoC profiles can be seen to change in a wave pattern (see figure 2).

ASSESSING STAGES OF CONCERN

The data for the research studies described above were collected using assessment instruments that had demonstrated a high degree of scientific validity, particularly the SoC Questionnaire form. While this instrument is extremely useful in practical applications, there are several alternative ways in which the staff developer can collect concerns data from the individuals involved in an ongoing innovation-adoption process.

FIGURE 2

Hypothesized Development of Stages of Concern

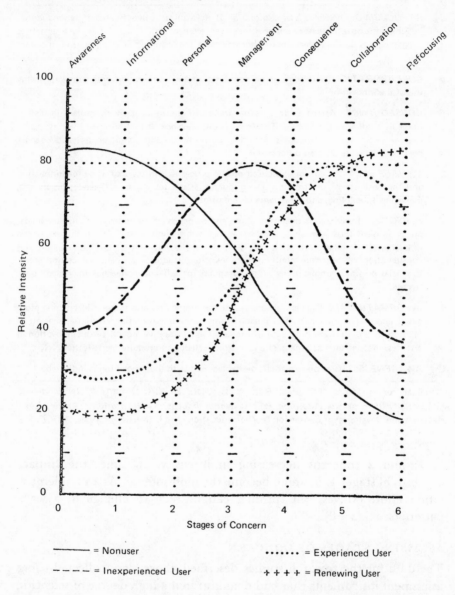

Conversational Assessment .The simplest is informal conversational assessment—in other words, talk about it. Ask leading questions, listen for clues in informal discussions, evaluate requests for input and support made by the innovation adopter. Experience has shown it is best not to ask directly what concerns the user or nonuser has, but to ask individuals to talk about what they are doing with the innovation *and* how they are using it. Also, questions about their perception of the innovation's strengths and weaknesses and what problems they are having typically elicit information about concerns. What conversational assessment lacks in scientific rigor, it makes up in ease of use and cost effectiveness. The method is also unobtrusive and does not readily solicit misleading information. This seat-of-the-pants assessment can be used to confirm or update more formal data and is most valuable to the experienced facilitator who wants to keep in "real-time" contact with the progress of an adoption process.

Open-ended Statement   More formally, an open-ended statement of concerns can be solicited by asking for a written response to the question: "When you think of [the innovation], what are you concerned about?" A manual[6] is available that gives instructions for administering and scoring this simple assessment device. Figure 3 provides an example of an open-ended statement and its scoring.

FIGURE 3

OPEN-ENDED STATEMENT OF CONCERNS (Sample)

WHEN YOU THINK ABOUT [*THE INNOVATION*], WHAT ARE YOU CONCERNED 'ABOUT? (Do not say what you think others are concerned about, but only what concerns you *now*.) Please write in complete sentences, and please be frank.

[Almost every night I wonder if I'll be able to locate and organize the material I will be using 3 the next day.] [I worry because I can't yet prevent surprises that cause a lot of wasted time.] 3 [I am not yet able to anticipate what things I will need to requisition for next week.] [Overall, 3 I'm concerned because I fell inefficient when I think about my use of the innovation.]   3 (2)

The open-ended response in figure 3 reflects statements made by an individual with Management (stage 3) concerns. This is reflected in complaints about time, efficiency, and planning. As are all open-ended responses, this paragraph is scored by considering each sentence, scoring it according to the definitions in figure 1, and then developing an overall picture of the paragraph. Care must be taken to consider the gestalt, the overall flavor of the responses (which often reflect more than one SoC) and not to focus purely on the numbers or arithmetical averages that result.

6   B.W. Newlove and G.E. Hall, "A Manual for Assessing Open-ended Statements of Concern about an Innovation" (Austin, Tex.: Research and Development Center for Teacher Education, The University of Texas, 1976).

The open-ended statement can be solicited any time new activities are being planned in an innovation-adoption process and can be used as a quick reference point to check the relevance of the activity. The change facilitator can easily flip through a batch of responses to get a feeling of the total group and to spot problem areas.

Stages-of-Concern Questionnaire The most formal and precise measure of Stages of Concern is the SoC Questionnaire.[7] The questionnaire consists of thirty-five items, each of which has a Likert scale (not true of me now . . . very true of me now) on which respondents indicate their present degree of concern about the topic described in the item. There are five items for each of the seven Stages of Concern. A sample item representing stage 5, Collaboration, is: "I would like to coordinate my efforts with others to maximize the innovation's effects."

The questionnaire takes about fifteen minutes to administer and can be scored either by hand, using percentile tables, or by computer. The questionnaire is psychometrically rigorous and reliable enough to provide both meaningful research data and information for planning change strategies. It is more efficient than the open-ended statement with large numbers of people, and provides more precise information on the basis of a larger quantity of data. More time is needed to process and interpret the responses, however, and the procedure costs more than the less formal measures.

SoC Questionnaire data can be interpreted in two ways. The first and simplest is by noting the stage that received the highest percentile score. This indicates the kinds of concerns that are most intense for the individual at that particular point in time. Assistance targeted at that particular concern may be warranted. A more complex interpretation of SoCQ data is possible by examining the "profile" of scores, that is, the percentile score for every stage for a respondent. The scores must be viewed as relative, with the highest and second-highest scores indicating areas of greatest concern and the lower scores as areas of least concern. Analysis of a concerns profile allows the staff developer to assess the relative value of alternative activities to the individual.

IMPLICATIONS OF CONCERNS FOR STAFF DEVELOPMENT

The data collected to date in research studies reveal a variety of implications that the concerns dimension can hold for the staff developer. First, it is clear from several samples with many innovations that nonusers of an innovation have their most intense concerns on stages 0, 1, and

---

7 Hall, George, and Rutherford, *Measuring Stages of Concern about the Innovation.*

2. They are most concerned about having general descriptive information about the innovation (stage 1) and the personal implications of the innovation (stage 2). Further, they are not as concerned, relatively speaking, about the impact of the innovation upon students (low intensity in stages 4, 5, and 6).

Analysis of SoC profiles suggests that staff-development activities for nonusers should address those initial informational needs and personal concerns, perhaps by representing general descriptive information about the innovation and by describing how the innovation will affect them personally. For instance, potential users should be told the time it will take and what they will have to give up if they are going to use the innovation. Additionally, their supervisor should show that it is important to him or her that the innovation be used. In dealing with nonusers, the staff developers might be well advised to downplay the consequences of the innovation for students. Nonusers are naturally somewhat concerned about the implications of an educational innovation for students but are *more* concerned about what the innovation means to them. Hence, the often-heard administrator's statement "You should do this because it's good for kids" does not address the concerns of the typical nonuser. Indeed, such admonitions may arouse Personal and Informational concerns in the nonuser instead of facilitating a positive resolution.

One sample of research findings is presented in figure 4. Figure 4 summarizes a cross-sectional sampling of 307 elementary school teachers in regard to the innovation, team teaching.

In these data, the "concerns profile" made by connecting the "0" points is again typical of what is found for nonusers of an innovation. Their most intense concerns are at stages 0, 1, and 2, and their least intense concerns are at stages 4, 5, and 6. First- through tenth-year users of teaming have their most intense concerns at the Management level, stage 3. Second-year teamers also had their most intense concerns at the Management level, as did third and fourth through tenth-year users of teaming.

In the innovation of teaming, Management concerns are apparently not resolved quickly. Clearly, these individuals need staff-development activities to resolve Management concerns. In the field sites where these data were collected, very little or no in-service support had been provided to the teachers implementing teaming. Thus, teachers were left on their own to "discover" how to organize and operate their teams more efficiently. Since teaming is a process innovation, it does not have clearly defined products that can simply be plugged in. Rather, users of teaming need to develop process skills, both as individuals and as teams. To accomplish

FIGURE 4

Distribution of Teachers' Concerns about Teaming according to Years of Experience with Teaming

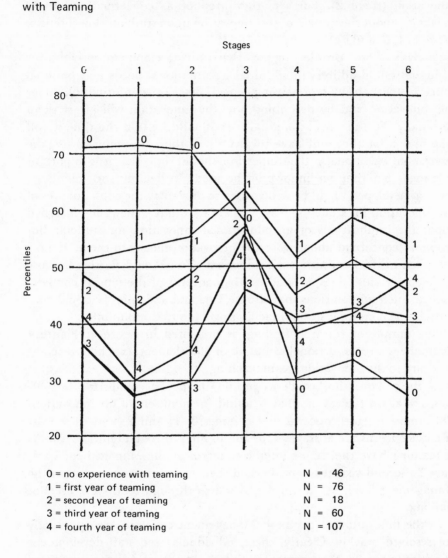

```
0 = no experience with teaming        N  =  46
1 = first year of teaming             N  =  76
2 = second year of teaming            N  =  18
3 = third year of teaming             N  =  60
4 = fourth year of teaming            N  = 107
```

this through the discovery approach or through on-the-job training would surely require an extended period of time. Not surprisingly, a great deal of time can be lost through inefficiencies. Comments such as "We never seem to get even simple decisions made" and "I have to do all my planning at night because our team planning time is consumed in administrative tasks" were frequently heard in the research sample cited above.

It may be that users of teaming with high Mangement concerns would benefit from an Organizational Development (OD) workshop on agenda setting, decision making, and other basic teaming or group-skills training.

Interestingly, such a workshop would likely provide too much detail for the nonuser, who wants general descriptive information and information about potential personal implications, not all the nitty-gritty detail that the Management-concerned user wants. In a concerns-based implementation, the OD workshop on agenda setting would not be provided to team teachers until their Management concerns were more intense than their Self concerns.

In looking at the sample data on team teaching, the diagnostic and prescriptive powers of the concerns concept become apparent. The staff developer who assesses individual concerns data relative to an innovation in the adoption pipeline possesses valuable information with which to plan relevant and effective staff-develoment activities. Guesswork is thus removed from the planning process. "Gut feelings" about training needs are replaced by a reliable yardstick of concerns. The SoC profiles provide both individual and group data that can be used in various ways: to plan interventions, to evaluate progress, and to spot individual problems. In the next section, an example of using a concerns-based implementation effort based on SoC data is presented.

AN EXAMPLE OF A CONCERNS-BASED IN-SERVICE TEACHER TRAINING PROGRAM

As an illustration of how the concept of Stages of Concern can be employed in a concerns-based staff-development program, we will discuss a concerns-based implementation study being conducted by the Texas R&D Center in a large suburban school district. The implementation study involves teachers in grades three through six of the approximately eighty elementary schools in the district. The innovation is a revision of the science curriculum. In the past, teachers have used the packaged science curricula that were nationally developed in the 1960s.

The revision of the science curricula has entailed development of a teacher's guide that incorporates specific activities from several of the packaged curricula (e.g., Elementary Science Study Units and Science Curriculum Improvement Study Units), as well as values clarification, outdoor education, environmental education, and health education. The materials have been combined into one large notebook referred to as the "teacher's guide." The teacher's guide was designed to address SoC 3 Management concern issues. The "how-to-do-its" of teaching are included, with information on where to locate the materials and organisms, how to order films, and what back-up references the teachers can locate.

The curriculum materials and the teacher's guide were developed and field-tested within the school system. After the staff developers and the science consultants for the school system had completed field testing, and as they were designing plans for implementation of the science curriculum throughout the eighty elementary schools, the Texas R&D Center became involved.

Initially, the plan was to use three released-time in-service days placed fairly close together early in the fall of the school year. The planned in-service activities were well designed and included the kinds of activities that science education has emphasized in the last ten years. The plans included having teachers participate in student activities, introducing them to the materials and the science content, and having them experience the science units. Model lessons and direct handling of materials as a part of the teacher in-service activities were planned; experienced teachers would be in-service leaders during the training period. In general, the plan was consistent with a concerns-based approach. However, as our collaborative effort developed, the school district's plan was adjusted with regard to Stages of Concern and other data collected within the school system.

Influenced by the idea of a concerns-based implementation, the first change in the plan was to extend the time between each of the released-time in-service days. In fact, rather than completing the in-service training before the school year started or within a six- to nine-week period, the in-service workshops were distributed over one and one-half school years. This was done because the teachers' concerns would not develop within six weeks from high Informational and Personal concerns to high-intensity Impact concerns. Rather, at least one or two cycles of use are required to resolve Management concerns and to move toward Impact concerns. By a broad distribution of the in-service training days, more concerns could be addressed.

A second decision, made early in the collaborative effort, was to clarify the goal of the implementation effort. The school system had a choice: to design interventions striving either for a portion of the teachers to teach science at a high level of quality (Impact concerns) or for all teachers simply to teach science using the new materials. It was not possible for both goals to be accomplished with the same staff-development plan, as the content of the staff development would be quite different for

FIGURE 5

Science Study SoC Profiles before In-Service

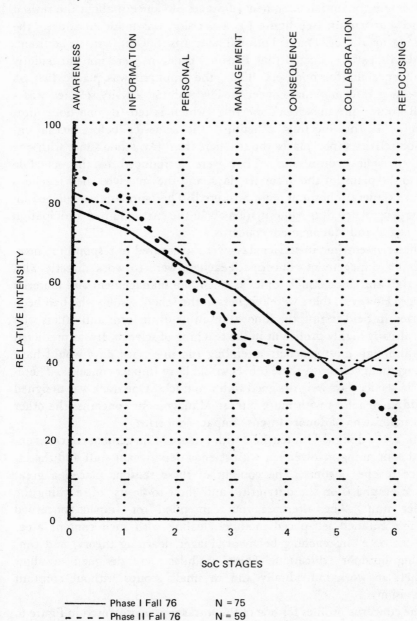

Phase I Fall 76   N = 75
Phase II Fall 76   N = 59
Phase III Fall 76   N = 69

different objectives. The school system's decision was to have "all kids receiving science instruction."

Based on the initial assessment of Stages of Concern about the revised science curriculum (see figure 5), a decision was made to address the Informational (SoC 1) and Personal concerns (SoC 2) first. In addition, the data clearly indicated that Personal concerns were not particularly high, especially for nonusers. Thus, the emphasis was placed first on addressing Informational concerns. The training activity selected was a small group "pre-in-service" meeting (which lasted for one hour after school). At this meeting, scheduled the semester before actual in-service activities took place, the teachers from two schools met with one of the science consultants. They were introduced to the schedule and to the plans for the in-service days, and they received their teacher's guides. General questions were answered. The emphasis was placed on giving general descriptive information about the curriculum in anticipation of Personal and Management concerns.

The released-time in-service days were structured to respond to "how-to-do-it" Management concerns. Teachers were to work directly with materials and discuss such topics as classroom management and material storage. However, there were teachers in the school system who had been involved in field testing the innovation in its draft form and others who were already highly proficient in the teaching of science. It was predicted that although most teachers attending the in-service days would have Management concerns, these others would have Impact concerns. Therefore, in-service days were designed with two tracks. One track was designed to address teachers with more intense Management concerns; the other for teachers who had more Intense Impact concerns.

The route designed for teachers with intense Management concerns entailed continuing involvement with science department staff and the in-service teacher leaders. The content of these sessions placed a great deal of emphasis on the nitty-gritty and "how-to-do-its" of teaching the science units. The alternate route intended for Impact-concerned teachers entailed self-paced modules dealing with such content areas as "wait time" in teaching behavior, Piaget, learning theory, and conducting outdoor education. These modules were designed to allow teachers to work individually and in small groups without constant supervision.

The concerns profiles for one of the workshops is presented in figure 6. As predicted, those teachers with higher Personal and Management concerns (SoC 2 and 3) stayed in the large group with the face-to-face

FIGURE 6

Phase I Grade 3

Worked with Modules   N = 23
Worked in Group Session   N = 18

contact and the how-to-do-it content. Those teachers who had lower Personal and Management concerns chose instead to move with the more independent, Impact-content, modular route.

The initial implementation of the concerns concept provided staff developers with an overall schema and with diagnostic data for planning further staff-development activities. The teacher's guide was sound and the training activities (which were planned initially) were worthwhile. The trick was to get these elements together with the teachers at the right time. The key to the timing was an assessment of the state of the change process using the SoC Questionnaire.

SUMMARY

The Concerns-Based Adoption Model remains the subject of a great deal of research and refinement. Manuals exist for use of instruments that measure its important dimensions, such as the SoC Questionnaire. Other materials are under development that will define more precise uses of the model for diagnosis and prescription in the process of innovation adoption. In the meantime, however, the base concept of concerns is a valuable tool available to anyone who wants to critically examine a particular staff-development situation and plan concerns-based staff-development activities. Much can be done with the Stages of Concern data and a little common sense.

In conclusion, we will summarize a few key principles that have been suggested by research with the Concerns-Based Adoption Model. These are, in many ways, brief summaries of what has been discussed above, but they will add further perspective on concerns-based staff development.

1. *Be sure to attend to the teachers' concerns as well as to the innovation's technology.*

There is an affective, or personal, side to change. Too often change facilitators and teacher educators become all-involved in the technology of the innovation and neglect to attend to the persons that are involved.

2. *It is all right to have personal concerns.*

Personal concerns are a very real part of the change process and they need to be acknowledged and recognized as legitimate. It is the responsibility of the change facilitators to attend to these early concerns, or the individual is not apt to be able to resolve these and move on to Impact concerns.

3. *Do not expect change to be accomplished overnight.*

Because change is a process, entailing developmental growth and learning, it will take time. Managers of the change process and other designers of staff-development activities need to acknowledge and anticipate that change is a process and, in response, they need to adjust their training activities accordingly. One-shot workshops will not implement a program; long-term follow-up is necessary. Policy and decision makers must also become aware of this fact, and, in response, stop assuming that their decrees and mandates will result in instantaneous cures out in the field.

4. *Teachers' concerns may not be the same as those of the staff developers.*

Staff developers probably hold their positions because they have Impact concerns. However, it does not necessarily follow that their clients (teachers) will have Impact concerns about staff-development activities. This difference will certainly be evident at the beginning of a change effort. Staff developers need to design and deliver their activities so that the concerns of the teachers are addressed, not their own concerns. Resolution of early concerns will allow teachers to develop the Impact concerns that most interest staff developers.

5. *Within any group there is a variety of concerns.*

Once people buy into the idea of concerns, a new dilemma appears. As with any group, groups of teachers are never at the same place at the same time. Rather, individuals with different kinds of concerns will be present. Therefore, the traditional, cost-effective format of providing common staff-development activities for all teachers is no longer acceptable. The problem becomes: how to individualize and personalize staff development in such a way that each teacher's concerns are spoken to, while attending to the fact that staff-development budgets and staff time have definite limits. Using small homogeneous groups, designing options within a staff-development session, and providing school-based programs all have potential for solving this dilemma.

Clearly, there is a need for creative, unique approaches to concerns-based staff development. And, this need presents a challenge to all sensitive, responsive staff developers. Up-front cost may seem higher, but the promise of efficient planning and accurately presented activities will represent a significant savings in the end. Furthermore, the satisfaction of contributing significantly to the professional development of individual teachers, which will ultimately result in higher quality learning for children, is what all staff developers strive for. The concept of concerns is offered as one tool for use in achieving our common goal — effective education.

The Social Realities of Teaching

ANN LIEBERMAN
Teachers College, Columbia University

LYNNE MILLER
University of Massachusetts, Amherst

We approach this article as field workers in schools for many years. Our vantage point is that of teachers on the elementary and secondary levels and participant-observers in many of the improvement projects of the 1960s and 1970s. We speak, recognizing both that we know a great deal about teachers and their world and that there is a great deal more to know. As practitioners, we are impatient with the gap that exists between knowledge and action. As researchers and theoreticians, we recognize the need to take time to synthesize current knowledge and to produce new knowledge that may guide and inform practice. Our intention here is to make meaning from "the field," that is from available conceptions, research, and experiences — however tentative — and to develop an understanding of the social reality of teaching from a teacher's perspective. Such an understanding, we believe, is a necessary precondition for addressing the conditions of schooling and improving schools through staff-development activities.

Our article is divided into three sections. The first two sections develop an understanding of the social realities of teaching. We begin with a review of our knowledge about teaching as a profession, presented in the form of social system understandings about teaching. We then describe the *dailiness* of teaching as an activity based on our own experiences and on the reportage of teachers with whom we have worked in schools.

In our final section, we use the understanding developed from the previous sections as the basis for drawing implications for the theory and practice of staff-development and school-improvement efforts.

THE NATURE OF TEACHING

We now have a fairly large group of people who have studied teachers as they live and work in schools and can talk about a set of phenomena we label "social system understandings." These understandings serve as a basis for discussing certain generalizations about the way the teacher learns the job and becomes a teacher. Drawing on the literature and reflection on our own experiences, we have formulated such understandings.

STYLE IS PERSONALIZED

In 1932 Willard Waller[1] wrote about the social world of teachers. His central insight has been documented by many. Teachers are faced with a major contradiction in their work life. The teacher must do something to the child—that is, teach him/her something. But at the same time, the teacher must make friends with the student. The teacher must control the environment, but also motivate, arouse interest, and find ways of engaging the student. This essential contradiction is what forms the basic context of the teacher's behavior in the classroom. In order to deal with this contradiction, teachers develop all kinds of strategies. Some quickly find a repertoire that works. But "style" is basically formed by trial and error and, as such, becomes highly personalized.[2]

REWARDS ARE DERIVED FROM STUDENTS

Most teachers learn their craft in isolation from other adults. Rewards come from the children, *not* from sharing, discussing, and reflecting on the nature of the work.[3] Dialogue about student and teacher learning styles, problems, alternate methodologies, and appropriateness is usually not a part of the school structure. Feedback, so essential to all people, comes from one source—the student. It is not difficult to see why teachers then become wary of new schemes, innovations, new packages, or even honest exhortations to do things differently.

TEACHING AND LEARNING LINKS ARE UNCERTAIN

The entire socialization of teachers is fraught with "endemic uncertainties."[4] High expectations are held for teachers that are often unrelated to the actual difficulties involved in teaching. Teachers often work without knowing that what they are doing will have the planned effects.

1　Willard Waller, *The Sociology of Teaching* (New York: John Wiley, 1952).
2　David Lortie, *School Teacher* (Chicago: University of Chicago Press, 1975).
3　Philip Jackson, *Life in Classrooms* (New York: Holt, Rinehart & Winston, 1968).
4　Lortie, *School Teacher*.

This is so in spite of plans, rational schemes, objectives, learning activities. One hopes that the children will get it — but one is never sure.

THE KNOWLEDGE BASE IS WEAK

It has been said that the profession of teaching has a weak knowledge base. For years teachers have complained about the irrelevance of their courses to the actual day-to-day work of teaching. We have not, as yet, been able to codify teaching under a variety of contingencies. This is not to suggest that many teachers don't continually take courses, in-service workshops, and so forth. Anyone who has ever taught knows that teachers constantly look for new ideas, new materials, new ways of reaching the students. This, in spite of the weak knowledge base.

TEACHING IS AN ART

Teaching is an art — in spite of recent efforts to scientize it. Some parts lend themselves to programming and rationalized efforts, but in the long haul much artistry is practiced as teachers struggle to adjust, readjust, or become routinized in an effort to deal with the ambiguous connection between what is taught and what is learned. This uncertainty complicates the work of teaching as it becomes for most a daily struggle to control the intangibles.

GOALS ARE VAGUE

There is currently much talk about goal specificity because of pronounced efforts at holding schools accountable for what they teach. Goals for schools are vague and often conflict. (Individualize and teach everyone in class.) And it is well known that many teachers are left to their own devices to somehow translate what these goals mean to themselves and their specific classes or subjects.

CONTROL NORMS ARE NECESSARY

Smith's[5] and McPherson's[6] ethnographies illustrate dramatically the teacher's day-to-day assault on gaining some sense of direction, control, and movement for the class. The teacher works hard to develop a set of norms in the classroom that both teacher and student can live with. This happens as the teacher moves through a cycle of giving orders, threatening, being tested by the students (Do you really mean it?), and finally

5 Louis Smith and William Geoffrey, *Complexities of an Urban Classroom* (New York: Holt, Rinehart & Winston, 1968).

6 Gertrude McPherson, *Small Town Teacher* (Cambridge: Harvard University Press, 1972).

working toward some standards that help move the class along. While this is proceeding, school-wide norms also affect teacher behavior. Some certainties appear to be necessary to deal with all the other ambiguities that make up the teacher's world. The establishment of control norms satisfies this need for certainty. So, such norms as "quiet classrooms mean good classrooms," and "teachers have to be tough at the beginning of the semester," and "don't try anything too far out" help maintain some order in an otherwise uncertain, shaky existence.

PROFESSIONAL SUPPORT IS LACKING

Many people have compared teaching as a profession to law, medicine, and even architecture. The one constant is the fact that for the other professions, the neophyte, along with learning the ways of being of his/her profession, also learns it with others. The shared ordeal or joy is buttressed by a peer group, a support system, and in many cases lifelong friendships. A strong sense of professional culture grows up as a result of moving from knowledge to shared experiences. This is not to say that all the professions don't share the huge gap between their schooling and the actual work of the profession. We all share this jolt. But teachers, unlike the other professions, move quickly from courses to being on their own, to struggling with the ambiguities alone. Apprenticeships are rare. Peer support groups are almost nonexistent (with the exception of team approaches and some recent personalized approaches to teaching). This leaves teachers with degree in hand, expectations that are high, and a fistful of methodologies, and few adults to share with, to learn from, and to grow with. Isolation best describes the teachers' work environment.

THE DAILINESS OF TEACHING

Our understanding of teaching as a profession has been deepened by our work in the field. This work has given us a perspective on the *dailiness* of teaching that adds to our knowledge about the nature of teaching. In describing the work life of the public school teacher, we rely on the notions of rhythms, rules, interactions, and feelings as our organizing frameworks.

RHYTHMS

Life in schools is marked by a rhythm of days, weeks, and months that are regular from year to year. The school day begins early, earlier than that of most other professions, and ends well before the rush hour of the rest of the adult labor force. For at least six hours a day, every day of the week, teachers are in a school building, that is, they are in a totally regulated and totally exclusive environment. For most of their day, they are time and space bound. In most elementary schools, teachers spend all day in one classroom with one group of students. On the secondary level, teachers often spend most of their time in one room with different groups of students. Free periods and lunch hours are usually spent within the school building, often with children. In a large number of schools, teachers need to sign out and have special permission to leave the school building during the school day.

In the course of the day, teachers' energy levels vary, but their formal task does not. Most secondary teachers consider the first and last classes of the day to be less effective for them and their students than the classes in the middle of the day and adjust expectations accordingly. Elementary school teachers learn to adapt the activities of the day to the pulse of their students and themselves. The school day is characterized by interruptions; announcements over loudspeaker systems often stop a teacher in mid-sentence. Requests for students to report to the office and various school activities continually disrupt the continuity of instruction in class. In addition, teachers spend a large part of their time involved in non-instructional activities—taking rolls, filling out forms, completing paper-work duties that are more clerical than professional.

The rhythm of days is embedded within the rhythm of the weeks. Monday is always a difficult day, as is Friday. The midweek is the optimal time for concentrated efforts toward teaching. Teachers accommodate this rhythm through their scheduling of activities. Mondays are often review days; Fridays are traditionally test days. In many urban systems, teachers will secretly admit that the school week has only three days and plan their lessons accordingly.

A rhythm of the months is also discernible, with high-energy teaching in the fall, tapering off to a steady and weary pace in the winter, and gaining momentum again in the early spring. "I always think of changing professions in February,"[7] says one teacher, naming the reality for many. The end of the school year is marked with the rituals of report cards, promotions, and graduation. Then, at an arbitrary date in June, the teachers and students part ways for two full months. The routines and adaptations that have taken form over ten months suddenly stop, to be created again in the early fall.

RULES

Like all formal organizations, schools are governed by rules—some

---

7 From field notes 1977/1978. All other quotes from teachers are from field notes and interviews 1977/1978, unless otherwise indicated.

formal and some informal. The informal rules that govern teacher behavior in schools are many. For our purposes, we concentrate on two of them: being practical and being private.

Being Practical[8]   Being practical can be best understood in terms of its opposites. Being practical is the opposite of being theoretical, and it is the opposite of being idealistic. Being theoretical is a mode of being that is associated with university courses and with university professors:

> Education courses in and of themselves are quite theoretical. To be sure, they are helpful as far as background material goes, but there is no substitute for actual *practical* experience. . . . My three-year stint of duty as a housemaster and teacher at a private school gave me a great deal of *practical* experience in learning more about young people and how to handle young people.[9]

The criterion for an idea's practicality is that it considers the circumstances of the school and that it can work immediately in a classroom. Practical school people are people who are or have recently been teachers. Practical school problems are problems of discipline, order, and achievement. Practical solutions require little additional preparation or work, are immediate and concrete, and can be effected with the resources and structures that presently exist. "No teacher ever does what she thinks is best. We do the best we can in the circumstances. What you think is a good idea from the outside turns out to be impossible in the classroom."[10] To be practical is to concentrate on products and not processes, to draw on experience and not on research, to be short-range and not long-range in thinking and planning.

Practicality as an opposite to idealism places a value on learning to adjust expectations to the present realities. Idealism is a quality that is identified with youth; it does not wear well in the adult "real world." New teachers are initiated into this ethic during their first year of teaching as they learn their "place" in the school organization, learn to keep quiet when private principles are violated by public practice in the school and to be politic about what they say and when they say it. To be practical in this sense is to accept the school as it is and to adapt. The striving to change the "system" is idealistic; the striving to "make do" is practical.

8   For a more extensive analysis see Walter Doyle and Gerald A. Ponder, "The Practicality Ethic in Teacher Decision Making," *Interchange* 8, no. 3 (1977-1978): 1.

9   Dan C. Lortie, "Teacher Socialization: The Robinson Crusoe Model," in *The Real World of the Classroom Teacher*, Report of the 1965 National TEPS Conference (Washington, D.C.: National Education Association, 1965).

10   McPherson, *Small Town Teacher*, p. 197.

The concern for the well-being and optimum learning of every student is idealistic; the acceptance of limitations on some students' potential is practical. The process of reflective self-criticism is idealistic; the expressed belief that "I do the best I can. It's the kids that don't try" is practical. Being open to change and to outsiders offering services is idealistic; being self-sufficient is practical. In essence, the value placed on practicality is a value placed on resistance to change and to expanding the possibilities of teaching.

Being Private The practicality ethic is linked to the privacy ethic; it is practical to be private about teaching. Being private means that teachers do not share experiences about their teaching, their classes, their students, or their perceptions of their roles with anyone inside the school building.

> I don't know what it's like in business or industry. It may be the same. I don't know how friendly co-workers are, how honest they are. It just seems that in teaching, teachers really are unwilling to be honest with one another, I think, to confide with each other about professional things and personal things. This gets worse on the high school level. I think they really see their role—I don't know—like their professors. You do your thing in your class and you leave and you don't talk to anyone about it.

> I don't know of anyone who talks about his teaching. There are always jokes, like he's the "Media Man" or he's the "handout man." But never serious conversation. Nobody really talks about his teaching.

When asked with whom he shared his teaching, this respondent paused and simply stated, "My wife."

By following the rule and being private, teachers forfeit the opportunity to display their successes, and they reserve the right to conceal their failures. To insure privacy, teachers rarely invite their peers into their classes and rarely visit others. Observation is equated with evaluation, and evaluation risks exposure. So, "it is safer to be private. There is some safety in the tradition, even if it keeps you lonely."

INTERACTIONS

Teachers interact with a variety of people in the course of a day. For our purposes, we concentrate on specific aspects of their interactions with (1) each other, (2) students, and (3) the principal. This discussion is, by necessity, brief and selective. It highlights the boundaries and content of what we consider among the most interesting and least studied of teacher interactions.

Teacher-Teacher Interactions As indicated previously, teacher interactions are far from open. Teachers choose to talk about nonschool themes with other teachers. They prefer to keep their distance as a way of preserving their autonomy in the classroom. They do not work collectively, even when there are strong unions. "It pays to be separate. We learn that in our isolation, we have strength. And from that comes a sense of peace."

We may characterize the daily teacher-teacher interactions that do exist as being of two types: *jousting* or *griping*. In jousting, teachers take a break from the demands of the classroom and engage in good-natured kidding, often making each other the butt of the jokes. When a serious question is raised, the initiator is good-naturedly dissuaded from continuing. In this way, serious conversation about professional concerns is transformed into modes of interaction that are more acceptable. "We need a 'time out' from the kids and classes and teaching. We need time to recharge for the next assault. We don't want to talk about anything serious. We want to take a break, kibitz, and then go back to our job."

Through griping, teachers find an avenue for the expression of negative feelings about their work in a safe and accepted form. The "gripe session" becomes an important structure in the teacher's life.

It doesn't matter what the issue is, and a lot of the time, it's a fake issue. It might be some bulletin the principal sent out. It can be most anything. It's something we can find unanimity in. We can all agree "that's BAD," and somehow that makes us good. It's something we can all agree on. And you feel better. It's never very serious, and it's never any thing you can do anything about.

Griping allows for the expression of anger with a time restraint on analysis and action. The gripe session serves as a ritual that builds group identity and is the way that teachers make themselves feel less alone and isolated.

Teacher-Student Interactions For teachers, relationships with students are primary. They spend most of their working day with students and, as stated earlier, receive almost all of their rewards from this audience. In talking with and observing teachers in their classes, we are always struck by how much importance teachers place on their relationship with their students. The relationship that is most gratifying to teachers seems to be personal rather than instructional. For many teachers, the personal interactions are not viewed as "professional."

I feel like I'm a role model for the kids. I mean, I'm not sure that's part of my job, not professional, you know? I mean, it's got nothing to do with teaching math, and that's what I'm being paid to do. But if I couldn't do that, then I wouldn't be much of a math teacher.

But professional or not, being a role model is a powerful position and one that demands a great deal of a teacher's attention.

> When you realize what you say in the classroom — even though you think the kid isn't listening — has an effect on a kid, you're kind of a role model — even though you might not think you're a role model. It's something I think about a lot. The kids take what you say and think about it, and they make decisions based on what you say. You have the influence because of your personality. When I stop to think about it, it's scary . . . but it makes me feel good. It's a big responsibility.

For some teachers, the role-modeling function is of primary importance and defines their role as teacher.

> If someone told me that my job was just to teach kids Business, I would quit. I couldn't stand to see myself as someone who teaches skills and nothing else. I have to feel that I'm doing more than that — something more lasting.

Whatever the degree of consciousness about the role modeling that characterizes the teacher-student interaction, it remains an important aspect of being a teacher. Unfortunately, it is an aspect of teaching that is continually underplayed in the professional literature and is seldom publicly acknowledged in the life of the school.

Teacher-Principal Interactions While we have written a great deal about the autonomy and isolation of the teacher, we do not believe that the teacher is unaffected by the issues of leadership and administration in the school. Teachers, too, are quick to acknowledge the importance of the principal in their daily activity. Although face-to-face interactions with the principal are not always common — especially in large urban high schools — the relationship of teacher to principal is of paramount importance. The principal has the power to make the teacher's work life pleasant or unbearable; that is quite a bit of power. A principal who makes teaching pleasant is one who trusts his/her staff to perform their tasks as classroom teachers, who observes classes only when formal evaluations are due. He/she is a principal who deals with parents and community in a way that supports the teacher's decisions and safeguards against personal attacks.

Teachers avoid "getting on the bad side of the principal"; such a positioning can make life unbearable. The principal has the power to make extra duty assignments, to criticize classroom practices and procedures, to assign class rosters. More importantly, on an informal level, being disliked by the principal has its psychological disadvantages.

If I see him in the hall and he doesn't smile or look at me, I'm upset all day. What did I do wrong? Why doesn't he like me? Will he listen to me if there's a problem? I know it shouldn't affect me, but it does.

When a teacher views a principal as critical and punishing, he/she is less likely to take risks and try new things in his/her classes. When a teacher views a principal as supportive and rewarding, he/she is more able to approach the principal for assistance in trying new things, in securing new resources, in gaining permission for special events. The relationship of the teacher to the principal is one of gaining privilege, and the privilege is arbitrarily in the hands of the principal. This is especially true for teachers who aspire to administrative levels themselves. The principal's recommendation about the potentials of his/her teachers is taken seriously. While many teachers profess they avoid or surmount the principal and learn to get around him/her, the importance of the office is never unacknowledged in the daily life of the school.

FEELINGS

Since teaching is so private a profession, it is often difficult to uncover teachers' genuine feelings about their role. We have found that, when gently pushed, teachers will talk about feelings of ambivalence, conflict, and frustration in the day-to-day activities of their work.

Feelings about Always Being with Children   Teachers are ambivalent about the fact that they are always with children and that they turn to their students as their only source of rewards. We have noted previously how we are struck by most teachers' feelings of genuine satisfaction in their interactions with children, especially as role models. The other side of those feelings is also quite powerful, and it most often comes to light in the company of other adults outside of teaching.

I had a disagreement with my mother-in-law the other day. I don't remember what it was about—taxes or something that's being voted on. Everytime I started to talk, she'd disagree and then tell me that I didn't live in the real world, that I spent all of my time with kids and that I just didn't know enough about business and other things.

I felt very angry. That kind of thing happens now and again. I feel that I do live in the real world, but people who don't teach don't think that's true.

To the rest of the adult world, teachers often seem to be living in a child's reality and are viewed as not being able to function as adults. This perception leaves teachers uneasy at best, defensive at worst, and ambivalent about their roles and their constant relationship with young people.

Feelings about One's Confidence   Teachers are in conflict about their own value as good teachers. The lack of peer support and adult interaction makes it difficult for the teacher to develop a clear sense of the quality of his/her teaching. Teaching is left to be evaluated by the students, who are neither direct nor accepted as trustworthy. Because of this, teachers deeply feel a lack of confidence inside and outside of the classroom.

> It took me ten years to feel that I was a good teacher. In fact, I would always try very hard not to miss a day of school. I thought that if I missed and a substitute came in and taught my classes that all of the students would find out how bad I was and how good someone else could be.

Lack of confidence, then, is linked to feelings of vulnerability, of being "found out." These feelings are exacerbated by the privacy ethic that dominates the school. The teacher has no "safe place" to air his/her uncertainties and to get the kind of feedback that will reduce the anxiety centered around being a good, or at least adequate, professional.

Feelings about Control   Teachers are frustrated about the quantity and quality of control they have—or don't have—in a school. Control is territorial; it exists for teachers in the classroom but not in the larger organization of the school.

> When I'm in my classroom, I know I'm in control. I can teach the way I want to teach, do what I want to do.

But even in the classroom, the teacher's control is tenuous. It depends on a mutual adaptation between teacher and students. When a teacher loses control of a class, he/she subordinates all teaching activities to the reestablishment of order and control. Keeping a class under control is the only visible indication that one is, in fact, a good teacher; losing control means the loss of one's professional role.

Once outside of the classroom, all of the teacher's control disappears. Within the formal organization of the school, the teacher has little authority in making decisions that control his/her environment. The teacher, then, is always moving from a level of almost complete and always necessary control to a level of powerlessness. This being at once in-and-out-of-control leads to feelings of frustration in regard to trying to effect change outside of the classroom as well as to feelings of "resignation to the way things are and will always be."

IMPLICATION FOR STAFF DEVELOPMENT/ SCHOOL IMPROVEMENT

We strongly believe that any staff-development/school-improvement effort has to be grounded in the social realities of teaching. In the previous two sections, we have presented our accounting of what these realities entail. In this final section, we develop a framework for utilizing these understandings in staff-development/school-improvement programs. Central to our discussion are the issues of order and legitimation. That is, we accept that in schools as in other organizations "an order which enjoys the prestige of being considered binding, or as it may be expressed, of 'legitimacy' "[11] is most stable and most effective in effecting desired changes. It is essential, then, that teachers and all of those who work with teachers build such a legitimate order in their enterprises, that the forms and approaches that are used in staff-development efforts recognize the authority of all of the actors and draw on those authorities in the design, implementation, and daily activities of the projects.

Again, looking to the "field," we can make some general statements about how staff-development/school-improvement efforts can be legitimated. We draw on the growing number of investigations that focus on issues of legitimation in school-improvement efforts for our recommendations.

ADOPTING A PUBLIC RELATIONS FACADE

Sussmann,[12] in her description of three elementary schools attempting innovations, describes how innovators, much like salespeople, become advocates of their ideas. They do this because they must come to believe in what they sell and they must also evoke enthusiasm from the teachers. This is not meant in a pejorative sense. Rather, the need to engage in public relations derives from acknowledgement of the weak knowledge base of teaching, the personal style forged in isolation, and the practicality ethic that inhibits innovative behavior. Therefore, one must be

11 Max Weber, *The Theory of Social and Economic Organization* (New York: Free Press, 1947), p. 125.

12 Leila Sussmann, *Tales Out of School: Implementing Organizational Change in the Elementary Grades* (Philadelpia: Temple University Press, 1977).

energetic, enthusiastic, and a salesperson to engage teaching staff in a new enterprise. The public relations facade is a precarious one, however. At its most extreme, the facade makes an interventionist appear to be a "true believer,"[13] so zealous about an innovation that she/he neglects the reality of schools and loses credibility and legitimacy.

TAKING A REACTIVE STANCE

Related to the public relations facade is the notion of the reactive stance, or what has been called "a non-model" for change.[14] Although interventionists become representatives or salespeople of a cluster of ideas about school improvement, activities related to these ideas must be tempered by a more reactive stance that considers starting from where the people are — not where we would like them to be.

This stance of responding to where the people are in their understanding of themselves as teachers, their own histories, and their particular social settings considers the way teachers come to learn their jobs as personalized responses to practical and immediate concerns and also considers the fact that we have no really clear conceptions of what is better. What we do have is a professional commitment to struggle together to find more effective ways of working. This is a value position that must be mated to an understanding of the complex work of teachers.

GETTING PERSONALLY INVOLVED IN IMPLEMENTATION

Recent studies[15] are documenting in different ways the same pattern of implementing progressive change in schools. These studies show that the product/process argument is no longer helpful in our understanding of the complexities. We clearly need both! But what is less clear is when products are needed and when process is needed and how these two essentials are handled and by whom. What we do know is that im-

13 Louis Smith and Pat Keith, *Anatomy of an Educational Innovation* (New York: John Wiley, 1971).

14 For example, see John Emrick and Susan Peterson, *A Synthesis of Findings across Five Recent Studies of Educational Dissemination and Change* (San Francisco: Far West Laboratory, 1978); David A. Shiman and Ann Lieberman, "Non-model for School Change," *Educational Forum* 38, no. 4 (May 1974): 441-45; Neal Gross, Joseph B. Giacquinta, and Marilyn Bernstein, *Implementing Organizational Innovations* (New York: Basic Books, 1971); and Smith and Keith, *Anatomy of An Educational Innovation.*

15 See Sussmann, *Tales Out of School*; Emrick and Peterson, *A Synthesis of Findings across Five Studies of Educational Dissemination and Change*; John I. Goodlad, *The Dynamics of Educational Change* (New York: McGraw-Hill, 1975); Mary M. Bentzen, *Changing Schools: The Magic Feather Principle* (New York: McGraw-Hill, 1975); and Gross, Giacquinta, and Bernstein, *Implementing Organizational Innovations.*

provement efforts must be carried on by people who care and understand the ideas they present as well as the work life of teachers. This means that canned programs won't work. Packages won't work, unless a personalized involvement with school staffs melds into the social system, gets the staff itself to help define direction, and encourages, rewards, and makes possible fresh ways of looking at what teachers are doing. Teachers have always called out for additional resources. What they mean is people, time, materials, and expertise in a mix that engages them, educates them, and makes their growth possible. This is not meant as sentimentality toward the teacher, but rather as dealing with where the teacher finds himself/herself—isolated, cut off from ideas, not involved with adults, left usually to his/her own resources to make do.

DISCARDING THE "TRAINING MODEL"

Our field-work investigation leads us to conclude that the notion of "training" is one that needs to be discarded. Based on a deficit model of teacher education, training does not acknowledge the complex social realities of teaching, assumes that one group (the trainers) is more able than another (the trainees), and does not establish legitimacy in the life of the school and of teachers. It is time to consider alternatives to training.

Emrick has used the term "guided activity." Bentzen has used the concept "re-socialization." Berman and McLaughlin have described the necessity for concrete activities, regular meetings, and the building of group cohesion. Sarason speaks to the necessity of changing existing regularities. Sussmann describes the differences between "underdeveloped innovations" that leave a staff to struggle on its own to determine how to do it and linear innovations that may not engage people in any meaningful way. What all this means to us is that working with school people means that one needs to:

a. have a personal approach to the particulars of a school staff;

b. have ideas that are pregnant with possibilities, related to what teachers see as meaningful and doable given the real constraints of time, energy, and the dailiness of school;

c. think developmentally about the engagement of teachers with ideas in the same way that a teacher would with his/her class;

d. have the ability to work collegially with school people, recognizing the fact that it is not the teachers' problem but "our" problem;

e. have the understanding and ability to become a part of the process of improvement.

ESTABLISHING SUPPORTIVE CONDITIONS

The rejection of the training model and its replacement with developmental activities require that we closely examine the complex social structures that support development. It has now become very clear that there are certain conditions that we can identify as necessary to make school improvement a realistic possibility. These conditions include:

1. A principal who is supportive of school improvement, because it is the principal who can act as facilitator for what goes on at the local level.

2. Resources that may mean personnel used in different ways; time available to learn and practice; use of expertise when needed; materials are necessary, either original materials created by teachers or commercial materials reworked by teachers and others.

3. The energy drain is huge and must be complemented with words, smiles, encouragement, and the growth of peer support.

4. The district must support what the local school is trying to do.

5. Activities (meetings, workshops, etc.) should be scheduled on a regular basis, where the group learns to struggle collectively and where teachers learn to gain professional rewards from their peers.

6. The growth of a professional supportive culture for teachers may come about for the first time as teachers face each other with their *collective* problems.

CONCLUSION: TEACHING AS AN ART REVISITED

If one accepts teaching as an art, one might entertain the possibility that school improvement and staff development are artistic processes. That is, the interventionist, or whoever takes the role of initiating and maintaining school-improvement/staff-development projects, needs to think about his/her work as a teaching problem.

One must engage teachers: yoke them out of their dailiness, sell, but not oversell, be empathic rather than sympathetic, construct and reconstruct depending on the development of the group.

Staff Development and School Change

MILBREY WALLIN McLAUGHLIN
The Rand Corporation, Santa Monica, California

DAVID D. MARSH
University of Southern California

INTRODUCTION

The desultory status of staff development as education's neglected step-child is changing. Until recently, there was little interest in the professional development of experienced teachers. Teacher-training institutions were preoccupied with preservice education and local school districts were struggling to accommodate burgeoning student enrollments and build new schools. But now issues related to staff development have moved to center stage. One reason for the new status of staff development is the recognition that many of the "Great Society" education reform efforts fell short primarily because planners seriously underestimated teacher-training needs. In retrospect, it was unrealistic to expect that classroom teachers could bring about significant change in the services provided to such special student groups as the disadvantaged and the bilingual without substantial in-service education. In the absence of such training, it is not surprising that the result of many reform efforts was, disappointingly, more of the same. An important lesson of the so-called "Decade of Reform" (1965-1975) is that even the "best" educational practice is unlikely to fulfill its promise in the hands of an inadequately trained or unmotivated teacher. We have learned that the problem of reform or change is more a function of people and organizations than of technology.

A second reason for the current interest in staff development is that the last decade's period of unprecedented growth has been followed by an equally dramatic decline in pupil enrollment. The market for new teachers is practically nonexistent and — for the first time in many years —

local school districts find themselves with a stable, and tenured, staff. Thus, teacher-training institutions are confronted with the need to move from a focus on preservice education; local school districts can no longer rely on "new hires" to bring fresh ideas into district classrooms and must face the problem of how to upgrade the skills of the teachers they already have.

However, the only consensus that appears to exist about staff development is that what we have now is ineffective and a waste of time. The general feeling is that most staff-development programs have benefited neither teachers nor students.

If effective staff development is not an isolated workshop or an evening extension course, what is it? Rand's study of federal programs supporting educational change looked closely at the local process of change—and at the factors that support teacher growth.[1] The Change Agent study deals with a number of issues that are central to the design and implementation of staff-development programs—for example, what motivates teachers to acquire new skills? What helps teachers to retain these skills? What can the principal do to support and sustain teacher change? What is the role of the central administration in the efforts of classroom teachers to improve their practices? This essay draws on the Rand Change Agent study to suggest issues that will be central to rethinking both the nature and the role of staff-development programs.

1 Rand has just completed, under the sponsorship of the United States Office of Education (USOE), a four-year, two-phase study of federally funded programs designed to introduce and spread innovative practices in public schools. This study of federal programs supporting educational change is often referred to as the "Change Agent Study." The first phase of the study addressed those factors affecting the initiation and implementation of local "change-agent" projects. The second phase of the study examined the institutional and project factors that influenced the continuation of innovations after special federal funding terminated.

The study collected extensive information from superintendents, district federal program officers, project directors, principals, and teachers about the local process of change. In the first phase of the study, 293 local projects were surveyed and fieldwork was conducted in 24 school districts. The second phase of the study involved a survey of 100 projects in 20 states and fieldwork in 18 school districts.

The results of the first phase of the study are summarized in Paul Berman and Milbrey Wallin McLaughlin, *Federal Programs Supporting Educational Change, Vol. IV: The Findings in Review* (Santa Monica, Calif.: The Rand Corporation [R-1589/4-HEW], April 1975). The findings of the second phase of the Change Agent study are reported in Paul Berman and Milbrey Wallin McLaughlin, *Federal Programs Supporting Educational Change, Vol. VII: Factors Affecting Implementation and Continuation* (Santa Monica, Calif.: The Rand Corporation [R-1589/7-HEW], April 1977).

Also see *Making Change Happen?* a series of articles on the Phase I study in the *Teachers College Record* 7, no. 3, February 1976.

THE RAND FINDINGS

The Rand study examines staff development in the context of broader changes in schools associated with various types of federally funded projects. The study is rich in implications for in-service education for several reasons. The study used "outcome" measures that correspond directly to the anticipated results of in-service education. These outcomes include change in teacher practices, pupil growth, and the retention of teacher change in the form of continued use of project methods and materials following termination of federal funds. The study also included many of the process variables considered in in-service education such as teacher commitment and involvement, staff reward structures, skills training and classroom follow-up, and the role of the principal or school climate in teacher growth and the maintenance of change. Finally, in the view of the study's respondents, "successful change" and "staff development" were essentially synonymous.

The Change Agent study identified four clusters of broad factors as crucial to the successful implementation and continuation of local change efforts. These clusters are: *institutional motivation, project implementation strategies, institutional leadership,* and certain *teacher characteristics.* This section will discuss each of these clusters of factors and examine its relationship to the extent of project goals achieved, the extent of teacher change, the extent of student growth, and the continued use of teacher methods and materials following termination of federal funds.[2]

INSTITUTIONAL MOTIVATION

Institutional motivation is the first cluster of factors that the study found to be critical to project outcomes. A school district may undertake a special project, and a school or teacher may agree to participate in the project, for very different reasons. A district may initiate a change-agent project to address a high priority need — or it may start a project to ameliorate community pressures, or to appear "up-to-date," or simply because the money is there. Similarly, teachers participate in a special project effort because they are "told to," or because it is their own idea, or because of collegial pressure, or because they see the project as an

---

2 These five dependent measures as discussed in this article (percentage of project goals achieved, total teacher change, total student performance gain, continuation of teacher methods, and continuation of project materials) were continuous variables derived from the teacher questionnaire. Berman and McLaughlin, *Federal Programs Supporting Educational Change, Vol. IV,* chap. IV, describes these measures and their validity in detail.

opportunity for important professional growth. The institutional motivations that characterize a planned change effort significantly influence both project implementation and the extent to which project methods and strategies are eventually incorporated into regular school or district practice.

Not surprisingly, the commitment of project teachers is very important. The Rand Change Agent study found that teacher commitment had the most consistently positive relationship to all the project outcomes (e.g., percentage of project goals achieved, change in teachers, change in student performance, and continuation of project methods and materials). The importance of teacher commitment to the achievement of project goals is axiomatic: Project success is unlikely unless teachers want to work hard to make it happen.

Though few disagree that teacher commitment is a necessary ingredient to project success, there is debate about the extent to which the commitment of teachers can be affected by policies or program strategies. A number of practitioners and planners—perhaps turned somewhat cynical by a parade of disappointing change efforts—have come to believe that teacher commitment is essentially "immutable": Some teachers are eager to change and learn new practices, and some simply are not. The policy implications of such a perspective are discouraging—that is, efforts to improve educational practice should be limited to those teachers who evidence strong initial interest and motivation. The Change Agent study suggests a much less deterministic view. Both the fieldwork and the survey analysis suggest that teacher commitment is influenced by at least three factors: the motivation of district managers, project planning strategies, and the scope of the proposed change-agent project. How does each of these factors affect teacher commitment?

Motivation of District Managers The attitudes of district administration about a planned change effort were a "signal" to teachers as to how seriously they should take a special project. The fieldwork offers numerous examples of teachers—many of whom supported the project goals—who decided not to put in the necessary extra effort simply because they did not feel that district administrators were interested. In the absence of explicit district support for their efforts, many teachers felt that the personal costs associated with a change effort were not in their professional self-interest and were unlikely to make a difference in the long run. Consequently, few of the projects that were initiated by the district primarily for opportunistic or political reasons were effectively implemented; none were officially continued after the end of federal funding. As one respondent put it, "The superintendent had better believe in the project—give it his personal backing and support. Teacher confidence is essential; teachers should see in the beginning that top administration believe [in the project] and are committed to it."

The Change Agent study further suggests that administrative support must be generated at the outset. Given the multiple demands facing district administrators, local project planners cannot expect to secure this interest and backing once the project activities are under way. But even were this possible, the initial disinterest of the district leadership will likely leave a negative legacy upon the commitment and attitudes of project teachers.

Project-Planning Strategies   The commitment of both district administrators and teachers was also influenced by the way the project was planned initially. Four general patterns of project planning characterized change-agent projects and had very different implications for staff commitment and project outcomes. One could be called a "top-down" strategy. In this case, project plans were made almost entirely in the central office and announced to would-be implementors. A second pattern, "grass-roots planning," was just the opposite—plans were devised by teachers or school-based project staff with little involvement of district administrators. A third planning strategy was one of essentially "no planning." A project plan and project funds were imported into the district with little or no involvement from district staff at any level.

"Collaborative planning" characterized the fourth general planning strategy. In this mode, project plans were made with equal input from teachers and district managers. Although this style was rarely characterized by conscious notions of "parity," participants at all levels in the system were treated as partners in the process of planning for a special project effort. Of these four planning strategies, a collaborative planning style was necessary to both the short-term and long-run success of a planned change effort.

Top-down planning strategies typically resulted in indifferent implementation and spotty continuation even when district officials were committed to project goals and serious about the change effort. Top-down planning usually met with indifference or resistance from the school staff. Teachers felt that such projects were not "theirs" but the central administrators' and had little personal investment in project objectives or success.

Top-down planning strategies often resulted in disappointing projects for another reason: Central office staff were insufficiently aware of the needs and practices of particular schools, classrooms, and teachers. One teacher made this revealing comment:

This project hasn't worked out and its main effect has been to cause a close, well-organized faculty to turn to distrust each other. This was the result of forcing a program on a school, using an outside coordinator unfamiliar with the school and faculty, and not having the full support of teachers. I personally felt the project ideas were good and could have worked if the teachers in our school had been involved in the planning.

Or, as another teacher in an unsuccessful project complained, "The project was planned and designed without the knowledge and consent of the teachers at the school . . . the planner had hardly ever been to our school." Top-down planning generally fails even with the best of intentions both because it cannot generate the staff commitment necessary to project success and because this planning style does not incorporate the special knowledge and suggestions of the staff who will be responsible for project implementation.

The second planning strategy, grass-roots planning, was only a little more successful. Projects that were conceived and planned at the school level with only cursory review by central office staff often evidenced high initial teacher commitment. But, in the absence of explicit support from district managers, that commitment waned over the course of project implementation. Project teachers found it difficult to sustain initial enthusiasm and motivation when there was little indication that district officials also cared. In the long run, grass-roots projects generally disappeared as completely as top-down projects. Though teacher-initiated project practices and methods could be found in isolated pockets of the district, without district support, even successful projects withered away because of factors such as staff turnover, indifference, or lack of information on the part of building principals.

Only the fourth (and more time-consuming) planning strategy, collaborative planning, generated the *broad-based* institutional support necessary to effective implementation and to the continuation of successful practices. Projects adopting this planning style actively engaged both teaching and administrative staff from the preproposal period through implementation, thereby gaining consensus and support from teachers, principals, and central office personnel. Evidence of the Change Agent study on this point gives the lie to the conventional wisdom that teacher-initiated projects are usually more successful than are those conceived downtown. "Who" originated a project did not matter. For example, teacher change and the continuation of project strategies were not significantly different in schools that had originated the project from what they were in schools that had been asked to participate. What did matter was "how" project planning was carried out, regardless of the source of the idea.

Scope of Change A third factor that influenced teacher motivation is the scope of change proposed by a project. The Rand study found that the more effort required of project teachers, and the greater the overall change in teaching style attempted by the project, the higher the proportion of committed teachers. Complex and ambitious projects were more likely to elicit the enthusiasm of teachers than were routine and limited projects. The reason for this, we believe, is that ambitious projects appeal to a teacher's sense of professionalism. Evidence from the Change Agent study indicates that a primary motivation for teachers to take on the extra work and other personal costs of attempting change is the belief that they will become better teachers and their students will benefit. Fieldwork observation and interviews with practitioners suggest that the educational promise of an innovation and the apparent opportunity for professional growth are crucial factors in generating teacher commitment.

The importance of professionalism, or intrinsic motivation, to teacher motivation (and thus to project success) raises questions about the utility of extrinsic rewards as a project strategy. Many groups have proposed extrinsic rewards—credit on the district salary scale, extra pay, and so on—as possible solutions to the "problem" of teacher motivation. Although the Change Agent study did not consider this issue comprehensively, it did examine the effects of extra pay for attending staff training sessions. Sometimes this strategy was used "to get the teachers to go along" with a project, or to "sweeten the pill." Teachers who received extra pay for training (about 60 percent of the sample) were *less* likely than others to report a high percentage of project goals achieved. These teachers also reported *less* improvement in student performance, especially academic performance, than did other teachers in the study.

These findings support the idea that instrinsic professional rewards—such as those implicit in the proposed scope of change—are far more important in motivating teachers. To this point, a number of project directors commented that although the teachers appreciated the extra pay, the pay alone did not induce teachers to work hard to learn new skills if professional motivation was absent. As one teacher remarked, "I'll go [to the training session], and I'll collect my $30, but I don't have to listen."

PROJECT IMPLEMENTATION STRATEGIES

The second critical factor affecting the outcomes of local change efforts was the project implementation strategy. Among the most important choices made during the initial planning period were those about how to put the project into practice. Local planners had considerable discretion in selecting project implementation strategies. For example, similar reading projects utilized very different staff-training strategies and project-governance procedures. The most important of those local choices were those that determined the ways in which the school staff would be assisted in acquiring the new skills and information necessary to project implementation — staff-development strategies.

Project strategies that fostered staff learning and change had two complementary elements: (1) *staff-training activities*; and (2) *training-support activities*. The study found that well-conducted staff training and staff-training support activities improved project implementation, promoted student gains, fostered teacher change, and enhanced the continuation of project methods and materials. These training and support variables alone accounted for a substantial portion of the variation in project success and continuation.

This in itself is not a surprising finding. After all, teachers have to acquire new skills or behavior if project-related changes are to influence student performance and if project strategies are to be continued. But the very different contributions made by these two activities — staff training and support activities — furnish important insights for staff-development planners.

Staff Training   Staff-training activities were typically skill specific — instruction in how to carry out a new reading program or introduction to new mathematics materials, for example. As such, this component of a project's implementation strategy corresponds most directly to the traditional focus of many in-service teacher education efforts. Skill training usually involved project workshops, and could occur prior to project implementation, during the first year of project operation, or after the first year. By themselves, staff-training activities had strong, positive effects on the percent of project goals achieved, and on student performance in the areas of both achievement and behavior. However, skill-specific training had only a small and not significant effect on teacher change and on the continuation of project methods and materials. In other words, skill-specific training alone influenced student gains and project implementation *only in the short run.*

This finding is puzzling at first glance. After all, if staff-training activities significantly and positively affected student performance during the period of project operation, why didn't this effect continue after special funding was terminated? The Change Agent study results suggest a straightforward explanation for this apparent anomaly. Skill-specific training activities only have transient effect because, by themselves, *they do not support staff learning and teacher change*. Skill-specific training enabled teachers to implement new project methods and materials under the aegis of special-project operation. But this implementation was often mechanistic and did not necessarily constitute teacher assimilation of the new techniques and procedures. Thus, when the supports of the funded project operation were removed, teachers discontinued using the practices that apparently enhanced student performance because they had never really learned them in the first place. Skill-specific training, in short, can affect project implementation and student outcomes, but it does not affect the longer-term project outcomes of teacher change and continuation. Staff-support activities are necessary to sustain the gains of how-to-do-it training.

Staff-Support Activities Projects pursued a number of activities to support teacher assimilation of the skills and information delivered in training sessions. In particular, the study examined the contribution of classroom assistance by resource personnel, the use of outside consultants, project meetings, and teacher participation in project decisions. Taken together as a support strategy, these activities (when they were seen as useful by the school staff) had a major positive effect — as did staff training — on the percentage of project goals achieved and on student performance. But in contrast to staff-training activities, these support activities also had strong positive and direct effects on the longer-term project outcomes — teacher change and continuation of project methods and materials. Well-conducted staff-support activities not only reinforce the contribution of staff training, but they also make their own important contribution to promoting teacher change and to supporting staff assimilation of project practices.

Training is essentially an information transfer — providing teachers with necessary techniques. But, as the first phase of this study found, the process of implementation is a process of *mutual adaptation* in which teachers modify their practices to conform to project requirements and project technologies are adapted to the day-to-day realities of the school and classroom. Staff-support activities, in particular classroom assistance from resource personnel and project meetings, can provide the feedback project staff need to make these modifications. Through these support activities, skill-specific training can be "individualized" for project teachers in terms of timing and content modification.

Staff-support activities can also aid teachers in understanding and applying complex new strategies in ways that standard training—in terms of both form and content—usually cannot do effectively. For example, even a carefully planned staff-training program usually cannot anticipate the nature or the timing of project staff-assistance requirements, especially as they relate to particular classroom problems. Likewise, staff often cannot perceive what they need to know until the need arises. For both reasons, the needs of project staff are not always predictable or synchronized with scheduled training sessions. The utilization of local resource personnel or consultants to provide "on-line" assistance can help remedy these inevitable deficiencies. However, it is important to note that the *quality* of this assistance is critical. The study found that the *amount* of classroom assistance from local resource personnel did not matter when teachers perceived their help as useful or very useful. But the frequency of classroom visits did have an effect when it was *not* perceived as helpful. Numerous visits to the classroom by district or project staff were counterproductive when teachers did not feel they were being helped. This assistance actually interfered with project implementation.

Similarly, it was better for projects to use no outside consultants than to use poor ones—and much better than to use poor ones often. Good consultants helped by providing concrete practical advice to project teachers—showing them how to adapt project methods or materials to their own situation. Good consultants assisted teachers in learning how to solve problems for themselves, rather than by solving problems for them. Ineffective consultants often furnished advice that was too abstract to be useful. In making a recommendation for improving project implementation, one teacher advised, "Be sure consultants know [the project] goals and some specific things to tell the teachers and not a lot of worthless generalizations and theory." Another teacher remarked, "I found most [of the consultants] to be completely lacking in their exposure to, familiarity with, and willingness to come in and work with young children. Many were good philosophically, but not practically, in the day-to-day approach and follow-up."

Ironically, even "good" consultants actually diminished project outcomes in some cases. Consultants often unintentionally preempted staff-learning opportunities and prevented teachers from learning to implement project strategies for themselves. One superintendent attributed the failure of a project to this factor: "The first year, teachers came in from other communities and worked with our teachers. The following year, our teachers were alone and it was impossible to fully implement the program." The negative effects of consultants that appear in the Change Agent data can be interpreted both as a result of too little and too much help from consultants.

Frequent project meetings were another support strategy that aided teacher efforts to adapt project precepts to their classrooms and assimilate new strategies. Project meetings provided a forum whereby teachers could learn from one another's experience. Project meetings also supported the affective needs of teachers as they attempted to implement change. As one teacher commented, "Regular monthly meetings are absolutely critical for reinforcement and building interpersonal relationships for co-workers." However, like consultants and classroom assistance, if meetings were not perceived as useful, they had a detrimental effect on project operations. Frequent meetings that were not judged useful by teachers were strongly associated with less successful projects in the survey sample. The fieldwork suggested that meetings were unproductive when they dwelled primarily on details of project administration and record keeping and rarely included opportunities for staff to share their problems and reports on process. Such meetings did little to enhance classroom implementation, and teachers found them irritating.

All of these project activities to support training — classroom assistance, outside consultants, frequent meetings — contributed to project outcomes in yet another and equally critical way. These support activities were necessary for the development of *clarity* concerning the goals of the project and the implications of project strategies for ongoing classroom practices. It is important to note that clarity was not the same as *programmatic specificity*, nor were these factors necessarily related.

The analysis showed that specificity of goals had a major effect on implementation: The more specific the teachers felt the project goals were, the higher the percentage of goals the project achieved, the greater the student improvement attributed to the project, and the greater the continuation of both project methods and materials. Program planners and grants-makers, hoping to enhance special project outcomes, have placed increasing emphasis on the careful specification of project objectives. However, such programmatic specificity is only one component of the broader specificity so important to project success. Even more important is the second component of specificity — namely, *conceptual clarity*, or the extent to which project staff are clear about what they are to do and understand the rationale underlying project activities.

Programmatic specificity is fundamentally a project-design issue and, by itself, does not guarantee staff clarity about project operations. There were many projects in the study in which even clearly stated project objectives made little sense to project staff in terms of their day-to-day responsibilities. Furthermore, programmatic specificity of the type advocated by grants-makers and planners is often not feasible for many ambitious projects, such as projects that focus on change in classroom organization. Conceptual clarity may be fostered—but cannot be assured —by specific project-goal statements or by the use of packaged materials or by lectures from outside consultants. The conceptual clarity critical to project success and continuation must be achieved during the process of project implementation—it cannot be "given" to staff at the outset. Frequent staff meetings and timely classroom assistance by resource personnel are strategies that provide staff with this practical understanding concerning the project goals and methods promulgated in training sessions and project designs.

The effectiveness of both training and training-support activities was enhanced by another project-implementation strategy—teacher participation in project decision making. Decisions and choices during implementation would not be necessary if projects were always carried out as originally planned. Most projects, however, particularly successful projects, underwent modification in their initial plans and objectives, and these adaptations were almost always positive improvements.

The strong, positive effect of teacher participation on the percent of project goals achieved suggests that teacher inputs can significantly improve implementation. Teachers, because of their day-to-day involvement with project operations, are in a much better position than district specialists or even the project director to identify problems and recommend feasible solutions. To this point, one elementary school principal advised, "Give the classroom teacher a strong role in planning any project that he or she is going to be working with. Then listen and change when things do not go as planned on paper."

Teacher participation in decisions about the project had an important *instrumental* value: Teacher suggestions improved the implemented project, and staff participation in reviewing and modifying project procedures significantly enhanced staff clarity. Teacher participation also made an important *affective* contribution to project implementation, namely, development of teachers' "sense of ownership."

INSTITUTIONAL LEADERSHIP

Institutional leadership is a third important factor for the successful implementation and continuation of a local change project. Indeed, the Change Agent study suggests that project planners need to enlarge their notion of the leadership critical to project outcomes. District planners invest considerable time in identifying competent, enthusiastic leadership for special project efforts, because their concern about leadership typically focuses on the project director. Research underscores the importance of project director leadership to project outcomes. The Change Agent data show that the more effective the project director (in the view of teachers), the higher the percentage of project goals achieved, and the greater the student improvement observed as a result of the project. An effective project director has significant instrumental value to project implementation — a director's special skills or knowledge can foster staff understanding of project goals and operations, minimize the day-to-day difficulties encountered by classroom teachers, and provide the concrete information staff need to learn during the course of project operations.

The data also indicate, however, that effective project leadership plays only a short-term and circumscribed role in the outcome of local change-agent projects. The effectiveness of a project director had no relationship to project continuation or to teacher change. Both the fieldwork and the survey analysis point to other components of school district leadership as critical to these important longer-term project outcomes.

The support and interest of central office staff was, as suggested earlier, very important to staff willingness to work hard to make changes in their teaching practices. Though a skilled and enthusiastic project director may be able to effectively implement a special project in the absence of explicit support from "downtown," project staff are unlikely to continue using project strategies unless district administrators express interest.

The attitude of the building principal was even more critical to the long-term results of a change-agent project. The support of the school principal for a special project was directly related to the likelihood that staff would continue to use project methods and materials after special funding is withdrawn. Furthermore, principal support positively affected project implementation. The Phase II survey asked teachers to indicate the attitude of their principal toward the project. Few of the projects in which the principal was perceived to be unfavorably inclined toward the project scored well on any of the study's outcome measures — percent of goals achieved, teacher change, student improvement, or continuation. Some projects with neutral or indifferent principals scored well, particularly in the percent of goals achieved, but these projects typically focused on individualized instruction or curriculum revision — activities that could occur almost completely "behind the classroom door" and in which highly effective project directors could compensate for lukewarm principals.

Projects having the active support of principals were most likely to succeed, and to be continued.

Why is the principal, not the project director, so important to long-term project outcomes? At the end of federal funding, the principal must take a stance toward the project and make a variety of decisions that explicitly or implicitly influence what happens to project methods and materials within the school. In particular, the principal is chiefly responsible for establishing the school's educational policies and philosophy. A project that is in agreement with the school's general operating style would be more likely to be sustained than one that was not. For example, the fieldwork examined an open-classroom project that operated in a very traditional school as part of a district-wide project. Once the umbrella of project authority was removed, the principal made it clear to project teachers in the school that he wished to see their classrooms returned to the traditional pattern; he also strongly discouraged nonproject teachers who expressed interest in trying some of the project ideas in their classrooms. In the same district, however, the principal at another school strongly supported the open-classroom approach. After the project ended, this principal encouraged the use of project methods in other classrooms and allocated discretionary money to purchase the necessary materials.

In short, the building principal gives subtle but nonetheless strong messages concerning the "legitimacy" of continuing project operations in the school — a message that teachers cannot help but receive and interpret in terms of their professional self-interest. Support from the principal is also important to the longevity of special project strategies because of the staff turnover experienced by most schools. If project methods are not to dissipate over time, the principal will have to familiarize new teachers with project concepts and techniques. As one superintendent observed. "A large turnover in staff [makes it hard to] sustain volunteer activities. If you get a principal who isn't in agreement with project philosophy, it can be difficult to keep a program in a school."[3]

One way in which principals demonstrated their active support for project activities — as well as gained the information necessary to promote continuation of project strategies — was to participate in project training sessions. Involvement in project training updated their classroom skills

3   The enthusiasm of principals is also an important element in introducing project methods to additional school sites. A superintendent commented, "This project has really been sustained through the direction and enthusiasm of principals. They were tremendously enthused, at first particularly, and so the project spread to other schools."

and knowledge, and equipped them to lend advice and a sympathetic ear to project teachers. But equally as important, the attendance of principals in project training imparted some important messages to teachers—notably, their personal commitment and their view that the project was a school effort in which everyone was expected to cooperate and work hard. In this way, principal attendance at project sessions helped undermine the "deficit" model that sometimes colors staff-training activities and builds resentment of the project as something done "to" teachers.

In summary, the quality of the leadership available to project staff was critical to the successful implementation and continuation of change-agent project efforts. However, it was not enough simply to provide the special project with a skilled and enthusiastic project director. The efforts of even a talented director were likely to be ephemeral unless central-office leadership supported the efforts of project staff and unless the school principal actively engaged in project activities. Evidence from the Change Agent study suggests that the task confronting planners in establishing effective leadership for project activities must be construed in broad, institutional terms, not in narrow, special-project terms.

To this point, the study found that the school climate was as important as the principal as an influence on continuation of project methods and materials once the federal funding was terminated. The Rand data indicate that good working relationships among teachers enhanced implementation and promoted continuation of project methods and materials. Good working relationships and teacher participation in project decisions were correlated: The development of the one helped the development of the other. And, in addition, the quality of the school's organizational climate—whether teachers felt their school was a good school to work in, had esprit de corps, was efficient, and was managed effectively by the principal—influenced the quality of project relationships. The correlation between participation in project decisions and good staff working relationships draws attention to the implementation strategies chosen for the project; in particular the influence of the general school climate—a background factor not directly related to project operations—underlines the significance of district site selection. Good project working relationships could develop in "average" schools when teachers participated in project decisions; and, conversely, "good" schools could develop good project working relationships without teacher participation in decisions. However, projects combining a supportive organizational environment with a strategy of teacher participation in project adaptation were most able to implement effectively and continue their innovations.

TEACHER CHARACTERISTICS

The fourth general factor that the Rand study found had major influence on the outcome of planned change efforts is teacher characteristics — the attitudes, abilities, and experience teachers bring to a special-project effort. A "conventional wisdom" has developed concerning the effects of various teacher attributes: that older teachers are less willing to change, that the best ideas come from younger teachers, that teachers with high verbal ability are more able to achieve gains in student performance, and so on. Such beliefs suggest that the personal characteristics of project teachers could have significant import for the outcome of planned change efforts. The study collected information on several teacher attributes most often cited as significantly influencing both student performance and the outcome of innovative projects: age, educational background, verbal ability, years of experience, and sense of efficacy.

Three teacher attributes — years of experience, verbal ability, and sense of efficacy — had strong and significant, but very different, effects on most of the project outcomes. Specifically, the number of years of teacher experience was *negatively* related to all of the dependent variables, with the exception of teacher continuation of project techniques, where there was no relationship. In other words, the more experienced the project teacher, the less likely was the project to achieve its goals, and the less likely was the project to improve student performance.

These relationships in large part are attributable to the fact that the more experienced teachers also were less likely to change their practices as a result of project participation. Moreover, both the fieldwork and the survey analysis suggest that teacher tenure has a curvilinear relationship to project outcomes. That is, teachers seem to "peak out" after five to seven years of teaching — either maintaining their level of effectiveness (in the best cases) or actually becoming less effective. For many teachers in the Rand study, the passage of time on the job seemed to diminish their capacity to change and to dampen their enthusiasm for innovations and for teaching. This "calcifying" effect seemed less an intrinsic characteristic of teachers or of the teaching role than testimony to the way schools are managed and the way professional development activities are provided for staff.

In particular, the professional-development needs of experienced teachers are different from those of new teachers. For example, the workshop approach that may be useful for teachers still mastering the classroom craft is not sufficiently relevant or challenging to more experienced teachers. After several years in the classroom, teachers want to explore new areas and take more responsibility for their professional growth.

District-wide—or even school-wide—in-service education activities that only elaborate on present practice usually are seen as a waste of time by experienced staff. But few schools or districts explicitly address the professional-development needs of their tenured staff. Thus, it is not entirely surprising that experienced teachers sometimes feel there is little challenge left for them and "turn off" from teaching.

A second teacher characteristic, verbal ability, was significantly related to only one outcome measure—total improvement in student performance.[4] However, when student performance was broken down into its cognitive and affective components, the data indicate that teacher verbal ability affects only achievement; it apparently had no significant effect on student affective development.

The most powerful teacher attribute in the Rand analysis was teacher sense of efficacy—a belief that the teacher can help even the most difficult or unmotivated students.[5] This teacher characteristic showed a strong, positive relationship to all of the project outcome measures. Furthermore, the effects of a sense of efficacy were among the strongest of all the relationships identified in the analysis. Teacher sense of efficacy was positively related to the percent of project goals achieved, the amount of teacher change, total improved student performance, and the continuation of both project methods and materials. Teachers' attitudes about their own professional competence, in short, appear to have major influence on what happens to change-agent projects and how effective they are.[6]

---

4 Teachers' verbal ability was measured by a self-administered Quick Word Test consisting of a fifty-question, multiple-choice, vocabulary-type test. The test, developed by Edgar F. Borgatta and Raymond Corsini (*Quick Word Test* [New York: Harcourt Brace Jovanovich, nd]) as a measure of verbal abilities, has high reliability and is correlated highly with more complex measures of intelligence. See Berman and McLaughlin, *Federal Programs Supporting Educational Change, Vol. VII,* p. 137.

5 The measure of teachers' sense of efficacy was based on two questions. One asked whether the teacher felt that "when it comes down to it, a teacher really can't do much because most of a student's motivation and performance depends on his or her home environment." The other asked whether the teacher thought that "if I really try hard, I can get through to even the most difficult or unmotivated students." Responses to these two questions were combined into a single measure of efficacy—the extent to which the teacher believed he or she had the capacity to affect student performance. Ibid.

6 A Rand study of the School Preferred Reading program in Los Angeles drew heavily on the instrumentation and design of the Change Agent study and reached similar conclusions. Specifically, it concluded that "the more efficacious the teachers felt, the more their students advanced in reading achievement." See David Armor et al., *Analysis of the School Preferred Reading Program in Selected Los Angeles Minority Schools* (Santa Monica, Calif.: The Rand Corporation [R-2007-LAUSD], August 1976). This study used, as the dependent variable, the change in individual students' scores on a standardized reading test.

An important question for planners is the extent to which a teacher's sense of efficacy can be affected by project-design choices, or whether teacher perceptions about their competence is simply a "given." The study did not measure this teacher attribute before project activities began, and so cannot report "before and after" findings. However, the information that was collected furnishes important insights for planners of in-service education. First, teacher sense of efficacy was not significantly related to years of experience or to verbal ability. In other words, a highly verbal, experienced teacher is no more or less likely to feel a sense of efficacy than are other teachers. Second, teachers having a high sense of efficacy tended to be part of projects that placed heavy emphasis on the staff-support activities discussed earlier. That is, projects that involved teachers in project decision making, that provided timely and ongoing assistance in the classroom, and that had frequent staff meetings were more likely to have teachers with a high sense of efficacy than were projects with narrowly defined goals, that had little teacher participation, or that relied heavily on the use of outside specialists to implement the project.

An obvious question is whether low efficacy and high efficacy teachers were "selected into" these different project types. Did project directors, based on their assessment of a sense of competence on the part of project teachers, encourage or discourage teacher participation in the project? Or, did "low efficacy" teachers tend to avoid projects in which they would have to play a major role? Though such self-selection undoubtedly occurred to some extent, the fieldwork suggests that project training-support activities functioned to enhance teacher efficacy. Staff-support activities seemed to promote teacher efficacy in several ways. They provided timely assistance to teachers and a forum in which teachers could talk through project strategies in terms of their own classrooms and thus feel confident in utilizing new ideas. Furthermore, they allowed peer encouragement and development of a sense of ownership in project activities. Staff-support activities provided teachers with crucial collegial support in their efforts to change and grow.

Projects that sought staff participation and involvement in project decision making also conveyed the message to teachers that school administrators viewed them as competent professionals — able to make important decisions about project activities and objectives. A "Pygmalion effect" of sorts may operate in projects where teachers are given a responsible role. Teachers who are given an opportunity to make decisions about project activities and take responsibility for the substantive direction of their decisions soon acquire such skills.

In summary, the Rand study confirms much of the conventional wisdom concerning the importance of teacher characteristics to the outcome of a planned change effort. But, more importantly, this study also suggests ways in which project-design choices and district leadership can influence these important factors.

IMPLICATIONS

The Rand study presents a fundamentally different view of staff development or in-service education from that typically found in the literature or in practice. The study moves away from a traditional view of staff development as a concern about the governance, financing, staffing, delivery, and reward structures for "those workshops" or as a problem of technology transfer. Instead, the Rand study emphasizes learning for professionals as part of ongoing program building in an organizational context. This *view* of staff development is one of the most important implications of the study.

As part of this view of staff development, the Rand study suggests a number of new assumptions to guide the design and implementation of staff-development activities. First, the study suggests that in terms of knowledge about the practice of teaching, teachers often represent the best clinical expertise available. For example, in teaching as in other clinical settings, the appropriate strategy to resolve problems is unclear. To this point, the state of educational research is such that it is difficult to reach consensus concerning the value of most any set of teaching strategies. For teachers, the learning task is more like problem solving than like mastering "proven" procedures. Consequently, outside experts and tightly structured training are relatively less helpful than they are in technology-dominant activities such as industry. The instrumental value of involving classroom teachers in identifying problems and solutions is clearly expressed in the Rand study.

Second, the Rand study describes the process by which an innovation comes to be used in a local setting as adaptive and heuristic. This mode of implementation exemplifies the professional learning process for the projects in the Rand study. In a sense, teachers and administrative staff need to "reinvent the wheel" each time an innovation is brought into the school setting. Reinventing the wheel helps the teachers and administrative staff understand and adjust the innovation to local needs. Learning occurs throughout this adaptation process as staff come to understand their own needs for additional information. Even clarifying the purpose of the innovation is a learning process in itself. Conceptual clarity about project goals in the study evolved as staff learned to understand the implications and nuances of the innovation.

Besides having training that is individualized according to learning rate and learning style, the study found that training and staff support play different roles in this professional learning process. Skill training typically provides the cognitive information and general skills, which then must be adapted within individual classrooms. Outside consultants typically had a difficult time in meeting the learning needs of staff within the training and support staff framework. Whether intentional or not, consultants typically upstaged staff.

A third and related assumption communicated by the Rand study is that professional learning is a long-term, nonlinear process. In the study, innovation sometimes took one or several years to achieve full implementation. Over this time, teachers and administrative staff needed to learn what innovation was needed and what the innovation ought to look like in their particular school setting. They needed to learn what help was needed to implement the innovation as well as the new ideas and skills contained in the skill training. They also needed to learn how to apply these skills or ideas in their classrooms and even how to retain these skills or materials once federal funding had terminated. The continuation of project methods and materials can be seen as a learning problem where the methods and materials are used under new conditions—the absence of the supporting structure provided by federal funds.

A fourth assumption suggested by this study concerns viewing staff development as part of the program-building process in schools. In the Rand study, the process of adoption of a specific innovation helped define the program-improvement goal for teachers, administrators, and project staff. It helped to coalesce the commitment and energies of these groups around the implementation of this innovation and focused the resources and expertise needed to complete the learning process. The three groups —teachers, administrators, and project staff—did not necessarily see the goals of the project in congruent terms for several reasons. Moreover, as described above, conceptual clarity evolved as people came to understand the innovation more thoroughly. Consequently, the innovation process helped to focus the energy, commitment, resources, and expertise for staff development even though the perception of the project evolved over time and differed, to some extent, by role group. But it was important that professional learning be related to ongoing classroom activities. Staff-development activities undertaken in isolation from teachers' day-to-day responsibilities seldom had much impact.[7]

7 See, especially, Appendix A in Peter W. Greenwood, Dale Mann, and Milbrey Wallin McLaughlin, *Federal Programs Supporting Educational Change, Vol. III: The Process of Change* (Santa Monica, Calif.: The Rand Corporation [R-1589/3-HEW], April 1975).

Viewing staff development in the context of program building also helped to shift staff development from a deficit model where teachers are seen as needing in-service because they lack professional skills. In general, the deficit model of staff development is characterized by the view of other educators that teachers need staff development because they lack the necessary skills to teach successfully. This characterization has several elements that need to be understood if the deficit-model approach to staff development is to be changed. First, the deficit model is a collective view supported by members of diverse role groups such as principals, school district administrators, university professors, state department of education officials, and legislators. This leaves teachers with the belief that everyone is critical of them. Secondly, these outside groups bring to bear administrative regulations, credential requirements, university degree requirements, and state law as a network of rein-forcement for their belief: The critical view of other educators is being powerfully communicated to teachers. Thirdly, teachers have typically been excluded from any discussion of their "deficit" or any discussion about how to carry out its removal and, finally, the deficit model has been built based on the dogmatic belief of other educators that they know, and can justify, their statements about what consitutes good teaching. Though educational research developed over twenty-five years has not resolved the dilemma of what constitutes good teaching, deficit-model outside experts or central office specialists often act as though they know.

A number of features of staff development as part of program building at the school site help to displace the deficit-model view of staff development among teachers and administrators. In the Rand study, staff development became part of a program-improvement process where many role groups needed new skills: Teachers were not the only group involved in project-skill development activities. Such an approach helped to spread and lessen the psychological risks of change. Teachers also were major decision makers about the innovative process; outside groups were no longer deciding what teachers ought to know. Moreover, teachers perceived that change was possible on a broader scale because the implementation process itself brought about changes in administrative structures, curriculum, and instructional-materials strategies as well as in teacher behavior. In fact, integrating teacher improvement with other aspects of school change such as curriculum development and adminis-trative reform increased the effectiveness of the staff-development efforts.

In this context, the intrinsic motivation associated with teacher professionalism was fostered. This is in sharp contrast to traditional thinking about staff development where the debate seems to focus on which form of extrinsic motivation should be used to get teachers to attend one-shot workshops or other almost ritualistic forms of staff development. In the context of staff development to support the innovation process, the Rand study found that the teacher motivation issue was no longer one of persuading teachers to attend staff-development meetings to remedy their deficiencies.

A fifth broad assumption suggested by the Rand study concerns the importance of seeing staff development in the context of the school as an organization. Within the most successful projects, the project was not a "project" at all, but an integral part of an ongoing problem-solving and improvement process within the school. In a sense, good staff development never ends. It is a continual characteristic of the school site.

The importance of the organization context was apparent in all phases of the change process. Projects that sought federal dollars to address an important concern in the entire school were much more successful than were those that were more opportunistic in their search for money. Successful implementation was also dependent upon the organizational climate and the leadership of the school as well as upon implementation strategies that provided staff with new skills and information but also provided classroom follow-up and other staff support. Extensive teacher participation and a critical mass of school staff needed to bring about change were also necessary ingredients.

Yet it was at the continuation phase of the project where the linkage between staff-development activities and the organizational characteristics of the school became most important. In successful projects, continuation was a dynamic process that helped maintain changes in teacher practices. Active involvement of both the principal and school district leadership was vital to the maintenance of these changes. Contrary to the common belief that the availability of district funds is the main factor in determining whether successful innovations are retained, the Rand study found that district and school-site organizational factors were more important than were financial factors. From the initiation to the effective institutionalization of an innovation, organizational factors play a vital role. The implementation and especially the long-term effectiveness of in-service efforts are very much influenced by these same organizational forces.

In summary, the Rand study suggests that effective staff-development activities should incorporate five general assumptions about professional learning:

Teachers possess important clinical expertise.

Professional learning is an adaptive and heuristic process.

Professional learning is a long-term, nonlinear process.

Professional learning must be tied to school-site program-building efforts.

Professional learning is critically influenced by organizational factors in the school site and in the district.

These assumptions support a view of staff development emphasizing learning for professionals as part of program building in an organizational context.

The broad view of staff development given by the Rand study has a number of implications for teachers, teacher organizations, school and school district leadership, and universities. For teachers, this approach to staff development implies long-term teacher responsibilities, collaborative planning, and implementation of significant change in schools. In many ways, this is the positive opportunity teachers have asked for for some time. Yet in the past, the invitation for teachers to participate in collaborative planning and implementation of significant change has been a mixed message. Teachers were invited to participate without having significiant decision-making power and without time being given for them to participate meaningfully. Moreover, school district administrators and colleges often set up a host of bureaucratic regulations that made authentic teacher participation quite difficult. The current financial, legal, and political tension within school districts means that the current invitation for teacher participation is a complex one. The spring of each school year is better symbolized by dismissal letters and budget cuts than it is by opportunities for new collaborative planning around program improvement.

Teachers will also have to overcome a resulting tendency to feel that they are the victim of external forces. Currently, teachers seem impatient with the long and often arduous process of collaborative planning, learning, and adaptation necessary to make innovations successful. Ironically, teachers currently want to give priority to their role as classroom teachers when the Rand study suggests that their role as collaborative planners has become increasingly important in the context of creating ongoing problem-solving capabilities within schools.

The Rand study also suggests that more experienced teachers may need a different approach to their professional growth than is contained in staff development as part of the implementation of innovations. Some experienced teachers continue to grow personally and professionally, and their contribution as teachers is well respected. In general, however, the Rand study suggests that teachers with many years of experience find it more difficult to bring about change in their own teaching behavior and to maintain the use of new teaching strategies and new teaching materials over time. Lortie[8] also found that many older teachers had shifted a good deal of their energies to family or other outside-of-school interests, either out of frustration or weariness. We believe that a more personal approach to professional growth may be important for more experienced teachers. This personal approach should emphasize new cognitive frameworks for looking at teaching practice and at their effectiveness as teachers. The apparent mutability of a teacher's sense of efficacy suggested by the Rand study suggests that experienced teachers need not peak out, but can continue to learn and grow.

The Rand study has several implications for the teacher center movement. Our view of staff development emphasizes professional learning as part of program building in an organizational context. Current thinking about teacher centers emphasizes many of the qualities and many of the characteristics of professional learning that we have described above. Yet, some of the writing about teacher centers lacks sufficient concern about program building within schools or the organizational context for staff development, which we feel may hinder the ultimate effectiveness of teacher centers as vehicles for staff development. However, teacher centers have a number of features we find very attractive. The insistence on extensive teacher participation, the call for practical training that is perceived as useful by teachers, and the linkage of teacher behavior and curriculum materials are all strongly supported in the Rand findings.

The Rand research has a number of implications for the roles of principals and school district leadership. The Rand study gives new meaning to the role of instructional leadership for school principals. This instructional role usually connotes activities such as clinical supervision with individual teachers or conducting staff meetings at the school site. The Rand research sets the role of the principal as instructional leader in the context of strengthening the school-improvement process through team building and problem solving in a "project-like" context. It suggests that principals need to give clear messages that teachers may take responsibility for their own professional growth. The results also

8   Dan Lortie, *School Teacher* (Chicago: University of Chicago Press, 1975).

emphasize the importance of principals and school district leadership giving special attention to the task of continuation of teacher change and innovation at the school. Administrative involvement for such continuation includes early support for the continuation phase of the innovation cycle, administrative participation during the implementation of the innovation, and attention to the organizational as well as financial consideration for program continuation. We have learned that innovation is more a learning process than a systems design problem. Administrators enamored with a systems design or technology transfer notion of change will find little encouragement in the Rand research. On the other hand, the role of administrator was not merely managing the educational enterprise in a static fashion. Successful local projects were part of a dynamic, problem-solving organizational framework headed by a committed administrator.

The Rand research also points to the need for staff development for principals and district administrators. Ironically, these groups have been ignored in federal legislation concerning local educational reform — in part because staff development for administrators would make the federal government appear to be taking too heavy an intervention role in local district affairs. The staff-development needs of middle-level managers are usually ignored in most school districts as well. The Rand study suggests that staff development for principals is critical. It is needed to strengthen their ability to carry out the many facets in the innovation process in the context of building an ongoing problem-solving capacity at the school.

Finally, the ineffectiveness of outside consultants in the implementation process raises serious questions about the roles that universities can play in school-based staff-development programs. It is clear that packaged in-service programs, especially those offered without extensive classroom follow-up and teacher participation, are not likely to be effective according to the Rand research. In turn, however, universities could play several creative roles. First, they could prepare administrators and other school leaders who are able to carry out the innovation process as described in this study. Secondly, in their preservice teacher education programs, they could prepare teachers to play the secondary role of collaborative planner within a problem-solving dynamic organization. In any role that universities are to take in support of school-based staff-development programs, it is clear that they need to be part of the ongoing developmental process at the school. This means that they will need to be a part of the collaborative planning and implementation process at the school site. They would need to provide concrete, timely training that is perceived as useful by the teachers and be willing to help in the classroom follow-up process. University faculty would also need to be credible in the school setting and themselves be willing to undergo an adaptation process as they take on these new roles. In short, the Rand study suggests that universities will have to implement significant change themselves if they are to be effective partners in school district staff-development efforts.

A Political Perspective on Staff Development

RICHARD C. WILLIAMS

University of California, Los Angeles

Staff development in education is a curious phenomenon; it resembles the world's search for eternal peace. The citizens of the world seek the end of war and violence, yet somehow it always eludes their grasp. Similarly with staff development — everyone extolls its merits and sees the need for it. Many even agree on what characterizes an effective staff-development program. Yet the lament from the vast majority of those who are subjected to staff-development activities is that they are ineffective and generally a failure.

Why? Given the apparent interest and somewhat general agreement on desirable characteristics, one would expect staff development to be a roaring success. Many explanations have been given, ranging from the lack of sufficiently interesting and skilled "staff developers," to pointing out that the structure and culture of schools do not properly allow staff development to function adequately, to the belief that teachers are not sufficiently interested in staff development or capable of changing their behavior through staff development. These structural, sociological, and psychological explanations have their merits and likely explain some of the reasons for the ineffectiveness of staff-development activities. Somehow they do not completely account for the dilemma.

The purpose of this article is to explore this problem from a political perspective. At the outset I should confess that I am using the term *political* in a very general, imprecise, and unsystematic way. I will not be discussing political systems theory, or analyzing power configurations, or trying to place this analysis within a larger theoretical setting. I will be using the term *political* to mean essentially economic or organizational self-interest. No doubt a more sophisticated analysis would be

The author acknowledges the assistance of Joyce Brooks in the preparation of this article.

useful, but I do not feel particularly competent to attempt such an undertaking, nor do I feel the state of our knowledge of the dynamics of staff development to be sufficiently defined so as to lend itself to such precision.

My thesis can be summed up in a nutshell: A partial explanation of our seeming inability to launch effective staff-development activities lies in the fact that the various parties who are engaged in the designing, providing, and receiving of staff development often, in spite of their public utterances to the contrary, behave in ways that are at least as responsive to their own self-interests as they are to their official positions regarding what constitutes a desirable development program. I do not wish to make any value judgments about this behavior. I only wish to point out that the interaction of these several groups behaving in this way can partially explain the ineffectiveness of staff-development programs. Knowledge and consideration of this political dimension would seem to be essential to anyone who is seriously considering the renewal of the schools through staff development.

As a means of attacking this topic, I propose to:

1. briefly review two major studies of school renewal and innovation and synthesize their findings into a hypothetical staff-development model. This hypothetical model will be used as a tool for exploring the political dimension of staff development.

2. identify several organizations and groups that have historically had a significant role in staff-development activities.

3. explore, for each of those organizations or groups, the basis for its interest in staff development and discuss what I would predict to be its behavior toward this hypothetical staff-development model based on what is known about the realities of their political "self-interest."

Before beginning this discussion, I wish to emphasize the speculative nature of the analysis: The hypothetical model as such does not actually exist (although the major components of it have received wide discussion and endorsement in other contexts). It follows that the political interests of the various groups vis-à-vis this model must be derived from what is known or believed known about their present political and economic situations.

HYPOTHETICAL STAFF-DEVELOPMENT MODEL

In Western Los Angeles, approximately ten freeway miles separate the Research Division of the Kettering Foundation's Institute for the Development of Educational Activities (/I/D/E/A/) and the Rand Corporation. These two organizations have no formal or pragmatic working relationship; indeed one rarely acknowledges that the other is involved in related educational research. This is not to imply that there is a hostile relationship — only that they are functionally independent. Yet both of these organizations have conducted very comprehensive studies of educational innovation and school renewal. The studies are quite different in terms of research design and when and how the data were collected. Yet the findings and recommendations of the principal researchers of these studies regarding the design and functioning of staff development in school renewal are remarkably similar. Because of the importance of these studies and the similitude of their recommendations, I am taking the liberty of deriving a *Hypothetical* /I/D/E/A/-Rand Staff-Development Model that, for purposes of this discussion, will serve as a common element against which we can examine the political interests of various groups and organizations in staff development.

THE /I/D/E/A/ STUDY

The /I/D/E/A/ Study of Educational Change and School Improvement (SECSI) was conducted during the years 1967–1972; it was a five-year longitudinal inquiry into the process of change in selected elementary schools in Southern California.[1] Eighteen school districts each "donated" one elementary school to a League of Cooperating Schools. Each school agreed to undertake a major change effort during the ensuing five years. A central /I/D/E/A/ staff worked with the schools in assisting them in implementing change and, at the same time, studied the process of change as it was reflected in those schools. The /I/D/E/A/ staff's approach to this research was both deductive and inductive. They began their study with some hunches about how the process of change and school improvement might best be accomplished; however, during the course of the five-year project, they modified and adapted their ideas to meet the problems they encountered. There were a number of findings and recommendations that came from this study and that have been reported in considerable detail elsewhere. For purposes of this paper, I will only briefly summarize the major components of an effective school-renewal effort that resulted from the study and are related to this topic:

1 A series of books was published as a result of this study. The two summary volumes were: Mary M. Bentzen, *Changing Schools: The Magic Feather Principle* (New York: McGraw-Hill, 1974); and John I. Goodlad, *The Dynamics of Educational Change* (New York: McGraw-Hill, 1975).

1. The individual school site should be the locus of school-renewal efforts. Staff development, as the term implies, means the improvement of staff collectively, not of individual teachers. Because of the structure of our schooling system, the unit that potentially has the greatest unity, common purpose, and ease of communication is the school site.

2. The individual school staff should be so organized and led that it has effective problem-solving skills. School sites differ in the configuration of staff, students, community, purpose, emphasis, etc. It follows that each site has unique problems and conditions for which general solutions are inadequate. Also, solutions to problems will most likely be implemented if the school staff and principal have been actively involved in the identification of problems and the determination of solutions.

3. School staffs need assistance in developing problem-solving skills. The structure and culture of schools are such that the individual school site does not typically behave in this way. Teachers work independently or in departmental configurations, and principals seldom work with the entire faculty in a problem-solving mode.

4. School staffs are not sufficiently aware of the in-service or staff-development activities that can be made available to them to solve their problems. Also, they do not typically look to other principals and teachers as a rich source of expertise that can be used in solving their problems.

5. In renewing schools, there is a need for a central coordinating group that can both work with school staff in helping them to become more effective problem solvers and assist in identifying staff-development resources.

THE RAND STUDY

The Rand study, conducted in 1974, was a large-scale inquiry into the effectiveness of several federally funded projects aimed at school improvement and educational change.[2] Data were collected through conducting interviews and field-site visits and distributing questionnaires at 225 federally funded projects across the United States. A main purpose of this study was to determine why some school sties were more effective

---

2 A series of volumes was published as a result of this study. Readers who are interested in an overview of the study might refer to: Paul Berman and Milbrey Wallin McLaughlin, *Federal Programs Supporting Educational Change, Vol. IV: The Findings in Review* (Santa Monica, Calif.: The Rand Corporation [R-1589/4-HEW], April 1975).

in initiating, designing, and implementing change than others. This was an *ex post facto* study, and the researchers had no expressed preconceptions about the central research questions, although they had developed some theoretical notions to guide their data collection.

In a yet unpublished paper,[3] the principal authors discussed, on the basis of this research, what they considered an effective federal strategy for school renewal. The following are some of their recommendations regarding staff development:

1. Staff development should have a school-site component. Such an approach allows teachers and administrators to identify and address *their* interests as well as the needs particular to their student bodies and classrooms.

2. Funds should be used to develop the school districts' capacity to provide staff development. Schools and school districts are not usually skilled in problem solving and in selecting staff-development and in-service activities that will help them solve their problems.

3. Staff development should be peer based; teachers and administrators should consider their colleagues as major resources for staff development. This utilization of peers makes it more likely that the services will be appropriate and those who provide them will be credible. Staff development should utilize staff exchanges so as to emphasize collegial contact in the transfer of information.

4. Some regional agency or agencies should be given the responsibility for helping local school sites in developing a problem-solving capacity and in identifying and effectively utilizing staff-development and in-service resources that are available.

In summary, /I/D/E/A/ and Rand, in almost total independence from each other, and utilizing somewhat different research methodologies, have conducted large-scale inquiries into the process of school renewal and change. Their recommendations for the effective use of staff development in school renewal programs have many similarities. They are:

1. The school site should be an important component of the change process.

2. Teachers and administrators should be provided the skills and time necessary to focus their attention on school-site problem solving.

---

3 Paul Berman and Milbrey Wallin McLaughlin, *Rethinking the Federal Role in Education,* Rand Working Note (Santa Monica, Calif.: The Rand Corporation [Rand/WN 10004–HEW], 1978).

3. Staff-development activities should flow from and be related to the problems identified by the staff. The staff should play a major role in determining the staff-development and in-service activities that it needs.

4. Teachers and administrators have within themselves a considerable amount of expertise to bring to bear on the problems they face. Collegial sharing within and among schools should figure prominently in staff-development activities.

5. Some regional or local agency should be used to help school districts and school sites in developing their problem-solving capacity and in identifying, designing, and effectively utilizing appropriate staff-development and in-service activities.

For purposes of this article I will refer to the above five components as a Hypothetical /I/D/E/A/-Rand Staff-Development Model.

POLITICS OF STAFF DEVELOPMENT

I shall now turn to the political or "self-interest" realities of implementing the Hypothetical /I/D/E/A/-Rand Staff-Development Model for the following groups and organizations: universities and colleges, private consultants, federal and state governments, school districts, and teacher organizations.[4]

UNIVERSITIES AND COLLEGES

One hears a good deal of discussion in departments and schools of education these days about the value and need for staff development in the public schools. While no doubt this interest in staff development reflects a genuine concern on the part of many about the need to renew schools through staff development, it is also an outgrowth of a hard economic and political reality that is facing these institutions. The demand for newly minted teachers and administrators has fallen off dramatically and this is being reflected in the declining number of students enrolled in these institutions.

Such institutions are remarkably inelastic. Their faculties are tenured and it is difficult to reduce the professional staff to reflect the decreased demands for their services. An alternative institutional response is to seek other ways of keeping their faculties busy — staff development would seem to be one way to accomplish this purpose.

The culture and norms of academic institutions are such that it is

---

4 One of the few "political" examinations in the literature is K.W. Howey, "Putting In-service Education into Perspective," *Journal of Teacher Education*, Summer 1976, pp. 101-05.

not likely that they will fit very well into the Hypothetical /I/D/E/A/-Rand Staff-Development Model. On the one hand, the model is based on school sites' identifying problems and seeking assistance on their own terms. Often they will be asking for sustained, intensive, and cooperative institutional relationships that are demanding in terms of time and commitment. The cultures of many schools and departments of education do not encourage or sustain that kind of an arrangement. The incentives in many institutions are for writing, research, and creative activities. What is more, the principal working norm is individualistic—that is, faculty members seldom engage in long-term sustained cooperative activities with each other, much less with external institutions. Finally, university and college faculties generally view themselves as having considerable wisdom as regards the determination of what is best for practitioners. They are not likely to accept the passive role that results when school sites play the major role in the determination of staff-development activities.

As a result, many schools or departments of education likely would not be able to contribute to the development of this hypothetical /I/D/E/A/-Rand model because it does not match their political and organizational realities. Academic institutions will likely press for staff-development activities on their own terms. One can already begin to see the form this is taking. A real weapon academic institutions have is the legitimizing function. That is, these institutions can confer degrees and certificates that are sought for their intrinsic or monetary value. Using these incentives, many institutions are launching "external" degree programs to bolster their regular academic activities. Generally these programs provide opportunities for working practitioners to obtain advanced degrees with a minimal amount of inconvenience. The institutions recruit groups of practitioners in a selected geographical area (sometimes hundreds of miles away from the main campus); faculty members visit these groups and provide "on site" programs for the student groups. The focus of the program, however, is the individual student and not the site where he or she works. Many times the students are required to spend a summer term on the campus in order to fulfill residency requirements. This development is more consistent with the norms and culture of the university and college and, with the exception of individual faculty consulting, will likely constitute the main "staff-development" contributions of many academic institutions.

PRIVATE CONSULTANTS

As is widely known, the job market for individuals with advanced degrees in education has dwindled considerably. Thus a large number of individuals who would have gone into professorships, research, or leadership positions in education have had to seek other forms of employment. Many of them have gone into educational consulting, either individually or as members of consultant firms. Presumably a large percentage of them are engaged in work that is related to staff development. This group will likely benefit considerably from the staff-development movement.

Consultants and consultant firms have considerable flexibility so that they can adapt their activities and mission so as to remain competitive in the market. Thus if the hypothetical model were to be widely used, one could expect that consultants would be able to provide the needed services and would prosper accordingly. Unlike academic institutions, they cannot rely on the conferring of degrees to attract clients; thus they will have to build their reputation on their competency and ability to provide the needed services. One part of the model would prove troublesome, however; that is, consultant services may not be in heavy demand if teachers and administrators increasingly turn to their peers for staff-development expertise, thereby reducing the need for outside help.

FEDERAL GOVERMENT

For purposes of this discussion, the federal government will be the U.S. Office of Education (USOE). USOE has been increasingly involved in in-service training and staff development. Much of this involvement has been a result of the mandatory provisions for staff development that are often a condition for the granting and renewing of federal funding. It has also been involved with a relatively limited number of school districts through the funding of Title IVc projects, some of which have a staff-development component.

USOE's relationship with districts has largely been that of monitoring compliance with either the law or the provisions of federal contracts. This monitoring function has been consistent with the national political realities that have become translated in part into fiscal and programmatic accountability.

As a consequence, USOE has developed a large bureaucracy that spends its time in monitoring activities. One of provisions of the Hypothetical /I/D/E/A/-Rand Staff-Development Model, as envisioned by Berman and McLaughlin, would be to move the direct monitoring of individual school districts' staff-development activities to the states. Under this model the federal government would provide funds to states, who would in turn be held accountable for the distribution of the funds in accordance with federal guidelines. The federal government would monitor state governments; it follows that the size of the federal monitoring bureaucracy would have to be reduced considerably.

This development would seem to be consistent with the often-expressed desire of federal politicians to reduce the size of the federal bureaucracy and to move responsibility and initiative to the lowest operating level. However, in the present unstable federal political environment, the reduction in size of the USOE bureaucracy would appear to be risky from the view of the USOE. What is more, organizations tend to be very protective of their employees; and USOE can, understandably, be expected to take those actions necessary to protect the occupational welfare of its employees.

Thus the Hypothetical Staff-Development Model would likely be opposed by many in USOE because it would shift many responsibilities from the federal level to the state, thereby causing a reduction in the size of the USOE bureaucracy and a loosening of its control over the accountability for federal programs under its jurisdiction.

STATE GOVERMENT

Under the Berman and McLaughlin model, the state educational agencies (SEA) would play an important developmental and monitoring role in staff development. They would receive and distribute federal and state staff-development funds and oversee the establishment of a statewide staff-development effort.

This role would be a further extension of the role that SEAs have been playing in the present distribution of some federal funds. The amount of autonomy and responsibility SEAs would have over the distribution of staff-development funds and the monitoring of staff-development projects would increase considerably. This presumably would be looked upon by SEAs as an opportunity to expand their operations and to have a greater impact on school-renewal efforts in the state. Likely, the political influence of SEAs would be increased accordingly. Also, this would serve to reduce the tremendous load of paperwork and number of communications problems that have resulted from the federal monitoring role. Thus it is assumed that SEAs would welcome and encourage such developments.

Problems would be likely to develop, however, in the shifting of these responsibilities to SEAs. Some SEAs have developed sizable consultant staffs that provide in-service training activities to school districts. It can be expected that these consultant staffs will want to continue in this role. This expectation could cause problems because under the Hypothetical /I/D/E/A/-Rand Staff-Development Model the determination of staff-development programs rests with the beneficiaries at the school site, not with the state or regional units.

In the early years of the /I/D/E/A/ project, the staff experienced considerable difficulty in adjusting to this more passive role. Traditionally educational staff-development and in-service training activities have been built on the assumption that the higher-level administrative units or the consultants themselves know what is best for beneficiaries. Engineering this shift in the thinking and operating of SEA consultants and departments will likely cause a difficult internal political problem.

SCHOOL DISTRICTS AND SCHOOL SITES

A fundamental assumption of the /I/D/E/A/-Rand model is that the school site will identify its problems, determine appropriate solutions, and seek whatever help is necessary in implementing its solutions. A critical element in this model is that the school site will have the sufficient time and skill to become a problem-solving entity. As schools are presently operated, this seems an unlikely prospect. Schools typically do not view themselves as problem-solving entities. The general operating norm is that the school faculty will organize and operate itself in such a way that it can achieve its ends more efficiently under a standard, acceptable operating procedure. The teacher's day is defined as spending the vast majority of his or her time in direct contact with pupils in the classroom. The remainder of the time is spent in preparation, informal conversations with colleagues, and occasionally in faculty meetings. Except at occasional workshops, little time is spent on intense, extended problem-solving discussions.

The changing of the school-site organization and functioning in order to accomplish such a norm would cause political problems for school district managers. Teachers are no longer willing to engage in these problem-solving activities on their own time. Thus the instructional program would have to be altered so that either teachers would be paid to attend such sessions after hours, or substitutes would be hired to release them from the classroom, or the students' classroom hours would be reduced. Each of these requirements would cause school district management political problems, especially today in an atmosphere of declining test scores and district revenues. The public would not be likely to look kindly on efforts to increase the budget or reduce students' classroom hours. A further problem would be developing the group problem-solving skills of school principals and teachers. Typically they have not worked together in that way. This would probably be more of a problem at the secondary level because of the greater size of those institutions and departmentalization based on academic preparation and responsibilities.[5]

This approach would also require a change in the typical "top down" attitude toward staff development and in-service training that is found in most districts. Typically districts have an individual or a staff, depending on the size of the district, who is assigned staff-development responsibilities. Those charged with such responsibilities generally determine what is best for the beneficiaries. They sometimes ask beneficiaries what they want, but the ultimate decision is made centrally and is generally provided to district cohorts, for example, reading teachers, and not on a school-site basis. The shifting of staff-development decision making to the school-site level would require a shift in the structure of the central staff-development staff and, more importantly, in their attitudes, so that they really believe that teachers and administrators are best qualified to identify their staff-development needs.

TEACHER UNIONS

For purposes of this discussion I will use the term *union* to include both the National Education Association (NEA) and American Federation of Teachers (AFT) and their respective state organizations. It is commonly acknowledged that teacher unions have changed considerably over the past fifteen years or so. This change can be marked in terms of their behavior (more militant), their involvement in the school decision-making process (from advising to bargaining collectively), their organizational relationship with administrators and school boards (more independent). A major concern that has traditionally absorbed the energies and strategic capabilities of teacher unions has been bread-and-butter issues, for example, wages and working conditions. There is a discernible trend, however, for teacher unions to expand their concerns beyond wages and working hours into other areas including instruction, curriculum, and staff development. At least two political realities are causing this shift: one, the deteriorating financial situation in many school districts, especially in urban areas, makes it risky for teacher unions to seek any major breakthroughs or to risk their organizational reputation on wage settlements that are significantly above increases in the cost of living; two, as teacher organizations have become more involved in the decision-making structure, they increasingly move from the position of outside critics of boards and administrators to that of active decision makers in

5   See Dale Mann, "The Politics of Training Teachers in Schools," *Teachers College Record* 77, no. 3 (February 1976): 323–38.

the educational establishment. If the public views the schools as ineffective and not worthy of their continued support, teacher unions are increasingly aware that they must share the blame and the consequences. Staff development is one strategy for renewing schools.

Thus, at least partly for political reasons, teacher unions can be expected to support staff-development efforts, especially if such programs emphasize the role of teachers in the design of the staff-development efforts and if such programs do not violate traditional union positions such as extra pay for extra hours.

It follows that teacher unions would find the Hypothetical /I/D/E/A/-Rand Staff-Development Model consistent with their political realities and that they would support the further development of this model. One can already see movement in this direction by the support teacher unions have given to the teacher-center legislation, many features of which are consistent with the general thrust of the Hypothetical /I/D/E/A/-Rand Staff-Development Model.

CONCLUSION

I have no pretensions that this effort represents anything more than a preliminary excursion into a largely unexamined topic. There are several limitations in this article that come to mind: No theory or conceptual framework was used in the analysis, the Hypothetical /I/D/E/A/-Rand Staff-Development Model by definition does not exist and this gives the examination a sense of nonrealism; there are other groups and organizations, for example, whose political interests could be chosen for examination, and the political interests of those groups that were chosen might be interpreted differently by other observers.

The value of this effort, I believe, is to look at a common phenomenon in an uncommon way. It is to make explicit something that we all know but seldom acknowledge, namely, that organizations and groups have both public and private positions on educational reform proposals. The public position generally is translated into "doing what's best for kids," but the overt or covert actions of the group are sometimes motivated by more political and private self-interest, which may or may not coincide with their public position.

Anyone who proposes plans for the renewal or improvement of schools through staff development must include in their implementation strategy consideration for the private political interests of the organizations and groups that will be participants in the staff-development activities and can thereby influence the success of the implementation strategy.

How Teacher Unionists View In-Service Education

MAURICE LEITER, MYRNA COOPER
United Federation of Teachers, New York

We write in behalf of some timely and sensible positions which are obvious to most elementary and secondary school teachers, namely, that in-service education should be, etiologically, a product of the practitioners who are to be serviced, that in-service education is neither tack-on nor ancilla but a priority that should be treated as the core of effective professional practice, that in-service education has failed largely out of irrelevance, diffusion, haphazardness, and superficiality, that in-service educational reform is tied to parallel reform in other aspects of teacher education (preservice, certification) as well as to the relationships among the constituents of the education community, that teacher unionists are uniquely capable of articulating the in-service needs of teachers and effecting change in the models which influence in-service education, that research has supported teacher-centered in-service education and researchers should direct themselves away from collation and regurgitation toward evaluation of the effect of this education of, by, and for teachers on performance, pupil attainment, and school improvement. These views will be related to and integrated with reference to union contributions to in-service education, cost-effectiveness, funding, adult learners, and the roles and performance of colleges, government education agencies, school boards, and supervisors in the area of in-service education. We will not always be kind.

THE TEACHER EDUCATION ESTABLISHMENT

To tell the truth teachers have, for a long time, been impatient with foreign solutions to domestic difficulties. Many of them are even unaware that, out there, members of the teacher education establishment are meeting to exchange views on in-service models, the organization of staff-development programs, cost-effective teacher training and the like. What most teachers know is that, come 8:30 on any Tuesday in January, they had certainly better be ready to teach, and that, if they have a problem coping with what that Tuesday will bring, self-reliance on Monday night is the way to professional development.

Of course, teachers, as a group, are citizens with positive social attitudes and are generally outer-directed in their thinking. They are interested to hear that many people who do not share their daily risks are concerned about their growth and their competence. They are impressed that almost 10 percent of the people connected with education are not connected with children and that these people cost about six billion dollars a year to employ, that among these are 45,000 professors who spend part of their time teaching in-service courses and 100,000 administrators who engage (occasionally) in staff development and 40,000 consultants and supervisors of instruction who are on the job, and some 20,000 school district superintendents who are concerned about effective instruction,[1] countless thousands of state education agency and U.S. Office of Education personnel are conferring about the delivery of in-service training to teachers, and that thousands of others engaged in budget and management supervision to assure, among other things, that the one-half of 1 percent of education money spent on in-service is being properly utilized.[2]

Some are, no doubt, reassured that there are people abroad in the land who are rethinking and reconceptualizing in-service education, seeking current perspectives and evolving trends, defining issues, comparing delivery systems, thinking ahead, modeling, collaborating, recording and describing effective patterns and practices, summarizing the state of the art, charting new directions, making recommendations, and, in short, meeting each other at popular tourist centers across the nation to share epiphanies of the obvious (frequently funded by our tax dollars) and convincing each other that something needs to be done and should be done about in-service education if only the money were there to do it. So much (in volume) is being said by so many so similarly and so often that, confronted with so vast and miasmic a dirge of words, it is no wonder that, occasionally, a concerned observer of the scene is prompted to suggest that in-service teacher education is to the literature and litterateurs in

1 Kenneth R. Howey, *Current Perspectives and Evolving Trends in Inservice Education in the United States* (Washington, D.C.: Department of Health, Education, and Welfare, [Contract #300-75-0257, 1977]), pp. 90–91.

2 *The Regents Statewide Plan for the Development of Postsecondary Education* (Albany: New York State Education Department, 1976), p. 62.

the field as is an impatient Liza Doolittle to the ponderous and prolix Professor Higgins.

WHOSE PRIORITY IS IN-SERVICE?

Notwithstanding the plethora of books, articles, and collections on the subject of professional development and the importance, for a variety of motives, of in-service education to all groups in the educational community, it continues to be no one's priority. If there is a thrust toward making in-service education a central concern, it comes from teacher organizations that are responding to teacher dissatisfaction with current in-service practices and teacher needs that have not been adequately met. Having expected too much from others and been disappointed, teachers are learning to assume the professional development responsibility themselves.

The degree of interest in professional development and the extent of commitment reflected by boards of education, school supervisors, colleges, and government education agencies are often a function of concerns other than the relationship of in-service training to classroom effectiveness. A staff-development person in a large school district may feel that evidence of successful in-service education consists of publishing a thick booklet of course offerings and in-service activities irrespective of the relevance (or the actuality) of the contents. A local school board will view in-service functions in terms of public acceptance and possible public criticism of expenditures, A superintendent may emphasize the appearance of innovation or may simply regard teacher training as a vehicle for the imposition of district program priorities. Colleges often see in-service education as a source of dollars, as a way of preserving the institution in the face of enormous fiscal problems. A school supervisor's perception of in-service may consist largely in surviving the next grade three conference by duplicating an article on techniques of building vocabulary. Each participant, functionary, and institution approaches in-service training with a complex of political and personal considerations which, while thoroughly understandable, often reduce in-service training to a repetition of what has not worked offered by people doing the only thing they are comfortable doing for people who are disaffected and alienated and cynical about the process, all occurring on a budget either meager or nonexistent.

In addition, there is the simple and timeless problem of power and authority. Efforts to alter the course of staff-development approaches are often frustrated because they are seen as attempts to usurp power, to wrest control from one or another player or role group in the establishment, and to, implicitly, subject those who are in control to criticism.

Teacher organizations encounter this frequently. Many school districts have not yet even adjusted to the collective bargaining process. Now, suddenly, teachers are *intruding* into matters of curriculum and professional development. The territorial imperative is under attack.

Yet, such conditions would not now exist if problems of the failure of in-service training had not caused teachers to abandon passivity and seek to affect their professional destinies. Consider that the public and the education managers and policymakers have placed so much emphasis on the profession's failures and shortcomings. Teachers are perceived in terms of deficiency. Ways to improve performance are secondary to the drive to "weed out" the alleged incompetent. Teacher's morale is at a low point. They can either accept the appraisal of their ineptitude and function as if they believe it, or they can do what anyone under such conditions should do—confront the problem and seek to engineer changes that will restore self-respect and facilitate effectiveness. Teachers' concerns would be better articulated if they, with the help of their own organization, could directly influence the nature of their professional-development activities.

IN-SERVICE ROLE OF UNIONS

However, the tendency has been to bar teacher organizations and teachers from school district, university, or education department efforts to develop in-service programs. There has been nothing approaching an equality or partnership for teachers in determining their own professional development. For district administrators, school boards, and university educators, the notion that teachers recognize the authority and legitimacy of their union's efforts to articulate their professional views is a source of discomfort.

Colleges tend to be elitist with regard to the needs of elementary and secondary teachers; school districts tend to be paternalistic. Is the teacher worthy of equality in educational planning? Do not administrators really know better what is best for the teacher? Much of this results from traditional American confusion about merit in relation to status and power. Someone is knowledgeable because that person's title commends this to us. Another is wise because his or her authority is imposing. Additionally, the teacher-organization role as adversary in negotiations has been, by extension, applied to union efforts to improve the level of in-service training and preparation of members and prospective members.

Happily, both history and logic are with the unions. In the first place, membership education has always been an organic part of the mission of the American trade union. Tied to the improvement of status and circumstance have been education and training for advancement, for mobility, to fill diverse jobs, to improve on-the-job performance and morale, for personal satisfaction. A teacher union gains practical increments from bringing about a professional situation with high entry and service standards, with successful and productive members who are good at what they do and are valued for their accomplishments, and with opportunities for monetary and task advancement objectively obtainable through experience and further training. These are conditions that yield a stable membership, one that is less costly to service for negative reasons, for example, unsatisfactory ratings, and one that will positively respond to the organization that created the desirable professional environment. Such a membership can then benefit from the use of the organization's resources more in areas of constructive professional concern, less in areas of defense and apology. A teacher organization has no stake in failure.

Thus, the teacher organization *is*, in fact, the appropriate source and "legitimizer" of the professional views of teachers. Teachers are more ready to trust those who represent them than those who rate them, and they identify more easily with the organization that has shared *their* trials and risks than with a degree-granting institution that is distant from the action and the stress. Nor should it be overlooked that a part of their confidence in their organization stems from their participation in the development of its policies and from the recognition that when all others abandon them, their organization faithfully maintains its respect for their efforts in the classroom and their value as professionals. Enlightened school boards, supervisors, and academic institutions appreciate the importance of the teacher organization in professional matters and its capacity to bring about well-motivated teacher improvement. Success in these areas does, after all, depend on teachers, and teachers will look to their union to channel participation.

COLLECTIVE BARGAINING AND IN-SERVICE EDUCATION

Contrary to a popular notion in management ranks and in the universities, the union's adversary role in negotiations, grievance handling, and due process representation of members has not blighted its capacity to be a constructive partner in matters of professional development. Nor does the union contract act merely to restrict efforts on the part of supervisors to bring in-service enlightenment to teachers as a result of time constraints written into collective bargaining agreements.[3]

Contracts, of course, have many purposes, and among them is the

3 The discussion in this section is based on experience within the United Federation of Teachers (UFT), the teachers' bargaining agent for the City School District of New York, and draws on present and past contractual contents in the *Agreement between the Board of Education and the UFT*.

description of the working conditions of employees in relatively un-
ambiguous language. Frequently, this documentation of hours of work,
scope of activities, and so forth, is based on practices already in existence
or procedures written elsewhere in by-laws, official circulars, or resolu-
tions of a board of education. While less ambitious than the U.S. Con-
stitution, in some respects, the United Federation of Teachers (UFT)
contract is mindful of that other document's prohibition on slavery and,
therefore, it was considered appropriate in the early years of contract
development to include a section that described the working time of
teachers and other personnel. In fact, it was the work day already in
existence and it incorporated a reference to board of education by-laws providing for additional working time under certain conditions. The contract
also provides teachers with a lunch period, "duty-free," a phenomenon still
lacking for employees in many U.S. school districts, and defines, subject
to innumerable erosions, the number of periods teachers may devote to
professional preparation, planning, marking, and other obligations that
are extensions of the teaching responsibility.

Many years ago, in the New York City schools, monthly faculty conferences that ran some three hours beyond the school day were not unknown. Some regarded this as professional development, but none of
these were teachers. Typical faculty conferences of that time consisted
either of a monologue by the principal or other administrators based on
pages of conference notes read verbatim or spiced with exegesis and concerned with such profoundly professional issues as bell schedules, test
schedules, lunch schedules, coverage schedules, traffic patterns, hall
patrol, drill schedules, attendance forms, bus forms, late passes, absence
notes, trip schedules, roll books, marking books, book collection, book
distribution, or, in schools with less sophisticated administrators, the
criticism of the faculty for its shortcomings (frequently in the nature of a
diatribe) delivered by an unassailable and self-righteous principal with a
devotion to autocracy. Rare were the conferences that dealt with professional matters and rarer still those reflecting the professional planning
and interests of teachers. The union was able to limit the length of these
exercises to forty minutes as the Board's by-laws had, in fact, provided
all along. This, in itself, did nothing to improve the quality of these
meetings; it merely relieved teachers of the physical and emotional burden of an unending assault on their valuable time and their human
sensibilities. Can this be what critics of the union contract mean when
they talk about tying the hands of those who wish to engage in staff-

development activities?[4] Or has a new breed of educational leader emerged who, unaware of the depredations of the recent past, presumes now to be prepared to bring in-service truth to the eager and all-suffering pedagogue so long as it be done in a required block of time after the school day? As teachers, we feel that our profession has already had too much of that "good thing" and it has not worked. One cannot impose staff development; one must generate and motivate it. And that generation must be with the recognition that a teacher's job is generally difficult, debilitating, and frustrating, and one does not help teachers by mandating that they participate in staff development after a long and wearying day.

UFT AND IN-SERVICE EDUCATION

The UFT has always had a more positive approach to in-service education and has attempted in its professional-development work and through its contract to reflect that attitude. The guiding principles have been teacher need, teacher involvement, incentives, practical benefits to instructional effectiveness, and renewal. Above all, the efforts have been realistic (see Appendix to this article).

The union view of what successful in-service programs require coincides with the teacher view and is supported by the research in the field.[5] It calls for individualized, teacher in-service-derived and teacher-delivered, that achieves high motivation and participation through intrinsic and extrinsic incentives and is supported with money and commitment on the part of the education establishment.

The whole issue of incentives needs to be thoroughly understood and its relationship to professional development appreciated. Incentives provide the climate and conditions that permit in-service education to be effective. Given the stresses and demands of teaching, given the fact that the rewards for teachers in salary and status are exceeded by other professional pursuits, to suggest that one can achieve willing and eager teacher involvement in in-service programs without a range of positive incentives suitable to each situation is naive. Making in-service education relevant and attractive costs money and that, of course, is what really accounts for many of the pieties about what teachers should be willing

4   A classically negative management view of this sort is found in Keith P. Eiken, "Teacher Unions and the Curriculum Change Process," *Educational Leadership* 35 (December 1977): 174–77.

5   Milbrey Wallin McLaughlin and Paul Berman, "Retooling Staff Development in a Period of Retrenchment," *Educational Leadership* 35 (December 1977): 191–94.

to do—for free—to improve their professional effectiveness. Nobody wants to pay the freight.

COST-EFFECTIVENESS AND OTHER SHAMS

The greatest single obstacle to adequate funding for a reformed in-service delivery system is the problem of demonstrating the relationship of in-service programs to teacher effectiveness and pupil learning. The evaluation of in-service models should be a research priority. Such research is necessary to overcome the resistance to allocating public dollars on the state and local level for this purpose. If you cannot prove in-service education cost-effective, you cannot sell it to the public. In addition, teachers, while anxious to see substantial funding for in-service education models that meet their needs, are interested in funding that *supplements* existing educational allocations and does not siphon money for training and incentives away from direct service delivery to children. Teachers do not wish to jeopardize manageable class size and pupil/personnel ratios or educational enrichment or supportive services to pay for in-service education. Such approaches make in-service funding punitive, occasion negative public attitudes, and demoralize the so-called beneficiaries of the programs.

The cost-effectiveness issue is knotty partly because it is formulated in a casually anti-intellectual fashion. Cost-effectiveness tends to be described in the context of the turn-of-the-century garment manufacturing sweatshop and concentrates primarily on the *ostensibly* measurable in education: test scores of the standardized reading and math variety, or pupil-teacher ratios, or percentages of defined working time spent in the classroom. By this approach, which is a stepchild of the industrial productivity concept, the allocation of one teacher to thirty pupils is more cost-effective than allocating one teacher to twenty-five pupils and, conversely, the teacher in the larger class is 20 percent more "productive." This, clearly, reduces the practitioner of education to a pieceworker, placing a dollar value on how many *head* of children are the responsibility of each teacher. In the same way, studies are made of cost-effectiveness as it translates to teacher time spent in the classroom and, naturally, the stock villain here is the preparation period. Conveniently, discussions of this sort limit themselves to the school day as legally defined because none of the slide-rule educators who are hot on the trail of out-of-classroom teacher time are really willing to assimilate into their tables the amount of time teachers spend after school and on weekends marking papers, planning lessons, developing materials, revising curricula, communicating with parents, or engaging in voluntary professional development such as courses, conferences, and reading. It is simpler to suggest that if teachers would give up preparation periods, the *head* count–dollar ratio would reflect a productivity increment. Needless to say, there are arguments on the same level of acuity concerning a teacher's right to eat lunch while not teaching. The final statistical panacea is the test score, and no quantity of effort expended in an attempt to place the standardized achievement measure in perspective has the faintest impact on those who see reading "retardation," whatever its actual statistical signification, as glaring evidence that the public isn't getting a dollar's worth of service for every dollar expended.

Accountability schemes surface periodically that link test scores to teacher evaluation and compensation. If children are short of the grade norm, the "thinking" goes, teachers and schools have failed. Few pundits in this territory concern themselves with the multiplicity of causes for reading or math shortcomings, or with the damage that is done by the minute stigmatization of each youngster with a "low" grade score, or with consideration of the individual child's relationship to his learning achievement, or with any effort to distinguish learning-disabled children from their peers in evaluating scores, or with the (well-documented) impact of economic and social deprivation on children's capacity to perform. The pillorying of the educator is, after all, a sport better attended than baseball, and no society can long survive that does not rationalize its inequities by resorting to the scapegoat.

PUBLIC PERCEPTION OF TEACHERS

The fact that education is a highly visible, publicly financed activity, one that every citizen has experienced to some degree, creates the additional complication of allowing all taxpayers to substitute themselves for the teacher and to determine the worth, the scope, and the appropriateness of a teacher's professional obligations. It is equivalent, we suppose, to awarding a medical degree to every survivor of an appendicitis operation or admitting three-time losers to the bar. Possibly, the public does not appreciate the reasons that we feel compel incentives to further in-service education because the adult public bases its perception of teaching on childhood memories combined with platitudes of the marketplace. The memories, naturally, are vague and undiscriminating, and there is a tendency to confuse the child's day in school with the teacher's. Ask a second grader what he did in school, and he will probably tell you about a ball game during the play period. Top that with the public view of an entire faculty departing from a school building at three or three-thirty, and you have a reading on what most people think of as the profession of teaching. Richard Cory seemed to have a pretty good deal, too.

So we come down to a defective perception (though self-righteous and highly proprietary) on the one hand and mammon on the other hand. Why are people so sure that the less education costs, the better it will be? We relate cost to quality in almost every area of the marketplace. We expect good doctors to cost more and good universities to drive us into debt in order to educate our children and good carpeting to cost an extra $4 a yard, but we want good teaching in the lower schools to be cheaper in order to be more measurably successful. Moreover, we make assumptions about effective teachers. An effective teacher, it is assumed, begins his or her career at a peak of expertise, is sustained on a mysterious inner nutrient called "dedication," and does not require even the preventive maintenance we would allow to R_2D_2. Being a consumer society dedicated to planned obsolescence and the discard of goods in order to maintain the production-consumption modality, we conclude that the teacher who falters, who encounters difficulties, who requires renewal, who "burns out," should be discarded as incompetent and inefficient. Frankly, our manufacturing and consumption system is not cost-effective, and our teachers are not toasters—any more than our children are.

Consider, then, the prospects for interpreting the value of professional-development expenditures in such a political environment. Yet, the effort must be made, for the benefits we see in effective ongoing professional development are the same benefits we have sought to convince the populace are inherent in a full, rich, and varied education for children: cultural awareness, personal growth, self-sufficiency and independence, discrimination and problem-solving ability, confidence, appreciation of one's own and others' potential.

There is a special kind of productivity in teaching, the productivity of a full and creative career—continuous and growing. This productivity translates into student learning, positive student attitudes, wholesome notions about school and society, and a reverence for life, for stability, and for social structure. The increment is the continuity of a culture that rests on order, balance, and the capacity for judgment based on knowledge. What, then, of cost-effectiveness in this connection? Is it cost-effective to save $4,000 per classroom on the pupil-teacher ratio only to pay for it later, directly, in the added cost of remediation for those children who needed the time the teacher did not have and, indirectly, in all the children whose adult lives will reflect the aridity and paucity of their school experience? And is it cost-effective when the teacher whose burden is 20 percent greater finds that his or her ability to function effectively is 50 percent less precisely because the burden is greater? And is it cost-effective to ignore the multitude of research findings that never filter down to the mass of practitioners because in-service programs are lacking, or to affirm that it is less costly to learn by one's mistakes than to avoid those mistakes by providing teachers with the conditions to perfect their skills and solve the range of new and lingering problems that beset the evolving educational scene? And is it really cost-effective in any other profession—or in industry, for that matter—to create obstacles to renewal, to assimilation of new methodology and new strategies and new materials, and to the confrontation of difficulties on the part of committed personnel?

The situation requires a commitment on the part of policymakers and lawmakers concerned with education to permit the nonvisible professional activities that make the visible happen to be carried on in a manner suitable to the needs of the profession. This means money and incentives and a recognition of the sophisticated importance of in-service professional development.

GOVERNMENT FUNDING

While, on the state and local level, teachers have had to confront resistance to funding for professional development, it is certainly true that legislative bodies, in general, have shown more recognition than school districts of the need for change and reform in areas of teacher preparation and continuing education. This is particularly true with respect to the federal initiative in in-service education. The federal government, involved as it is in a range of categorical educational programs, has, at least, accepted some responsibility for training teachers to make the programs work. The problem with the federal role is that it has both skewed and warped the system.

Basically, federal contributions to in-service education can be criticized as being frequently diffuse, limited in impact, and irrelevant to the teachers served. (Curiously, these are basic criticisms of in-service education in general.) The money is tucked into a wide range of program packages emerging from a variety of pieces of legislation, for example, vocational education, education for children with handicapping conditions, bilingual education, and so forth. This etiology of the funding guarantees that most federal aid will have no seminal effect on reforming in-service education but will act merely to finance a repetition of existing failed forms. What emerges in terms of program will be a function of someone's local priority and what is accomplished, if anything, will fall into obscurity— dissemination being another of the critical gaps in in-service education. The money is spread too thin, in too many places, with little lasting effect.

Ironically, the complex competition for funds that is a hallmark of the federal grant process is really not productive of relevant programs. Funding is often sought because it is available, not because a particular program is organic to a training or learning need. Moreover, we have placed education in the hands of the proposal writers. The real competition is not out of need or distinction of program or other meritorious educational criterion but between proposal writers, and an elite of fund raisers has arisen who, adept at exercises like threading their way through federal regulations, are capable of developing proposals that will justify any program, at least on paper.

Because the in-service training money is imbedded in an array of diverse and unrelated programs, in-service education gets the same level of concern and attention as it does in other areas of education, that is, it is treated as an ancilla. Thus, as is the case in typical school district budgets, when program funding dies or is cut back, the teacher training component is generally the first casualty.

Furthermore, because the funding is in response to a specific program whose primary *raison d'être* is some need other than in-service training (which is really tacked on to the program), the training offered will be linked to the program need rather than to the teacher's need. The two may not coincide.

What is needed on the state and federal levels is a basic funding reform that will involve aid targeted categorically to in-service education.[6] Localities should be rewarded for programs that are consortial in development. The funding agency should seek primarily to encourage a variety of approaches, to identify effective program models, and to disseminate information on such programs to encourage their adaptation and use elsewhere. The current federal legislation on teacher centers comes closest, at present, to a government program that recognizes in-service education as an independent priority, comprehends the teacher union as the authentic voice of teachers, encourages collaborative program development among teacher unions, local education agencies, and colleges, and enables teachers to influence their own professional development.[7]

Teacher organizations have seen collaboration, the ingredient of partnership, as the best means of meeting needs perceived by teachers. There is little concern about which bureaucracy is in control. It is more important to develop the mechanism to insure that all role groups respond, con-

6 An incentive approach similar to changes currently proposed for the Elementary and Secondary Education Act (ESEA) in 1979, wherein local expenditures for instruction of disadvantaged pupils would be matched by federal dollars, would serve as a model for one type of categorical funding of teacher training.

7 Eugenia Kemble, "At Last, Teacher Centers That Are Really for Teachers," in *Teacher Centers,* Commissioner's Report on The Education Professions, 1975-1976 (Washington, D.C.: Department of Health, Education, and Welfare, U.S. Government Printing Office, 1977), pp. 141-47.

tribute, and derive benefits that will act as incentives to sustain the working relationship. That teacher unions are exerting leadership is no longer in question. The aforementioned teacher center legislation is a teacher union–initiated reform containing rewards for collaboration that function to bring the role groups together and give them a stake in change — for a change.

IMPROVING PROFESSIONAL DEVELOPMENT

The process now taking place emerged in response to the process that failed. Professional development has become locked in and reflexive in manner. Approaches are obsolete and vestigial. To teachers, staff development does not respond to the everyday frustrations nor does it speak to basic problems they encounter. Required and imposed in-service is met with deserved cynicism. It is someone else's notion of what one needs. The deliverers are not viewed collegially, are considered, often, with suspicion (some may end up rating the teachers they claim to be helping), or, at best, are regarded as people who are in another line of work (administration, higher education) and cannot really understand the needs of teachers. Frankly, the sole remaining external incentive for teachers to expose themselves, wearily, to in-service experiences so often meaningless and irrelevant is the practical consideration that X number of credits equals Y number of dollars in increments and/or salary differentials. However, as the average teacher age increases, the pool of teachers who will respond for this reason decreases.

If teachers' needs and concerns are not being met, if certain role groups are not successfully contributing, if there is no compulsion to be current, if the classroom teacher is excluded from decisions as to what professional-development activities are required and will work, if appropriate incentives are wanting, if cynicism and resistance to traditional in-service education are widespread, then a new direction, a reform, if you like, is the only option. One cannot bail water forever.

A revision in our views might commence with the recognition that substantial numbers of potentially useful staff-development personnel are available. They need to be retrained to function in a staff-development capacity to assess needs, design programs and integrate them with curriculum, develop information systems and networks, and construct research on program and teacher effectiveness. Such a conception can be valuable for the field of in-service education. In considering this idea, we are reminded that the original model for the staff developer, less elaborately attired, of course, is with us now and has been all along. We refer to an army some one hundred and thirty-five thousand strong who are heads of schools, assistants to principals, and instructional supervisors. In our more innocent days, we thought to think of them as principal teachers or, even, as helping teachers. These are the people who *should have been* the staff developers, *should have been* the helping teachers. Many are still bravely trying and a few are actually succeeding because of their individual distinction. For the most past, however, they are otherwise engaged, partly because of the changing demands and obligations they face, partly because their role as supervisor has interfered with their effectiveness as teacher trainers, and partly because so many of them have attained their positions for reasons other than their pedagogical and pro-fessional-development expertise. Many simply could not do the teacher education job if they wanted to although they have the credential and are adept at other supervisory activities such as community relations or budgeting or politics. In fact, colleges need to reexamine the way in which they train supervisors, learning perhaps from teacher-centered in-service approaches what would contribute to supervisory professional-development effectiveness. It may yet be necessary to separate the teacher-training role from the teacher evaluation and rating role to make the relationship work.

What of colleges of education and *their* personnel? As unionists whose affiliates also represent college teachers, we are sensitive to their problems, convinced of their willingness to grow and adapt, and mindful of the many difficulties they face. We are also realistic.

We know that it is unlikely that education faculties would be as con-cerned as they are now with in-service education were it not for the eco-nomic crisis they have also encountered. We know that both preservice and continuing teacher education need reform in the same way that in-service education does. We know that faculties of education tend to be directed to issues of the larger society and less likely to devote intense commitment to confronting the microcosm of serious educational issues that teachers in the lower schools confront. We know that teacher educa-tors, generally, are not comfortable with their own status and seek en-hancement through writing and publication—that the training of teachers is lower on the priority list, research and working with graduate students being more attractive.[8] We find that, very often, courses that should be dealing with *how* to teach turn out to be courses that are content cen-tered because it is a bother to teach how to teach. We believe

---

8 Robert B. Howsam et al., *Educating a Profession,* Report of the Bicentennial Commission on Education for the Profession of Teaching (Washington, D.C.: American Association of Colleges for Teacher Education, 1976), pp. 105–08.

that education students need subject matter, but they need learning theory and technique at least as much. We feel that for both teachers and teachers of teachers, the preservice training should be rigorous and comprehensive. We want the best and most committed teachers for education students. College teachers, clearly, need incentives, too.

Finally, we are concerned with bringing together the college educator of teachers who is involved in continuing professional development and the teacher who is on the job in grades K–12. There are many obstacles here, not the least of which is the distance between provider and practitioner. They really are in different professions, aren't they? Teachers feel that college people cannot possibly understand their problems. The student populations are different, the instructional environments are different, one group suffers lunch duty and hall patrol, the other functions in an environment regarded as sheltered and relatively tranquil. And, of course, there is the problem of teaching what one knows best irrespective of its relevance.

In short, another look and much reform is needed to make college teachers of education more interested in training teachers, more equipped to do so, more identifiable with their teacher-students, and more willing to adapt instruction to teacher needs. This last involves reconsideration of how adults (in this instance, teachers) learn. Many negative assumptions are made about the capacity and inclination of adult learners. Staff-development programs appear to regard adult learners as below average in intelligence, requiring that they be talked down to and that they be asked to handle only the most oversimplified, predigested, and flimsy ideas and concepts. They are thought to prefer "hands on" activities, and the glossy or "turn-on" approach rather than the analytic and serious.

Some of this thinking stems from long-abandoned ways of dealing with all education. Formerly, the models for the education of children and for teacher education were highly mechanical and structured rote models — education as received doctrine. Concepts of the whole child and individualized education strategies brought a change in teaching children, but little of this has impacted on the training of teachers. Adult learning has not been given the same attention in terms of motivation, individualization, and self-selection of goals. Most adult learning situations presuppose that adults *ought* to want to learn because they *are* adults and, in teacher-learning, this assumption is then coupled with a low estimate of their capacity. The result is the species of superficial instruction that constitutes most professional-development work. What we respect about children — variety, individuality — we fail to apply to teachers, and what we often tell children — that learning is hard work and requires concentration and application—we do not apply to our expectations for adults. People do learn in different ways. Learning is serious business and more provision must be made in teacher-learning situations for reading, reflection, discussion, profound and thorough presentations of ideas and strategies, and for a flexible, positively expectant learning environment with sufficient motivation and adult-student involvement to create the climate for learning. When learning takes place, it becomes pleasure, too.

A TEACHER TRAINING PERSPECTIVE

In the final analysis, the essence of all teacher education, be it preservice or in-service, is to train teachers to train themselves.[9] In this sense, a creative, well-financed reform of teacher training will, ultimately, reduce the dollar burden of professional development. It will also alter the nature of the need for in-service education and make the imperatives for it less urgent.

Before that stage is reached, however, the structure of the process will have to be profoundly changed both in ways already suggested and in certain other respects not unfamiliar to those who have looked at in-service education.

A basic condition for successful in-service education is agreement on decisions between provider and participant. These decisions, and the extensive planning that should precede the delivery, must grow out of an assessment of teacher needs.[10] However, teachers are not always in a position to clearly define their needs, particularly where the environment is overladen with the deficiency approach, where there is an absence of incentives, and where candor might be misconstrued. It is first necessary that in-service education be given its rightful place as part of a total school and system design aimed at maximum instructional effectiveness and pupil growth. So long as it is viewed as separate and apart from "the real business" of the school, so long will it fail to flourish. Moreover, teachers need to be made aware of what is possible so that they will have the confidence that what they articulate is realizable.

Under such conditions, it must be recognized that the components of successful in-service programs are site-centered. This means that the school day must provide the core of in-service time, and that helping teachers and other resource personnel must be always available at the site

---

9 Frederick J. McDonald, "Research and Development Strategies for Improving Teacher Education," *Journal of Teacher Education* 28 (November-December 1977): 29-33.

10 "Needs Assessment," *New York City Teacher Centers Consortium* (Brooklyn: City School District of New York, 1978), pp. 108-31.

for follow-up and consultation. Such devices as intervisitation (and the money for substitutes to make it possible) and planned professional days are important ingredients of such an effective program. Structural changes and incentives have, basically, two primary goals: to obtain a high degree of participation and to create conditions for optimum professional growth.

There are various models available to deal with the problem—the model chosen should be dictated by its compatibility with program design. Most models, however, will emphasize components such as those previously mentioned.

One last seminal aspect of teacher training needs to be mentioned— the internship. We are convinced that internship as a part of preservice training and as a transition to in-service performance holds the key to substantially improved teacher effectiveness.[11] As yet, it is an idea in its infancy with little in the way of program design or content to accompany it, but it is tied to the lifeline of professional development. Under proper conditions, it can assist in producing teachers with greater confidence and a broader range of strategies and techniques early in their careers. A preservice internship (along with more adequate preservice screening of candidates by colleges) would make ongoing professional development more relevant to positive purpose, less a defensive activity. In-service education could then concentrate on communicating the results of current research in terms of instructional approaches, on curriculum, on maintaining currency amidst the explosion of knowledge and the social and legal changes affecting education. This approach would relieve the need to provide the correctives and palliatives that grew out of inadequate preservice preparation.

CONCLUSION

What has been a priority of no one group in education is now a priority of teacher unionists. This is most fitting, for teachers have always depended on themselves for professional growth and for confrontation of the real-world problems in the classroom. Practitioners have always known what specialists are coming to accept—teachers learn best from teachers, teachers respond best when they are participants in determining their professional fate, teachers have a stake in success.

If no one wants to make the investment in changing the scope, quality, and direction of in-service (and preservice) teacher education, then we will continue our *ad hoc* crisis-oriented relationship to teacher training

11 "A Teacher Internship Model" (Position Paper of The United Federation of Teachers, New York, June 1975).

and education service delivery. College-level educators, local school districts, researchers, administrators, government education officials, and, above all, practicing classroom teachers have much to gain from joining together in efforts to provide adequate funding and supportive resources to in-service education. The opportunity exists for collaborative, systematic professional development that is organic, relevant, and productive of real gains to the subjects of the educational process — our students. The need is obvious, the failures of current approaches legion, and the benefits of a change in approach compelling.

APPENDIX

Here are examples of contributions in the area of professional development made by The United Federation of Teachers:

A. Curriculum and Instruction
 1. Q.U.E.S.T. Minicourses — low-cost, voluntary
 2. Teacher Center — David Wittes Educational Lounge — courses, materials display, consultant service
 3. T.E.A.C.H., Inc. — The Teachers' Store — largest stock in the United States of educational materials and supplies
 4. Retraining courses for laid-off teachers
 5. Curriculum Guides — labor studies, black history, Puerto Rican studies, Jewish history
 6. Retired Teachers — a full range of minicourses and activities
B. Contractual Incentives and Professional Development Provisions
 1. Experimentation Clause — to permit innovative approaches
 2. More Effective Schools — now defunct; when part of contract, a nationally recognized approach to dealing with pupil achievement and teacher training on a total school basis
 3. Sabbaticals — study, travel (also unpaid leaves for study, outside experience)
 4. Salary Increments and Differentials for advanced preparation
 5. Rotation of Assignments — encourages renewal and diversity in on-the-job assignments
 6. Paraprofessional Career Ladder — incentives for study and advancement to teacher certification
 7. Released Time — professional conferences, intervisitation
 8. New Teacher Training Program
C. Collaborative Efforts
 1. New York City Teacher Centers Consortium — joint proposal (Board, Union, colleges) for teacher center funding

2. Mastery Learning—consortium (involving Board, Union, private industry) to fund teacher training in this instructional approach
3. Union committees and reports on teacher centers, internship, licensing and certification, restructuring the middle schools, etc.
4. State and national participation in educational task forces, conferences, educational organizations
5. Annual National Education Conference sponsored by AFT-Q.U.E.S.T.
6. Proposals and lobbying for funding and constructive legislation in such areas as Title I, Children with Handicapping Conditions, Bilingual Education, Teacher Centers, Teacher Corps (with emphasis on in-service training)

Guidelines for the Evaluation of Staff Development Programs

GARY A. GRIFFIN

Teachers College, Columbia University

There is a long history of practical and theoretical demands and sugges-tions for evaluation of school-related activities. This history illustrates, on the one hand, the rationality and logic of determining if what schools do is effective in achieving what they believe they are engaged in accom-plishing and, on the other, the political and social necessity for providing evidence that what schools do justifies the expenditure of limited human and material resources. Evaluation of school programs, whether at the instructional or institutional level, has been a persistent thread in discourse about schooling for decades. The recent emphasis upon accountability for school people and their activities is only one more piece of this pattern.

The intentions of this article are to present a condensed picture of what the author has observed as being the most usual goals and purposes of staff development over the past two decades and, inferring from that condensation, to present guidelines for evaluation of such programs that appear to be directly and reasonably related to those purposes. This is not a technical treatise on evaluation; there is ample literature available to the inquisitive reader that suggests specific techniques and analytical procedures for evaluation.[1] What is presented here is a direct attempt to alert the reader to some of the neglected evaluation issues that arise from

---

1 See for example Lee J. Cronbach and Patrick Suppes, eds., *Research for Tomorrow's Schools* (New York: Macmillan, 1969); Maurice J. Eash, Harriet Talmadge, and Herbert J. Walbert, *Evaluation Designs for Practitioners* (Princeton, N.J.: Educational Testing Service, 1974); Gene V. Glass, *Evaluation Studies Review*, vol. I (Beverly Hills, Calif.: Sage Publications, 1976); John Hayman, Jr., *Evaluation in the Schools: A Human Process for Renewal* (Monterey, Calif.: Brooks/Cole, 1975); and Phi Delta Kappa, *Educational Evaluation and Decision Making* (Bloomington, Ind.: Phi Delta Kappa, 1971).

the complexities of promoting the professional development of educators. All of what follows has emerged as a consequence of inquiring into and enacting evaluation studies of schooling generally and professional reorientation or development programs specifically.

PERSISTENT PURPOSES OF STAFF-DEVELOPMENT PROGRAMS

One of the requirements of a profession is that its members somehow continue to learn, to grow, to renew themselves, so that their interactions with ideas and with clients are reflective of the best knowledge and skill available to them. Although there are some convincing arguments that question the wisdom of calling educators professionals, teachers and other school persons consider themselves such and, *ipso facto,* create expectations within their professional groupings and in the public for acting professionally. Such expectations call for systematic attention to the acquisition of new knowledge, understanding and acting upon the latest and best of research findings, and giving precise attention to keeping up with the times as they influence the activities of schooling. These and other targets for professional development are called "conventional goals" in this article. These goals have as their complementary points of attention the publicly acknowledged phenomena of schooling. They tend to be client-centered and attend to what might be called the "commonplaces" of schools. Examples of such staff-development purposes would include giving specific attention to newly defined and demonstrably effective pedagogy, acquiring knowledge and skill in implementing innovative curricula, improving school-community relations, formulating efficient and economical school-management practices, strengthening positive student-teacher relations, creating rational pupil organization plans, increasing the meaning of pupil reporting procedures, and the like.

Obviously, this list is incomplete. The imaginative school person will add many items to it. The reason for including such an incomplete compilation is to present what are usually conceived of as the reasons for engaging in staff development. That is, such programs are mounted in order to somehow make better the offerings of the school to the clients and the patrons. Each of the items noted, and others that could be added, relate directly to the teaching-learning environment, a setting that is seen by most to be the core of the educational enterprise.

In recent years, however, it has become clear that there are other reasons being suggested for engaging in staff development, reasons that focus upon the educator directly rather than upon the educator's relation to students and parents. There appears to be an underlying assumption that attending to certain educator-directed phenomena will help to make the professional-client relationship stronger and better. These phenomena are called "individual-contextual goals" in this article. Examples of professional-development purposes related to enhancing the individual and collective capabilities of the educator include promoting greater collegiality, creating opportunities for self-actualization of educators, increasing teacher participation in school decision making, allowing for peer-group interaction, raising the level of cosmopolitanism of the professional community, and the like.[2]

As was true for the first goal area, this list of exemplars is incomplete and open to numerous additions. It does, however, illustrate the difference in emphasis that has begun to appear with increasing frequency in the school-culture literature. Implicitly, and often explicitly, a cause-effect compatibility between the two goal areas is suggested. Certain research and propositions have indicated a relation between, for instance, the degree to which a school faculty engages in systematic problem solving and the kind of pedagogy characteristic of the school. The level of cosmopolitanism seems, to some, to be related to the degree to which school persons will try out and carefully attend to the consequences of installing new curricula. School climate may be a partial consequence of the degree and kind of teacher leadership in school affairs.

It is not intended to argue the linear relationships of the pairings of phenomena noted above, only to acknowledge that they are present in either research findings or speculations about schools. What *is* intended is to draw attention to the fact that these examples of staff-development purposes and others like them are found again and again to be at the center of staff-development programs. More often than not, however, the attention is not to an agreed-to or speculated-upon relationship that matches specific items from each goal area but to one or more items in isolation, although assumptions about relationships may be present in the planners' minds.

STRUCTURAL PROPERTIES OF STAFF-DEVELOPMENT PROGRAMS

A third issue essentially different from the preceding two characterizes staff-development programs as they have been observed over time. This

---

2 See for example Carmen M. Culver and Gary J. Hoban, eds., *The Power to Change: Issues for the Innovative Educator* (New York: McGraw-Hill, 1973); Mary M. Bentzen, *Changing Schools: The Magic Feather Principle* (New York: McGraw-Hill, 1974); and Seymour B. Sarason, *The Culture of the School and the Problem of Change* (Boston: Allyn and Bacon, 1971).

is the creation (or re-creation) of an institutional structure to accomplish goals in either or both of the areas already briefly described. Although it is easy to criticize the more-than-occasional organizational naiveté of school persons as they attempt to institute organizational entities necessary to accomodate new and/or reconceptualized notions of "professionalism," it is most often apparent that these attempts are sincerely designed and promoted as ways to accomodate new knowledge, create favorable circumstances for individual and collective self-renewal, and improve the environment in which teaching and learning take place. In other words, when "business as usual" ceases to be the criterion for perceived success, school persons are forced either to provide a new structure to accomplish the new set of intentions and practices or to revise an already existing structure so that it, at least hypothetically, will assist in that accomplishment.[3]

Certain institutional phenomena, structural and ideological, appear to be necessary to bring about any of the worthy school improvements noted in the two goal areas above. These phenomena include, but are not limited to, the creation of a representative governing body, reconceptualizing rewards for participants (time, status, technical assistance, money, etc.), installing an effective communication system, establishing credibility of the program, attending to issues of evaluation, providing substantive and procedural support systems, developing linkages to intra- and inter-systems, and systematically monitoring and reporting upon the progress of the program.

As with the two goal areas, this list is illustrative only. The literature dealing with organizational health and effectiveness offers many more clues to the person who wishes to engage in the creation of a structure to support school change.[4] The purpose here is to note that in addition to substantive and personal alterations in staff behavior, it is considered necessary to attend to the ways in which the institution will support the efforts to accomplish those alterations.

What we have, then, is an amalgam of three sets of examples drawn from observed staff-development programs that together (1) indicate two areas of focus for the programs and (2) propose certain structural properties to accomplish the goals in an institutional context. This amalgam, in diagram form, might look like this:

---

3 The task of creating new environments for new work is discussed cogently in Seymour B. Sarason, *The Creation of Settings and Future Societies* (San Francisco: Jossey-Bass, 1972).

4 A comprehensive compilation of related literature is presented in J.V. Baldridge and T.E. Deal, eds., *Managing Change in Educational Settings* (Berkeley: McCutchan Publishing, 1975).

Two Goal Areas for Staff Development and Structural Properties Contributing to the Accomplishment of the Goals

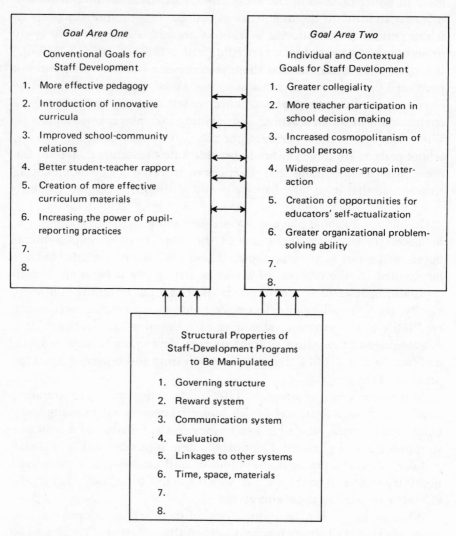

When one conceives of staff development in this fashion it becomes apparent that evaluation efforts should reflect the complexity represented and should, of necessity, move beyond such linear measures as pre- and post-tests of either knowledge or perceptions or summative measures of accomplishment of goals. The remainder of this article will offer guidelines that reflect the intricacies noted above and that, it is hoped, promote the revelation of important and meaningful data to both modify an ongoing program of staff development and judge it at its completion.

GUIDELINES FOR EVALUATION

What follows is derived in large part from an intensive study of a school-based research and development that has as its primary goal the promotion of an interactive model of collaboration among teachers, educational researchers, and teacher-educators for the design and conduct of research and development on teaching. This program, Interactive Research and Development on Teaching (IR&DT),[5] has many complex purposes and underlying assumptions about educational research and development. It focuses sharply upon creating both the circumstances for and the requisite behaviors related to role enactments different from those considered usual for school persons. It is, if you will, staff development of a new, different, and creatively defined order. In the course of studying this effort to reconceptualize long-held and broadly agreed-to roles of educators, certain requisites for evaluation became clear. These requisites and certain of the procedures for their realization are presented as they appear to be relevant to staff development as it was discussed above.

EVALUATION SHOULD BE ONGOING

The conventional evaluation of many school programs rests upon a determination at the end of a period of effort as to whether the effort achieved its purposes. Questionnaires, interviews, and other one-shot attempts are administered to decide whether or not staff development, in this instance, made any difference in individuals, programs, or a combination thereof. This certainly yields a desirable body of information and is a help to decision makers when they make judgments as to whether to continue, modify, or delete a program. A central purpose of evaluation as a tool for decision making is, to a degree, accomplished. The dependence upon some end measure, however, does not usually reveal to the decision makers what aspects of the program were more effective than others during the course of the program's life, what critical incidents were related to final perceptions, what models of operation altered over time and why such alterations took place, and other important and relevant issues. These pieces of information are necessary for decision makers and, importantly, for participants as they move forward with (or, in some instances, resign from) a program of staff development. The evaluation literature makes a distinction between summative evaluation (judgments made at the conclusion of a period of study) and formative evaluation (judg-

5 Interactive Research and Development on Teaching is a program of the Far West Laboratory for Educational Research and Development under funding from the National Institute of Education. Findings from the study of the program are anticipated as being available in March 1979.

ments drawn periodically to help redesign or modify a course of action).[6] It is the latter, formative evaluation, that is being promoted here as an important ongoing procedure. With the exception of controlled research of the process, staff-development opportunities are put in place for improvement, not just for making unilateral judgments as to effect or consequence. We *want* to improve as we move forward and appropriate evaluation procedures can help us to do that if the data are gathered over time and returned, along with conclusions drawn from them, to the participants in the process and to the planners and monitors of that process.

Useful procedures for gathering information as a staff-development program moves forward include direct observation by a participant observer who regularly and systematically records events of which he or she is a part or by a nonparticipant observer who does not interact with the other persons in the process but who serves as an observer only. Naturally, it is important to assure the credibility of whoever engages in either of these activities so that persons who are being observed are not made to feel uncomfortable, look at the evaluation processes from a distrustful viewpoint, or otherwise alter their authentic behavior.[7]

Another technique that has proved helpful in ongoing evaluation is having participants record on tape their interactions in formal settings such as meetings. These audio recordings (tape cassettes are both economical and efficient) afford an accurate account of what verbal transactions occur and can be analyzed from a variety of perspectives. Informal interactions and events that occur outside formal meetings can be captured by self-reports of participants in the forms of logs, diaries, or individual audio recordings. Although some persons may find these procedures cumbersome or time-consuming, it is a welcome surprise to discover how many others appreciate this opportunity to share individual self-reflection and idiosyncratic inquiry.

EVALUATION SHOULD BE INFORMED BY MULTIPLE DATA SOURCES

There has been a heavy reliance in the evaluation of school programs upon reports from only the so-called "subjects" of the programs. This, of course, is necessary and desirable, although it is considered incomplete.

6 Discussion and examples, drawn from classroom environment examples, are presented in Benjamin S. Bloom, Thomas Hastings, and George F. Madaus, *Handbook on Formative and Summative Evaluation* (New York: McGraw-Hill, 1971).

7 For a perceptive discussion of these methods from one who has "been there and back," see Gerry Dwight Jordan, "An Investigation to Determine the Nature and Degree of Influence of a Teacher Corps Project on the Social System of an Urban Elementary School" (Ed.D. diss., Teachers College, Columbia University, 1977).

There are others who are either involved in or affected by the programs. Consider, for example, a staff-development program designed to promote the use of new curriculum materials through a workshop format in which teachers and others try out the materials and consider them for use in classroom settings. Naturally, one would want to find out whether the workshop worked as a means for promoting the use of the materials and, therefore, one would use the participants in the process as a primary data source for evaluation of the degree of success of that format for accomplishing the purpose. There are others, though, who contribute to that degree of success and who could offer information to more fully explain the workshop's consequences: the support persons in the system who provide time and materials, the principals of individual schools who must accomodate teacher participation and subsequent tryout, students who may (one hopes) be involved in the process of determining the effectiveness of the curriculum materials, leaders and planners of the workshops who are privy to immediate and informal feedback from participants, teachers not involved in the workshop who are formally or informally affected by their colleagues' participation, and so on. The purpose here is to find out from as many sources as possible the consequences of a course of action and to determine from analyses of the data drawn from those sources the central *and* incidental reasons for those consequences.

EVALUATION SHOULD DEPEND UPON QUANTITATIVE AND QUALITATIVE DATA

The society generally and the school community specifically have been heavily influenced by the quantitative mode of determining where a person or a set of events stands in relation to other persons or events. Witness the dependence upon I.Q. scores, standardized achievement-test results presented in the form of percentile or stanine rankings, the rating scales of teacher performance that treat teaching as a score from 1 to 5, or the use of statistical procedures to determine significance of difference between groups. These quantitative methods are useful but are limited in that usefulness. They may tell us about an event or series of related events in summary fashion, but they do not give us descriptive information that helps to explain the summary. The use of qualitative methodologies, whether they be case studies or ethnographic observations or some other prose description of events, offers us explanatory power beyond that which is available from using statistical procedures solely.[8] The proposal here is not to abandon quantitative methods but to reinforce and enrich them with

8 See Robert E. Stake, "The Case Study Method in Social Inquiry," *Educational Researcher* 7, no. 2 (February 1978): 5-8.

descriptions of the events we wish to understand more fully. As was noted above, tape recordings of formal staff-development sessions were suggested to get at the ongoing interaction of participants and, subsequently, to be used to understand that interaction so that it might either be encouraged or modified in some fashion. It would be possible to monitor such recordings with a preconceived coding system and come up with scores that state categorically what percentages of total talk were devoted to curriculum, to personal issues, to professionally related issues, to professionally irrelevant issues, and to other areas of discourse. These scores would give us some indication of the broad categories of talk and, of course, that information would be useful. It would be even more useful, however, to be able to exemplify, using findings drawn from qualitative methodologies, the nature of the talk in each of the categories. We would be able to determine, for example, that the superintendent's bulletin that indicated the closing of yet another elementary school was the subject of professionally irrelevant talk, that a prominent community member's illness was a reason for an infusion of personal talk, that the curriculum issues considered were ones that might be fruitful for further staff-development efforts, or that there was a concerted effort on the part of one member of the group to divert the attention of the rest of the group from the central issues. Scores alone do not usually allow for these kinds of understandings. The addition of qualitative methods increases our explanatory power as well as provides us with opportunities for reasoned intervention and speculation for future work.

EVALUATION EXPECTATIONS AND PROCEDURES SHOULD BE EXPLICIT AND PUBLIC

Just the use of the word evaluation causes terror to strike in the hearts and minds of some individuals. The educational community has used the term so often in the context of making vital and long-lasting decisions about various individuals in schools (tenure, report-card marks, promotion, identification of persons in need of remediation) that the term itself seems to carry powerful negative connotations for many of us. Although staff development may seem to be, a priori, a worthy goal for a system to encourage, when one considers the items in goal area one above, one can see that it is possible for an individual to be somewhat tentative about being party to a program designed to help him or her to improve pedagogically if there is the belief that subsequent judgment will be not upon the efficacy of the program but upon him or her as a participant in the program. We see this phenomenon acted out in schools every day with students. Notwithstanding the broadside attacks upon schools from social critics, students who do not master a given instructional skill in school are most often viewed by teachers and others (including themselves) as failures. The programs of instruction that are believed to be powerful in promoting the skill in question move along with little or no modification. The person, then, is the failure, not the context in which the person exhibits lack of success. It should not be a surprise, then, that school persons often adopt the same set of negative expectations regarding evaluation and its consequences for people.

Given the argument above, it seems important to make very public and highly explicit the reasons for engaging in evaluation of staff development and to indicate how the procedures to be followed will help to accomodate those reasons. There should be no hidden agendas about the evaluation data. The data are there to provide information about the *program's* effectiveness, not the *participants'* capabilities or aptitudes as they help to accomplish or undermine the programs' expectations. (This is not to suggest that evaluation will not in many instances be focused upon individuals. For staff-development programs, however, it appears reasonable to assume that the program is on trial rather than the individuals who interact with it.) There will always be those persons who assume that any attempt to alter behavior will have hidden agendas. The only way to ameliorate this persistent belief is to go public, and stay there, and to continually demonstrate by explicit and implicit means that the data collected are for the purpose of program evaluation rather than for judgment about individual accomplishment.

EVALUATION SHOULD BE CONSIDERATE OF PARTICIPANTS' TIME AND ENERGY

Notwithstanding the arguments presented earlier about the intricacy of staff-development evaluation efforts, it is important to remember that participants in these programs are usually involved in the dailiness of school life. This dailiness is time consuming, energy reducing, and the principal focus of teachers' (or others') professional lives. The additional responsibility of entering into and dealing effectively and satisfyingly with staff development is often seen by many as, at best, one more way to become more proficient at what one already does well or as yet another institutional imposition that pulls one away from the "real world of classrooms." Even with the most well-intentioned participant in a program to improve the nature and quality of school life, it is unreasonable to assume that elaborate and time-consuming evaluation procedures are realistic. Lengthy questionnaires, afternoon or evening interviews, group reflections that follow a day of dealing with the almost countless interactions that occur in the normal classroom — each of these procedures is liable to be greeted with little enthusiasm, if not with outright hostility. The consequence of this lack of enthusiasm, of course, is that much of the information gathered may be suspect.

It is important to recognize that staff development is more often than not an additional layer on an already complicated and busy life. This recognition calls attention to the necessity to look at evaluation of staff development from a perspective that considers economic and efficient use of the participants' personal resources. Whenever possible informal techniques should be employed, ones that may depend upon some observation of normal behavior rather than upon out-of-context expenditure of additional effort by the participants. The tape recordings referred to earlier offer this opportunity. The effort called for from participants is really only the turning on and monitoring of the technical equipment. Further, products of the program, documents and other print materials, can be examined to determine their relation to the intentions of the program. "On the run" questions and answers can result in insights into the operation of the plan. The staff-development program evaluator should be aware of and willing to use unobtrusive measures and other techniques that emerge out of the natural setting rather than imposing yet another set of responsibilities on those persons who, willingly or unwillingly, are moving through the development activities.

EVALUATION SHOULD FOCUS ON ALL LEVELS OF THE ORGANIZATION

It was noted earlier that evaluation efforts should consider the use of multiple and complementary data sources. This point is expanded when one explicitly decides to focus on multiple levels of the organization in which the staff development occurs. There is often an oddly disjunctive relation between the higher levels of the school hierarchy, individual school or an entire school system, and other levels. It is not uncommon for staff development to be promoted for teachers while the roles played by principals, supervisors, and others in that effort are ignored. Yet, it seems reasonable to assume that changed behavior or altered expectations on the part of the teachers will have some effect upon others in the system, particularly those persons with whom they work most closely. Without belaboring the point, it is considered desirable to look at the activities and consequences of staff development not only as they relate to the primary target group, most often teachers, but to principals, central office personnel and other management staff, and so forth, and at the segments of the organization in which these persons function. It is not unusual, for example, to find that a program to increase the sensitivity of teachers to unfamiliar student groups does, indeed, result in greater understanding of and accomodation to social and cultural characteristics of the new students, but attempts to programmatically implement these understandings are thwarted because of administrative or community resistance. In such an instance, how does one determine whether or not the staff-development program was effective? Unless the gatekeepers and other authority figures in the schools receive some sort of attention from an evaluation there are few ways to understand why the program's purposes are not observable in the schools' classrooms.

Implicit in the discussion immediately above is the notion that the context in which professional development takes place is influential in the success of the program. It is a truism that complex organizations function as a consequence of individual effort, which is often masked by the layers of organization that impede clear vision of that effort. We are accustomed to hearing colleagues say, "They won't allow this," or "That's against policy," or "Our parents wouldn't stand for that for a minute." These statements, probably widely believed to be true, often have no explicit referents. When asked about the who, the policy, or which parents, we are often answered with blank stares or looks suggesting that it is believed we have just emerged from twenty years of deep sleep. There are unsubstantiated beliefs—call them myths if you will—that permeate most organizations. Schools are no exceptions and may, in fact, be exemplars of such phenomena. An important function that evaluation can perform for schools is to uncover these beliefs and reveal them to be representative of actuality or to be in some measure inadequate as explanations. These revelations will not occur if the evaluation process has a narrow focus or if it looks only at the immediate participants in staff-development activities. The evaluation should consider the individual, of course, but it should also consider the relation of the programs' intentions and activities within the broader context over time. This will result in cumulative data that will make more transparent those issues we too often understand incompletely or inaccurately.

In summary, then, the school context includes persons, belief systems, institutional regularities, a powerful and influential history, policies that impact upon practice, inter- and intra-agency agreements, hierarchical levels of power and authority, as well as new conceptions of how to get better at what it does. The evaluation design that is not sensitive to these phenomena is in danger of exhibiting markedly reduced explanatory powers and, ultimately, providing findings lacking in both credibility and reasoned directions for subsequent positive staff-development efforts.

EVALUATION REPORTS SHOULD BE PRESENTED
IN FORMS THAT CAN BE UNDERSTOOD BY
THE PARTICIPANTS AND PATRONS OF THE
PROGRAM STUDIED

The educational establishment, in much the same fashion as other occupational groupings, has developed into a series of specialty subsets. Although it is assumed that evaluators, supervisors of instruction, classroom teachers, educational researchers, and others are concerned with the teaching-learning setting but from different vantage points, the concerns manifest themselves in the formulation of different models, paradigms, theories, and methodologies. The consequence of this difference is often a sharply obvious breakdown in communication and, ultimately, understanding. There are too many obvious examples of this to require a lengthy discussion. Not the least of the examples that could be cited, however, is the more-than-occasional lack of communication power of evaluation reports.

It should be understood that it is perfectly reasonable for persons who share common knowledge and skills to develop language and other symbol systems to which they refer together and from which they draw meaning from a specialized section of a body of related phenomena. But, given the proliferation of specialized roles within a sociocultural setting— in this instance, schools—it is necessary to determine the most powerful mode of communicating across those roles if common understanding is desired. Consider this argument a call for a return to Standard English in evaluation reports that describe American efforts to promote, for our purposes here, positive staff development. If the work of evaluation is considered a way to understand the enactment and consequences of school-improvement activities, it is mandatory that the evaluator communicate clearly and precisely with all persons engaged in the enterprise studied. Leave the technical shorthand and the esoteric symbols to that group of specialists called evaluators. Speak to the clients and the patrons in language that has meaning for them and that—especially important—conveys the intentions of the evaluation effort as information for decision making.

CONCLUSION

This article has considered the complexity of staff-development intentions, attempted to clarify two broad and different areas of those intentions, suggested that the two areas are explicitly or implicitly related, and noted that certain properties of school organizations are manipulated in order to move toward goal accomplishment. This set of procedural and ideological relationships was used to justify the presentation of a series of guidelines for the evaluation of staff-development programs. Although direct relations between the guidelines and the goals and properties were not pointed out as one-to-one examples, it was assumed that the guidelines reflect the breadth and depth of staff-development issues when subjected to logical and situational scrutiny.

As others have noted, the times in which we engage in common cause toward the creation of more effective schools call for vigorous and sustained efforts of staff development at all levels of the school organization. Substantial pieces of those efforts are the determination of the consequences of our work and the use of that knowledge for the nurture and sustenance of more satisfying schoolplaces for children and adults.

STAFF DEVELOPMENT AT WORK

Overview

This section looks at the *practice* of staff development and describes and analyzes five current approaches, now or recently in use, which hold promise for future work in the field.

Lynne Miller and Tom Wolf in their chapter, "Staff Development for School Change: Theory and Practice," present a case study of an in-service Teacher Corps project where the purpose was to resocialize teachers away from self-contained classrooms to an open space high school. Their work draws heavily on the research and thinking of many of the authors in section I of this volume. Coming to their task with a recognition of the "tension between personal concerns of teachers and the institutional needs of schools," the authors develop a variety of structures using a multipath approach and administered under a system of "systematic ad-hocism." The approach presented here has many aspects that may be reproduced in other contexts and with less outside funding. The major shortcoming of the program as described is the total concentration on teacher resocialization and the absence of development activities on the leadership levels.

Patricia Zigarmi, Jeffrey Amory, and Drea Zigarmi present "A Model for an Individualized Staff Development Program," based on their work in South Dakota, which concentrates on individual classroom teachers as they cooperatively plan an improvment strategy with administrators and implement the plan with the assistance of a staff development agent. The authors clearly outline the roles of participants, the concept of matching resources that underlies the program, decision making and governance structures, and the role of the local coordinator. This chapter presents an approach to staff development that may have widespread usefulness in a variety of school districts. The major limitation of this program seems to be its concentration on the individual teacher, who is working outside a context of school-wide program planning and development.

Pauline Rauh in "Helping Teachers: A Model for Staff Development" describes a staff development approach that is very similar to the South

Dakota model. Based on the notion of experienced teachers providing assistance to his/her peers within a district, the Helping Teacher program encourages individual as well as school-wide development and improvement. The author discusses the phases of the model in practice—entry level, implementation, and self-renewal—and examines the dynamics necessary to make the model work effectively. She carefully draws attention to the pivotal role of the person serving as helping teacher and in so doing acknowledges the greatest strength and the greatest weakness of this approach. The need to develop ways to identify and train people to take on a new staff development role is suggested.

Patricia Zigarmi examines a new staff development approach that is being heavily supported by federal funds in "Teacher Centers: A Model for Teacher Iniated Staff Development." The author takes a comprehensive and critical look at teacher centers, their differences, their assumptions about teaching and staff development, and their possibilities as complements to other staff development activities. She discusses the questions of who and what are seen as resources, the kind of assistance centers provide, and the issue of responsibility. What distinguishes teacher centers from other staff development practices is the degree to which teachers themselves control the goals and the process of their own professional development. The extent to which teachers and teacher groups are successful in acknowledging the personal, social, organizational, and political realities that surround staff development, in responding to the authority prerogatives of the public and bureaucratic domain, and in utilizing existing knowledge about the importance of administrative involvement and support may well be the measure of the success of the teacher center movement.

The final chapter, "Faculty Development in Higher Education" by John Centra, explores issues of staff development outside the context of public schools. Colleges and universities, like the public schools, have reached a time of little growth and increased consolidation. This means that the majority of the faculty will, like public school teachers, remain in the same institution for a long time and that fewer younger colleagues will be hired. Thus "faculty development," like staff development, must deal with problems of funding, organization, volunteerism, and programs to encourage faculty improvement.* Research psychologist Centra reports

---

* Faculty development seems to be the term used by community colleges and universities. Staff development has been used by public schools. They appear to be talking about the same notions.

on a survey that sought to find out specifically what colleges are currently doing about faculty development and how effective are the practices undertaken. We find the discussion strikingly similar to the problems raised in the preceding chapters.

Staff Development for School Change: Theory and Practice

LYNNE MILLER, THOMAS E. WOLF

University of Massachusetts, Amherst

The approach to staff development described here has been developed as part of a federally funded Teacher Corps project, which involves a large state university and the public school system of a city in a collaborative effort to prepare teachers for change. The change, initiated and planned by the superintendent of schools, focuses on one school and is complex. It requires a change in space: there will be a move from an eighty-year-old high school facility to a new, flexible-space building in September 1978. It requires a change in numbers: the student population and staff will increase by one-third. It involves a change in orientation: the new school is designated a "community school." It requires a change in organization for curriculum and teaching: the flexible space of the new building requires a repertoire of new behaviors and materials. Finally, the change involves a change in role expectations and norms: the job specifications for the principal and teachers are noticeably different from those for other professionals in the school system. The task of the staff-development program, then, is to prepare staff in an existing school facility for their roles in a new flexible-space building. With a funded life of three years, the project is in its final year.

At this writing, quite simply, our approach to staff development involves a team of university-based educators in daily interaction over time with the faculty and administration of one urban high school. Our work is grounded in the social realities of public school teaching and in our own system of values and beliefs about change. *We define the goal*

An earlier version of this article, "Inservice Education and School Change," appeared in Sara Massey and Robert Henderson, eds., Iambic Inservice, Durham, New Hampshire: New England Teacher Corps Network, 1977.

of staff development as the promotion of change in educators and schools that improves the conditions for learning and teaching.

In the following pages, we describe and analyze our process of staff development in theory and in practice. We first develop the Staff Development for School Change (SD/SC) model and discuss the underpinnings of our implementation strategy. We then describe our program-in-practice, explaining the concrete operationalization of the model. Finally, we discuss the staffing of the program and our style of planning and management.

THE STAFF DEVELOPMENT FOR
SCHOOL CHANGE MODEL

Basic to the development of our model is an acknowledgement of the tension that exists between the personal concerns of teachers and the institutional needs of schools. In their article, Lieberman and Miller[1] discuss how teachers are constantly moving between institutional and personal levels of concern. This situation is exacerbated when the school in which they work is itself undergoing change. Our presence as "staff developers" initially served to increase the tensions that we were supposed to overcome.

Our response has been to recognize the contradiction of our role. We have also responded by accepting as a given the personal/institutional split as a starting point for our work. We are careful to develop a model of staff development that focuses on both levels of concern and need. Our staff-development efforts, then, have a dual focus: to impact on individual teachers and to impact on the social system of the school. We see teacher growth and school change as interdependent. That is, we believe individual change occurs most effectively and lastingly in a situation that supports organizational change. Conversely, we believe that organizational change is most effective and lasting where individual change is supported and encouraged.

In developing a model that legitimizes two levels of concern, we relied on two recent studies on teacher adaptation to innovation and school change. The Concerns Based Adoption Model (CBAM) developed at the University of Texas[2] presents a model for individual teacher adaptation of a teaching innovation. Developmental stages are documented based on levels of *concern* and levels of *use*. In the concerns domain, teachers move

1 See page 54 of this volume.
2 Gene Hall and William Rutherford, *Concerns of Teachers about Implementing the Innovation of Team Teaching* (Austin: Research and Development Center for Teacher Education, University of Texas, 1975).

from the need for information and personal meaning to concerns about strategy and implementation and impact, to concerns about collaboration, and finally to redefining goals. In the use domain, teachers go through a process of orientation to and preparation for the innovation, move toward a mechanical use, and then on to routinizing, refining, and finally integrating the innovation into their teaching repertoire. Finally, teachers begin a renewal process.

The /I/D/E/A/[3] studies indicate a similar process of development.

1. First people talk about the possibility of bringing about some kind of change within the school . . . . 2. Activity ensues. Some teachers begin to do something . . . . 3. Out of such activity, teachers begin to ask questions . . . . 4. The whole program begins to look shabby . . . . 5. The large philosophical questions are asked. Teachers begin to deal with goals for the first time. These questions open up others, and the process begins again.[4]

Formally labeled the Dialogue, Decision Making, Action, and Evaluation (DDAE) Process,[5] this sequence shows that change moves from the domain of personal meaning to the domain of individual action to a domain of shared or collaborative meaning, action, and evaluation. DDAE is important in another way; it is a measure of receptivity to change within a total school. Schools with high DDAE ratings were more receptive to change; schools with low DDAE ratings were resistant to change.

Taken together, the CBAM and /I/D/E/A/ studies provide a conceptual basis for the formulation of our model. The studies indicate an interdependent relationship between school change and teacher change. They justify a concentration on individual teacher concerns as a first step in a change process, and they provide a rationale for viewing change in terms of a development from individual to organizational concerns. Our model, represented below, provides for such development. We begin with individuals and their concerns, move to collaborations through the use of extensive dialogue, and then move to institutional change based on those collaborations. The institutional changes, so developed, provide a supportive framework for new growth and change — on both the

---

3 The /I/D/E/A/ studies are ongoing action research studies in schools supported by the Kettering Foundation under the direction of John Goodlad at UCLA.

4 Ann Lieberman and David A. Shiman, "The Stages of Change in Elementary School Settings," in *The Power to Change*, ed. Carmen M. Culver and Gary Hoban (New York: McGraw-Hill, 1973), p. 52.

5 Mary M. Bentzen, *Changing Schools: The Magic Feather Principle* (New York: McGraw-Hill, 1974).

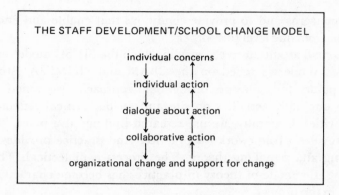

individual and institutional levels. The process is developmental and cyclical.

More concretely, we begin with individual teachers and engage them in a variety of personal interactions, most of them directed toward professional development as classroom teachers. We encourage and support individual teacher actions that change and improve upon instruction. We then enter into dialogue about the teacher's new behaviors, and we encourage dialogue among teachers who have taken similar individual actions. This dialogue is initiated and maintained through a variety of structures, some of which already exist in the school, some of which are newly invented.[6] Eventually, teachers who have been involved in dialogue decide to take collaborative actions. For instance, a group of teachers may design a new program; others may decide to team teach or to share classes; still others may decide to solve a problem that members have in common. These collaborative actions take hold, either on the formal or informal level, and become part of the social reality of the school. The school has, in effect, undergone a change, and in so doing has proved itself receptive to change. Such institutional change becomes the basis for and encourages more individual change; the process continues on the personal level, the group level, and the institutional level.

We call attention to the dialogical and dynamic nature of development within the model. We do not view development as linear. This means that at any given time a teacher or group of teachers may be at any level and is capable of moving to another level. It is the role of the staff developer to interact with teachers at their present

---

6 A more detailed analysis of structures, existing and newly invented, for this purpose appears in a later section of this article.

levels of concerns and to provide conditions that enable and encourage movement from one level to another.

We also call attention to the way in which the SD/SC model has been developed. While we relied on the CBAM and /I/D/E/A/ studies as starting points for conceptualizing our approach, we relied just as much on our daily activities on site and on our critical reflections on these activities. Generally, we use research findings as a place to begin; theory provides a framework for practice. And practice provides a basis for making and remaking theory. The process is dialectical. This style of working, the mode of theory-in-practice, has become characteristic of our work in the project.

IMPLEMENTATION STRATEGY

The complexity of the SD/SC model requires that we adopt an implementation strategy that allows for change to occur in individuals and in a school over time in varying degrees and in a variety of ways. In formulating our strategy, we depended on a gradualistic time perspective, using a social systems analysis.

We first came across the notion of gradualism in Smith and Keith, *The Anatomy of an Educational Innovation.*[7] Smith and Keith rely on an analysis of change, first presented by Etzioni, that is the distinction between the "alternatives of grandeur and gradualism." The alternative of grandeur is a "high risk strategy with potentially large rewards. One makes the large gambit by capitalizing on the high degree of system interdependence. If the pieces are finely honed and the machinery smoothly interlocked, the system takes off; if not, then the problems are momentous."[8] The alternative of gradualism, on the other hand, is based on the motto "aim high, score low; aim low, score high."[9]

The strategy is based on doing one thing at a time. There are nine elements in the gradualist approach:

1. amplifying the close: dealing with immediate and concrete concerns

2. phasing adjustments: taking small steps

3. phasing supranationality: allowing for the development of working subgroups

4. "stretch-out": extending periods of adjustment as needed

7   Louis Smith and Pat Keith, *The Anatomy of an Educational Innovation* (New York: John Wiley, 1971).
8   Ibid., p. 368.
9   Ibid., p. 373.

5. multipath approach: allowing for varied arrangements

6. locking-in systems: preventing regression

7. provision for institutional spillover: letting authority develop beyond expectations

8. provision for acceleration: accommodating to greater demands and faster progress

9. cushioning: providing escape clauses for individuals who need them

The central point here is to build on past strengths before moving into new areas and large-scale change. The gradualist strategy involves: "(1) lower levels of uncertainty and unintended outcomes, (2) decreased time pressure, (3) an increased interval for major change, (4) limited decisions related to the changes, and (5) decreased demand on resources."[10]

The gradualist strategy assumes an understanding of what is immediate for the people and the institutions we want to influence; such an understanding develops from viewing the school as a social system. Quite simply, a social system is a complex and interdependent set of "activities, interactions, and sentiments."[11] Schools as unique forms of social organization have unique social systems. Sarason[12] characterizes these systems as having a prehistory, programmatic and behavioral regularities, prescribed roles, a time perspective, and a modal process of change.

Our work on site often casts us as ethnographers, observing the dailiness of the school's activities, interactions, and sentiments and developing a critical interpretation of its social organization. We use this analysis as the basis for our decision making about how to intervene in the life of the school and how to promote changes.[13]

Our strategy for implementation acknowledges all of this and works to change it. The gradualist perspective allows us to work slowly and deliberately and prescribes the kinds of approaches we should use. The social systems analysis provides a framework for understanding where to direct our energies and how to begin.

---

10   Ibid.

11   George Homans, *The Human Group* (New York: Harcourt, Brace, and World, 1950).

12   Seymour Sarason, *The Culture of the school and the Problem of Change* (Boston: Allyn and Bacon, 1971).

13   The professional literature on schools as social systems is quite extensive. We depend on the works of Willard Waller, Matthew Miles, Seymour Sarason, Charles Bidwell, C. Wayne Gordon, and James Coleman as sources for our work.

THE PROGRAM-IN-PRACTICE

Our project's mandate is to prepare teachers for a move from a traditional and close-spaced secondary school building to one that is innovative and flexibly spaced by design. We have three specific goals for the project. They are:

1. To develop a variety of teaching/learning strategies that are necessary and appropriate for the new flexible-space school and can be initiated in the existing school site.

2. To develop norms within the faculty (sharing, collaboration, innovation, risk taking, school-community interaction, reflective thinking) that are necessary and appropriate for the new site and can be initiated in the current site.

3. To develop optional learning programs for the new site that can be piloted in the existing site.

The project goals reflect the levels of concern represented in the SD/SC model. The first goal corresponds to the levels of individual concerns/individual action. The second goal focuses on dialogues about action/collaborative actions. The third goal is geared toward organizational changes, which support other levels of change.

The structures that we use to meet these goals are of two types: existing structures or "regularities" in the school, and new structures that we invent. These two kinds of structures are discussed below as they are used in practice.

EXISTING STRUCTURES

In developing a social systems analysis, we take time to learn the daily procedures and practices of the school so that we can use them to our advantage. We gear many of our activities to the existing activities of the school. We work with guidance counselors on scheduling issues; we meet with teachers on specific teaching issues; we meet with administrators on administrative issues. When processes are vague, we help to clarify them. When procedures prove ineffective, we work with people to create procedures that are more effective. In effect, we embed ourselves in the existing formal and informal structures of the school, acknowledge the position of specific role groups, and work through procedures and processes that already exist.

This approach allows for "amplification of the close" and "phased adjustments" as well as other characteristics of gradualism. Among the existing structures we use are: individual classrooms, scheduled meetings, "mini-sabbaticals," and informal interaction.

Classrooms   Our work in classrooms involves us as coteachers, coplanners, observers, and evaluators. Upon request, we enter a teacher's classroom and provide assistance according to his/her wants and needs and our own abilities. In some instances, we are asked to observe and give feedback. In other cases, we help to carry out specific classroom innovations such as individualizing instruction, using learning contracts, designing learning stations, using small-group instruction, or reorganizing classrooms. We have access to videotape equipment and are oftentimes asked to tape classes for later analysis.

Our presence in classrooms serves to alleviate some of the isolation endemic in teaching. We encourage teachers to share the experiences they have with us, with each other. The result has been teacher exchanges of observations and visits to classes. Such activities lay the foundation for collegial interactions on a wider scale in the school.

Scheduled Meetings   We take part in regularly scheduled meetings at the school, sometimes as passive observers, other times as active participants. In the various department meetings held monthly, we have provided assistance in writing course descriptions, initiating new courses, and designing curriculum. We have brought in outside consultants to assist on specific tasks. At the all-faculty meetings, also held monthly, we have worked with the principal in doing a needs assessment survey of students and faculty, and we have led group discussions on aspects of innovative education.

We have also taken a leadership role in district-wide released-time programs. The school system has three full days of released time for professional development. Working closely with our principal, the district's director of staff development, and the various subject-matter supervisors, we have led workshops and discussions, arranged visits to other sites, planned large-group presentations, arranged for speakers, and worked with task forces on specific programs.

Our activities in scheduled meetings have allowed us to encourage collaborative problem solving as well as work with individuals. By fulfilling a need of the system and working through the system's structures, we are able to influence activities and policies and work toward our own goals.

The Mini-Sabbatical   Initiated almost five years ago by the director of staff development in the system, the mini-sabbatical provides additional released time for teachers to work in small groups around common concerns. Teachers leave the school and travel to a neighboring university or conference center and spend their time in professional-development activities. Originally designed as a week-long sabbatical from teaching, the program has been modified to meet budgeting restrictions.

We have used the mini-sabbatical structure as a way to "phase supranationality." Our version of the mini-sabbatical has small subgroups of teachers working together to develop new learning options for possible implementation in the school. We identify teachers who have common interests and who have expressed a desire to develop a specific kind of program and invite them to participate in a one- or two-day sabbatical. During this time, they conceptualize a new program and prepare a proposal for consideration by school administrators.

Our involvement in the mini-sabbatical has allowed us to modify an existing innovative structure and to use it to our advantage. The mini-sabbatical as we use it becomes a place where school-wide changes are initiated by teachers with a shared investment.

Informal Interactions Much of the meaningful interaction among teachers in a school occurs outside of formal meetings and structures. This interaction take place over lunch, in the teachers' room, in the corridors, in shared coaching and extracurricular responsibilities, in faculty sports competitions. We spend a great deal of our time "hanging out" with teachers in informal ways. Our presence around the school in ways that are goalless and natural allows us to penetrate the social system of the school in ways that outside consultants usually do not. In so doing, we share in the immediacy of teacher concerns, involve ourselves in idea sharing and *ad hoc* planning, develop a wide range of relationships, and gather information and perspectives that influence our more formal staff-development activities.

INVENTED STRUCTURES

Our almost daily involvement in the school not only makes us sensitive to how existing structures operate and can be used to our advantage, but also to the way in which what exists is ineffective, blocking change on both individual and institutional levels. In those instances, we invent new structures to reach our goals. Invented structures are most necessary in effecting our second and third goals (changing norms and developing new programs). The school as presently structured lends itself more easily to individual changes than it does to collaboration and group change. The structures we have invented in the project are: the Resource Room, Peer Group Structures, and an Instructional/Portfolio Program.

The Resource Room One of our initial tasks on site was the establishment of a teacher Resource Room. The Resource Room is central to our project; it serves as a base of operations for our staff and is identified by teachers as a place where personal and institutional issues around change may be addressed. The Resource Room was clearly a new invention; we renovated an old coal bin located in the basement of the old section of the school. The room was established to promote a set of norms that differ from those that prevail in the social system of the school as we found it. In organizing the Resource Room, our aim is to encourage collegiality and collaboration in place of individualism, to develop a future-orientation that replaces presentism and to encourage risk taking on personal and institutional levels as a counterforce to conservatism. In short, we use the Resource Room as a place to develop an alternative professional ethos for teachers who are preparing for work in an innovative setting.

The norm-changing function of the Resource Room is effected through a wide variety of activities, or a multipath approach. As usual, we begin with the immediate and the concrete. Our initial Resource Room activities involved teachers in individual and group discussion, demonstrations, and presentations geared toward the production of teaching materials and the solution of classroom problems. The room is equipped with typewriters, ditto machine and thermofax, cutting board, laminating machine, transparencies, overhead projectors, tape recorders, scheduled videotape equipment, and a variety of materials and resources. We organized discussion groups around discipline, attendance procedures, classroom organization, and other immediate concerns that teachers identified. We brought in a variety of consultants: university professors, system administrators, the school administration, teachers from other cities and schools, community people, social workers, and so forth.

In the beginning, we structured the Resource Room very highly. Every month a calendar of events was published. Teachers were sent personal invitations to join in activities scheduled during their preparation periods. Over time, we tried to take less responsibility for Resource Room activities and to encourage more teacher initiation and involvement. We have had mixed success in this effort. The utilization of the Resource Room varies. In a way, the room serves as a barometer of the sentiments of teachers toward change and their readiness to deal with the realities of the new school.

The Resource Room serves as the place where teachers can move from personal to collaborative to institutional concerns. This movement is made possible through our almost daily presence in the room, the variety of activities that are encouraged, the provisions for spillover the room allows, and the rhythm that is maintained providing for "stretch-out" and "acceleration."

Peer-Group Structures Essential to our work in changing norms and developing new programs have been peer-group structures for teachers. We have two structures, both situated in the Resource Room. The first structure is teacher-support groups, which are composed of teachers who gather in the Resource Room during their preparation or free periods to engage in conversation around emergent issues. The groups function as temporary systems, providing support and "cushioning" for their members for short periods of time. Though not task oriented by design, some groups have taken on clearly defined tasks for a time; for example, polling teachers on their concerns, documenting unnecessary interruptions in teaching time, developing new attendance procedures. Primarily, however, support groups serve as a place where teachers can share concerns, feel less isolated, and receive and give support from among their peers.

The other peer-group structure is more goal-directed and more permanent. This structure takes the form of planning and implementation teams. Having been initiated during the mini-sabbatical, these teams are composed of teachers who have developed and are currently involved in implementing new learning programs. At present, two such teams exist. They work together over a full year engaged with a constant group of students. Each team has a common preparation period; they meet daily to plan together, to make adjustments in their program, to evaluate student progress, and to assess their own strengths and weaknesses, resources and needs. These teams are involved in gradual change; they phase supranationality as well as provide for stretch-out and spillover, acceleration, locking in, and cushioning. Because the teams function as semiautonomous and protected subgroups within the school, they can develop new norms. In fact, the teams tend to merge tasks and roles and to become affectively involved with their students and with each other. These teams provide the major vehicle for instituting school-wide change and they are the primary place for practicing the new behaviors and norms that the move to the new school requires. In a significant way, the measure of the success of our program is the number of planning and implementation teams that are developed in the school before the faculty moves to the new school.

At present, we are working to develop a third peer-group structure with teachers — task forces. These task forces will be composed of teachers who volunteer to devote time to work to implement some of the structures of our project in the new school. Still in their formative stages, these task forces would carry over the structures and concerns of the SD/SC model that are judged most valuable for the new school. Task forces concentrating on teaming, establishing a Resource Room, materials development, new programs, and community education are being developed.

The Instructional Program   The instructional program is the most highly formalized of our invented structures. Designed to introduce teachers to alternative approaches to teaching and learning, the program also provides opportunities for group work and collaborations. Involvement in the program may earn teachers graduate credits, which are granted through the university or the school district's equivalency credit program. The instructional program may seem the most traditional aspect of our staff-development efforts. It delivers staff development in a way that is most familiar to teachers. In reality, however, the program has many innovative features and differs significantly from the traditional ways in which universities make outreach to public schools. The program has three basic components: (1) *modularized/site-based courses,* (2) *independent study,* and (3) *a graduate degree/portfolio program.*

1.   *Modularized/Site-Based Courses:* All courses offered are site-based; that is, university professors and other instructors travel to the school and hold classes there at the end of the working day. Usually, the instructors spend the earlier part of the day at the school, visiting classes and meeting individually with teachers. Thus far, about ten university graduate faculty members have offered courses on site. These faculty are self-selecting; by and large, they are the university people most concerned with practice and are the people most able to work with teachers in schools. The very fact that the faculty are willing to travel over an hour each way to teach their courses alleviates most of the mistrust that public school teachers express about professors of education.

All courses are modularized to allow for maximum teacher participation. There are multiple points of entry and exit throughout the school year. Such an organization allows teachers to commit themselves for short periods of time or to make a long-term investment. The flexible modular schedule is particularly appropriate for public school teachers whose after school activities vary throughout the year. In addition, the schedule allows for the development of new courses that are responsive to needs as they emerge. Courses vary in length from five weeks to a full semester, earn from one to six credits, and are staggered throughout the year. They also vary in content from teaching strategies to problems of school change.

Course content varies, but can be characterized as concentrating on theory and its application to practice. Pedagogic approaches vary also. Evaluation is used to plan further offerings.

2. *Independent Study:* Independent study involves a teacher or a group of teachers in a specific project that is contracted over time with a staff member or university faculty member. Contracts vary in terms of time commitment and the nature of the work to be done; contracts earn from one to six credits. We have two types of independent study options.

The first option, called "Applications," has a teacher or group of teachers contract to make a concrete change in the organization of their classes or programs. Most applications contracts provide for classroom observation, feedback and sharing with others.

The second option is termed "Institutional Research." Problems such as the tracking of students, guidance procedures, the use of the school intercom system, and discipline and attendance irregularities have been investigated by teachers. In some instances, the research has prompted actions that have changed school-wide procedures.

3. *Graduate Degree/Portfolio Program:* Finally, teachers may elect to enroll in a formal degree program, leading to the M.Ed. or Certificate of Advanced Study. The degree program may be completed in two to three years. The program adheres to all university regulations in regard to admissions, course work, and residency requirements. The program differs from traditional advanced-degree procedures in the type of courses that are offered, the varying options for instruction that are available, the way in which the program relates theory to practice, and how the degree candidate is evaluated.

Evaluation involves a review of all candidates by a board of their peers, in addition to the accumulation of a specified number of course units. Each degree candidate keeps a portfolio of his/her work. Included in the portfolio are a statement of goals and a description of how the goals were met, a listing of all formal course work and informal involvements in staff-development and school-change activities, a bibliography of all readings related to education, a listing of all resources used over the course of the degree program, samples of written work, samples of curriculum developed, an accounting of all applications to practice made as part of the program, and a description of involvements in the planning, implementation, and assistance in new learning programs. Only after an oral review of the portfolio by peers and Teacher Corps staff/faculty is the candidate recommended for the degree.

STAFFING, PLANNING, AND MANAGEMENT

In this final section we comment on our staffing patterns and the style of planning and management in use in our project. Our staffing and management operations were not predetermined; they developed in the first year of the project and have been altered to meet needs as they emerged in the two years that followed.

STAFFING

Our staff is composed of six people, four full-time and two part-time. Each staff member has responsibility for a particular aspect of the project; all staff members are involved in all aspects of the project to some degree. The project director, connected to Washington, D.C., and the university, is responsible for the overall operation of the staff. The field-based instructor has responsibility for the design and implementation of the SD/SC model and supervises the delivery of all staff-development services to the schools. This is a university person with faculty rank. The team leader is employed through the school district as the chief representative of the district in the project. The community-based instructor has charge over all community-based activities in the project. The two part-time people are graduate students at the university who share responsibility for the research and evaluation activities of the project.

A unique feature of our staff operations is our sharing in implementing *all* aspects of the project. For instance, all staff members (with the exception of the Participant Observer) have been involved as teachers in the Instructional Program. Each staff member has worked extensively with individual teachers in their classrooms and each has been involved in at least one team-planning mini-sabbatical. All staff participate in Resource Room activities and facilitate support groups during the day. In addition, all of us have worked with parent and community groups over the course of the project.

As a staff we share assumptions about the power of being present, and the importance of openness to change. For us, being present does not mean showing up at the close of the school day to work with teachers in courses that have merely moved the university to the school for a period of time. Nor does being present mean being somewhere at a specific period of time with the goal of carrying out an activity that enhances only the objectives of the change agent and does not enhance the objectives that teachers have for themselves or the school. Rather, presence means a willingness to commit oneself to large amounts of time on site, with no specific goal in mind and with no specific activity to be structured. This "goalless presence" is an essential ingredient in our project.

An openness to change on our parts means that "our intervention is already beginning to change us as well as the situation."[14] While it may be tempting to see oneself as helping others to change, it is impossible to do this without changing oneself in the process. In many ways, the most important work our staff does is to model norms of personal involvement, risk, and learning. In this way, the notion of presence takes on great meaning. In addition to being present to "witness" and facilitate the change in teachers, we are present as a staff of people, willing to extend ourselves in the process of school change and to commit ourselves to a journey whose end is unpredictable.

PLANNING AND MANAGEMENT: "SYSTEMATIC AD HOCISM"

There is the temptation to call the kind of planning we do nonplanning. In fact, our style of planning has been the source of some conflict within our staff. While we call the kind of planning-into-action that we do "systematic ad hocism," others think that it's "seat of the pants" management, which rarely is systematic and always gets done at the last minute. However, the project has been marked more by programs that have gone smoothly and by feelings of satisfaction than it has by poorly executed programs, disinterest, and dissatisfaction. The conflict that we have about the nature of our planning and management style is a microcosm of a longer, more protracted dialogue about planning and management theory and techniques in a variety of fields, including education.[15]

There are four attributes of systematic ad hocism: (1) having a map rather than an itinerary, (2) being long-range, (3) being adaptive, and (4) being value-based. For most of these attributes, we have looked to social theorists and, at times, borrowed their terms.

1. According to Getzels, Lipham, and Campbell,[16] *itineraries* are series of prescriptions for management or planning. They have no understanding of the country through which they travel. Emphasis is on

14   R.D. Laing, *The Politics of the Family and Other Essays* (New York: Vintage Books, 1972), pp. 39–42.

15   Among the authors engaged in this debate are William Scott, "Organizational Theory: An Overview and an Appraisal," in *Organizational Systems: General Systems Approach to Complex Organizations*, ed. Frank Baker (Homewood, Ill.: Richard D. Irwin, 1973); Jacob W. Getzels, James M. Lipman, and Roald F. Campbell, *Educational Administration as a Social Process* (New York: Harper & Row, 1968); Henri Fayol, *General and Industrial Management*, trans. Constance Storrs (London: Sir Isaac Pitman and Sons, 1949); and Donald Schon, *Beyond the Stable State* (New York: Random House, 1971).

16   Getzels, Lipham, and Campbell, *Educational Administration as a Social Process*, p. 3.

the empirical, the practical. *Maps* are conceptualizations, theories about the way organizations work, the ways individuals work within them, and the ways in which systems connect to one another.

Advocates of this position argue that ultimately administration will be improved by empiricism less than by conceptualization—less by collecting empirical solutions to operational problems than by understanding administrative and organizational processes in more fundamental and necessarily more abstract terms.[17]

The authors argue, not for abstractions that have no relevance to reality, but for the development and use of a theory grounded in practice. It is the application of prescriptions, the inflexible adherence to itineraries, that limits freedom and that becomes immobilized by the inevitable unexpectedness of complex open systems. On the other hand, the map allows the traveler flexibility in working out alternate routes in the case events make the original path unworkable.

2.   In the face of complex systems, many theorists have found the exercise of forecasting alternate futures to be a helpful one. This is what we mean by being "long term." It is important to remember that the forecast is not made with the assumption that it will enable the future to be foreseen or controlled.

It is not masterminding the future. Any attempt to do so is foolish; human beings can neither predict nor control the future. If anyone still suffers from the delusion that the ability to forecast beyond the shortest time span is given to us, let him look at the headlines in yesterday's paper, and then ask himself which of them he could possibly have predicted ten years ago.[18]

The generation of alternate futures is often used as an important way of understanding the complexities of the system as it exists now and the important decision points that will be reached in the future. For example, role play is used much in the same way as we use long-range planning—not to predict and control the future but to better understand both the values and the systems we operate in and to equip ourselves to choose amongst what may be unforeseeable and surprising alternatives in the future. Many of our predictions come true—we have strategy sessions devoted to the solution of difficult short-range problems. We feel that our short-range planning, our ad hocism, is much more systematic as a result

17   Ibid., p. 5.
18   Peter Drucker, "Long Range Planning: Challenge to Management Science," *Management Science*, April 1959, pp. 238-49.

of the long-range planning. There is a clearer understanding of the open system in which we operate than we would have if all our time were spent reacting to short-term issues.

3. The third aspect of systematic ad hocism is adaptive planning. We use the phrase in two ways: The first is being adaptive to the kinds of decisions we face. The second meaning is responsiveness. It is important to respond to the people and situations in the environment of the school. Part of systematic ad hocism is the understanding of the difference between a passive response to the environment, one in which the staff simply adapts its behavior to the environment, and an active response, one in which the staff attempts to challenge the environment with choices that reflect the full intent of organizational issues.

4. Finally, systematic ad hocism is value-based. Our work is not neutral; we have convictions. As a staff, we have found the work demanding, enjoyable, engrossing. The project has become a laboratory in which we are confronted with and test out our most deeply held values about personal, institutional, and political change. The intensity of the work and its engrossing personal nature have changed us. Whether we planned to or not, we risked ourselves and served as change models to other participants in the project. Thus, our meetings become more than an arena for theory and model building, long-range planning, and adaptive planning. They become a place where we can share and explore the learnings and growth we as individuals are experiencing; we believe this process is an important facet of systematic ad hocism in that it enables us as a team and as individuals to have confidence in our ability to make informed choices in the complex system in which we operate.

A Model for an Individualized Staff Development Program

PATRICIA ZIGARMI
University of Texas, Austin

JEFFREY AMORY
Nova University

DREA ZIGARMI
Miami University

The individualized staff development program described in this chapter was cooperatively planned by teachers and administrators who had come to realize that their own staff development had not been as effective as it might have been. The purpose of the individualized program they designed is to provide individual participants with advisory assistance and resources for planning, implementing, and evaluating their own in-service programs. With help from the staff development coordinator, an individual participant identifies a need and a set of resources to address that need, develops a proposal for review by a governance committee made up of teachers and administrators, carries out the staff development project, and interacts again with the coordinator to assess what was learned from the experience and to plan what to do next. The steps participants follow in planning their staff development projects are simply a framework that is based on a set of beliefs about the need for an individualized staff development program. This chapter describes that framework and the beliefs on which it is based.

A RATIONALE

Perhaps the single most important reason why this individualized staff development program merits attention is that it focuses on the day-by-day problems individual teachers struggle with that other staff development programs, which are geared to meet the needs of large groups of teachers or of a district as a whole, ignore. A number of educators would say that staff development programs have to be planned on a district-wide basis to address the large problems facing education today—such as declining achievement scores and desegregation. In these cases the district defines the problem(s) to be worked on. And yet, it may be that these sorts of problems can be tackled only if they are related to each staff member's understanding of his/her needs in relation to the overall problem. The individualized program is based on the assumption that staff members bring different experiences to the development activities they participate in and that these shape the way they see the problem. It may also be that until teachers' concerns with day-to-day management problems in the classroom are recognized as legitimate and addressed through staff development programs, no real work on the larger problems facing school districts can be done.

The individualized staff development program described here encourages teachers to look at their classrooms, at the curriculum, and at their interactions with students and to identify practices that are ineffective or inconsistent with the beliefs they hold about teaching and learning. The staff development projects they plan as a result of this reflection are thus based on their own perceptions of need and assessment of what might be helpful learning experiences.

In contrast to staff development programs where teachers are not involved in planning or in deciding how district resources for in-service education should be spent, staff members who participate in the individualized staff development program are involved in planning their own projects and in reviewing proposals that are submitted to a governance committee, composed of peers, for funding. In contrast to many staff development programs where teachers have no choice about what to focus on, who the resource people are to be, or when the learning is to take place, participants in the individualized staff development program decide first whether or not they want to participate in the program, since it is voluntary, and subsequently, what, how, and when they want to learn. Furthermore, the individualized program, in contrast to many staff development programs, recognizes that teachers learn and grow in different ways and through different experiences.

Finally, the individualized staff development program is based on the assumption that it is important for a teacher to engage in a self-examination problem-solving process and work a problem through to the point where she/he can see results in the classroom. Furthermore, the program is based on the belief that staff development must be continuous and that teachers need support if they are going to admit to a problem, seek help, and change what they do in classrooms. Most staff development programs do not provide for sustained self-examination or accommodate this sort of sustained learning. The individualized staff development program provides staff members with on-going support through the framework of the program, which shapes a staff member's thinking about needs and options.

To the extent that staff who participate in the program become more reflective about problems to be addressed, more critical of alternatives, more structured in planning a set of activities to address identified needs, and more concerned with applying what is learned through experiences in working with students, then the individualized staff development program described may be an interesting model that merits greater attention and provides a workable alternative to other staff development programs that may be too general to be helpful.

CONTEXT

The individualized staff development model described was initially proposed for ESEA Title III (IV–C) funding in 1974 by teachers and administrators in three small independent school districts in South Dakota. The planning was done by a group of 28 teachers and administrators with assistance from the State Department of Education. After the program was funded, the Director of Staff Development from the State Department of Education and the superintendents of the three districts continued to participate in decision-making meetings at the local level as nonvoting members, providing teachers and administrators who served on the governance committee with their perspectives on district needs and priorities and information on available resources.

Although the program was originally designed as a cooperative effort among the three school districts, the model is certainly adaptable to other settings. It could easily be managed by an office of staff development in a larger school district or coordinated on a regional basis by an intermediate agency.

FOUR COMPONENTS OF THE INDIVIDUALIZED STAFF DEVELOPMENT PROGRAM

THE STAFF MEMBER'S ROLE

The first component is the procedures that were developed so that staff members could make use of the program's resources in assessing their in-service needs and in designing, implementing, and evaluating their own in-service programs. Staff who desire to develop their own development projects start the process by consulting with a colleague who serves as an in-house advisor and program coordinator (Step 1). With assistance from this program coordinator, staff members assess their individual professional development needs (Step 2), screen possible resources, and plan a set of learning experiences to address needs that have been identified (Step 3). Staff members then develop proposals requesting a specific amount of financial support to carry out the activities they have planned, briefly defining the needs they have identified, specifying a series of learning experiences that will help meet those needs, and identifying ways of seeing how far they have come when the activities are completed (Step 4). Proposals are then submitted to a district-wide committee, which reviews them and allocates funds (Step 5). Proposals may be submitted by individuals or groups at any time during the school year and may include activities that occur any time during the calendar year. The committee has resources, such as substitute pay for released time and direct financial subsidies, to allocate in support of individual and small group projects. Once the activites outlined in a proposal are completed (Step 6), staff members review their entire experiences with the program coordinator to determine how what was learned can be applied and whether the experiences can be extended (Step 7).

This general process of developing a proposal and applying for funds is, of course, reminiscent of funding procedures used in a wide variety of settings. However, through these procedures, which are in large part new to teachers, staff members are being asked to take much more responsibility for planning and evaluating their own development experiences. Furthermore, the proposal development procedure itself reinforces many of the goals of the program, specifically those of encouraging staff members to plan development experiences on the basis of self-diagnosed needs (Steps 1 and 2), of developing alternatives to traditional college courses and in-service workshops (Step 3), and of encouraging follow-up (Steps 3 and 7).

MATCHING RESOURCES

The individualized staff development program has funds for consultants, workshops, certain kinds of materials, travel, and substitute teachers. These resources are allocated on a "matching basis."

Each proposal that is submitted to the district-wide committee includes a fairly detailed breakdown of time and dollars associated with the activities listed. On the basis of this breakdown, a "match" is established. In all cases participants are expected to invest from their own resources in proportion to the amount of release time and other financial support requested. In most cases, participants' contributions take the form of personal time, while the program's investment most often takes the form of substitute pay, workshop fees, and travel-related expenses.

The planning group for this program established this concept of a "shared investment" because it believed that the "match" would result in staff members demanding relevancy and quality from the in-service experiences they proposed. This concept also reflected the planning group's conviction that staff development is a responsibility shared by the district and the individual staff member. In that it was unreasonable to expect either staff members or the district to bear all the costs of engaging in in-service education, the "match" insured both contributions and provided staff members with enough assistance to make the program feasible.

GOVERNANCE

Once a proposal is developed, it is submitted for review to a district-wide committee composed of teachers and administrators. The committee assigns funds and establishes general procedural and policy guidelines for the program. This governance structure insures that a staff member's peers are reviewing his/her proposal and judging its suitability for funding. The planning group believed that teachers who served on the district-wide committee would develop new and valuable skills in planning and deciding how limited resources for in-service education should be spent. Finally, the governance structure provides a mechanism for district staff development needs to be effectively integrated with individual needs.

THE STAFF DEVELOPMENT COORDINATOR'S ROLE

The fourth component of the program is the role of the staff development program coordinator, who serves as an advisor and advocate for staff members who request program support. Traditionally one might expect the coordinator of a funding organization to provide technical assistance and advice to those seeking support; in the individualized staff development program, the coordinator provides more than just technical support. The coordinator is a nondirective counselor, a resource broker, an advocate, a monitor, an advisor (in the tradition of the open education or teacher center advisor) and, above all, a model teacher helping staff members become increasingly independent and "professional" in assessing needs and implementing changes.

The coordinator's role is rooted in many of the planning group's beliefs about staff development. Rather than serving as an "expert" or supervisor, the coordinator's role is to search out the client's own starting points for improvement and to support, nurture, and extend these beginnings. Similarly, the planning group felt that staff members proposing development activities need immediate reinforcement to the initiatives they take and then support as changes are first tried out. The coordinator provides support at both junctures. Furthermore, the coordinator helps staff members clarify and follow up on their development experiences. This role is consistent with the planning group's beliefs that staff development should include follow-up and be a continuous process of development.

In that the coordinator's role is the key component of this individualized program, it merits closer attention if an individualized staff development effort of this nature is going to be attempted in other school settings.

Client-Centered Counselor The coordinator is, firstly, a client-centered counselor, whose main function is to help staff members/clients be more perceptive about what is happening in their classrooms or offices and to help them clarify directions for their own growth. Since participation in the program is voluntary, the coordinator's first job is to be accessible to staff who take the initiative and ask for help.

In many staff development programs, needs assessment is initiated, at their convenience, by the people who are responsible for the program, and the results of the assessment are the basis for program planning. In contrast, this individualized model expects that needs assessment will occur whenever an individual feels it is right to begin exploring a new interest or working on an old problem. The particular needs assessment process used is also the choice of the client. While structured needs assessments may be used at the client's initiative to determine directions to grow in, it is important to note that the coordinator does not impose any procedures or perceptions on the individual. The coordinator's job is to clarify what a client can articulate about his/her needs and to understand what a client is willing to accept as a starting point for his/her own development. Charity James captured this aspect of the staff development coordinator's relationship to the individual staff member beautifully when she wrote:

> My work as a consultant has made me understand more fully than before what Socrates meant about the educator as midwife. . . . People in the field need time with someone like minded, time to voice their hopes and anxieties and to begin to think out in some detail about practical possibilities.[1]

1 Charity James, *Beyond Customs: An Educator's Journey* (New York: Agathon, 1974), pp. 61–62.

Resource Broker   The staff development coordinator plays an important role in the second step of process, resource identification, by helping clients identify and screen available resources and activity options. She/he uses a network of people who can help staff members identify available options in the form of workshops, resources people, and materials. Although the preliminary identification of resources is usually made by the coordinator, options beyond the information only stage are pursued by the clients themselves.

Although some staff seem prepared to consider a wide variety of resources in developing an individualized development plan, in many situations their initial reaction is to think only of workshops as legitimate vehicles for staff development. Many clients are surpised to learn that visits to established programs, planning sessions with other teachers, independent study, and observations by and consultations with specialists visiting their own classrooms are also viable options. While the coordinator will press an individual to consider all options, the final choice is left entirely up to the client.

Advocate   The third aspect of the coordinator's role is that of advocate. The coordinator is the client's representative in the decision-making process. Since the coordinator works closely with the review committee he/she also helps a client draft a proposal that will meet the review committee's expectations. Since a need has already been identified, resources reviewed, and activities decided upon, the focus in this step is on organizing this information in a way that will make the review committee comfortable with what the staff member is proposing. Although the coordinator plays only an advisory role in the staff member's written description of the need and proposed activities, he/she assumes most of the responsibility for drafting the budget and cost breakdown, which the client submits as part of his/her proposal to the review committee.

When the committee meets to review a staff member's proposal, a key responsibility of the local coordinator is to expand on and clarify the rationale for the proposal. Like a lawyer in a civil procedure, the coordinator makes the client's case to the review group by clarifying her/his assessment of needs and supporting his/her plan for working on those needs. In turn, the coordinator then relays the committee's decision about funding to the staff member.

Monitor/Advisor   The fourth aspect of the coordinator's role relates to his/her support for the client in evaluation and follow-up. The coordinator functions as a monitor/advisor in this phase. The designers of this individualized model believe that for any staff development program to be effective, it has to be prepared to help participants sort out and apply what they learn from the activities in which they are involved.

The coordinator's role as an advisor involves monitoring the staff member's proposed activities, helping (1) debrief his/her experiences, (2) think about curriculum or instructional changes he/she wants to make in his/her classroom, and (3) eventually assess whether or not the new strategies have worked as intended.

In certain respects, these follow-up activities may be the most unique aspect of the coordinator's role, even though the rhetoric of most staff development programs includes references to follow-up support. It is not the intention that is so unique here, but the reality. In many programs the investment of energy and thought "peaks" during the development and review of the original proposal. From there on, the client's activities are monitored, but, invariably, almost as an afterthought.

In this model the coordinator puts as much effort into follow-up as he/she does into the initial planning and subsequent review process, even though this usually requires an enormous amount of self-discipline on the part of the coordinator. Staff members proposing professional development activities receive immediate reinforcement to the initiatives they take in coming to the program coordinator. They receive support from the program in the form of direct subsidies for the activities they want to participate in. They also receive support from the coordinator as changes that result from the learning experiences are first tried out.

The coordinator's role in the whole sequence is consistent with a primary assumption on which the program is based, namely, that in-service education should be a continuous and cyclical process of development.

Developing Client's Self-Sufficiency and Independence This final aspect of the coordinator's role really permeates all of the stages of needs and resource identification, proposal development and review, evaluation, and follow-up. A coordinator is, above all, a model teacher. His/her objective is to help staff members become as self-sufficient as possible in planning, pursuing, and evaluating their own professional development. The coordinator, first of all, endeavors to make the entire process seem as straightforward and manageable as possible. She/he tries to clarify what is happening in each of the steps of the process, so that each client over a period of time (perhaps through a number of proposals) will be increasingly able to use the coordinator as a resource and ally without feeling dependent on him/her. In the first round, it is often necessary for the coordinator to take on much of the responsibility, at least until an individual is convinced that the process can work for him/her. From then on, however, increased independence is expected and worked for.

Other Aspects of the Coordinator's Role Although the five roles of the program coordinator are fairly comprehensive, a number of additional activities are clearly implied in the preceding discussion. Obviously staff development coordinators need to let prospective clients know of their services; they need to become part of a resource information network; they need to understand and be able to manipulate the mechanics of the contract review process; and they need to follow up with staff after they have started activities to see if plans need to be modified. In addition, a coordinator has to be concerned about developing and maintaining credibility with administrators and board members. This means taking the time and care to insure that administrators and board members are informed, that they understand what is happening, and that they are not bypassed at junctures that might seem critical to them.

ADAPTING THE INDIVIDUALIZED STAFF DEVELOPMENT MODEL TO NEW SETTINGS

REQUIRED SUPPORT

It almost goes without saying that a district adopting the individualized staff development model must make funds available for the coordinator's position and for underwriting staff activities. The amount itself is probably less important than the fact that the amount is a line item in the budget and that the means of access to these funds is well defined.

It is also important that the coordinator not be connected in any way with the formal staff assessment or evaluation process. Even though the coordinator may observe a staff member to help him/her assess his/her needs, the observation occurs at the staff member's request, and the coordinator should not be asked to gather data to contribute to administrative decisions concerning reemployment, transfer, or promotion.

NEGOTIABLE AND NONNEGOTIBLE ASPECTS OF THE MODEL

Furthermore, in adapting this model a district should be aware that there are negotiable and nonnegotiable, or essential, aspects of it. The negotiable aspects are those primarily associated with forms, formulas, and time-tables. If local politics dictate, for example, the composition of the review committee might provide for greater administrator participation. Or an across-the-board dollar limit might be placed on any single proposal, if local circumstances seem to call for it. Likewise, the frequency of proposal reviews might be increased or decreased. In a particular case, a district's budget might make it necessary to call for a sixty-forty or seventy-thirty match of client and district resources, instead of the model's provision for a fifty-fifty split.

The *essential* aspects of the model, on the other hand, are related to the goals the program holds for participants and to the process it prescribes for needs assessment, resource identification, proposal development and review, follow-up, and evaluation. The model is designed to help staff become increasingly more reflective about their work with students in the classroom and more responsible for planning and evaluating their own professional development projects. The individual's involvement in each step of the process is far more important than the number of staff members served. Finally, the importance of the coordinator's role in the model cannot be overemphasized. Our experiences in working with and observing the evolution of the model in three school districts have confirmed this over and over again.

These essential aspects of the model may create a tension between the district's criteria for success of the project in relation to the number of people served and the project's long-term goals in relation to the quality of support staff members receive and between the client's needs for short-term solutions to problems and immediate access to the project and the project's long-term goal to encourage sufficiency and responsibility.

POSSIBLE TENSIONS BETWEEN THE STAFF DEVELOPMENT COORDINATOR AND THE DISTRICT

Administrators, board members, external funding agencies, and evaluators tend — when they are reviewing a program's development — to emphasize their interest in quantity more than quality. They reason that the program has merit if it serves a large percentage of teachers and administrators in a district.

In most cases, board members want to know how many proposals have been developed, how many approved, how much money has been committed to them, how many teachers and administrators are involved, and how many "repeaters" there have been. Their emphasis is on the first five steps of the model process, through proposal development and review. Follow-up assessment — a review of what the staff gained from the experiences, a statement of what changes are planned for the client's classroom or office, and subsequent assessment of the impact of those changes on students — is usually taken for granted. Likewise, staff themselves are usually much more concerned about getting help to participate in a learning activity than they are in getting help to sort out the implications of that activity for their own work situation.

This creates a problem for the coordinator of an individualized staff development program that asserts that follow-up is the *most important feature* of the entire operation.

It is understandable, therefore, that coordinators sometimes become so involved in proposal development activities that insufficient attention is paid to follow-up. This tendency to short-shrift evaluation and follow-up in many ways compromises a key component of the model.

POSSIBLE TENSIONS BETWEEN THE STAFF DEVELOPMENT COORDINATOR AND STAFF

The basic dilemma the coordinator encounters in interacting with the client in each step of the process is that the individual may define his/her problem or interest in a general way (for example, to improve his/her teaching of reading); be unwilling to examine alternative activities and resources; and yet want to participate in the program and take advantage of the available funding. The coordinator has a difficult task under such circumstances; that is, to balance his/her response to clients in such a way that their perceptions of their needs are not denied, yet overall growth toward self-sufficiency in needs assessment and planning professional development is encouraged.

One of the coordinator's main tasks is to convince staff members that the resources of the program are indeed accessible, although not automatically available. It is not that the program demands that staff follow all seven steps of the process exactly, but that the process of self-examination is important. The coordinator values getting a client to become more reflective about the nature of the problem to be addressed through a staff development experience, more critical of possible resources, and more structured in planning a set of activities and assessing their impact. When clients feel they know what they want to do (for example, attend a particular workshop), the coordinator might ask them to restate their need in terms of their expectations for change in their classrooms (in terms of ends, not means) and then not require them to review a variety of learning activities before settling on specific activities to be included in the proposal. However, the next time one of these same clients wants to develop a proposal, the coordinator might push for more careful and extensive resource identification.

Another tension between staff and the coordinator may build up when the client is asked to write up the proposal. The individual may feel hassled by that step in the process. In short, it often seems more expedient for the coordinator to draft the page to page-and-a-half proposal than to insist that the client do it. Again, the tension here arises from the juxtaposition of clients' impatience to get going with their development plans and the program's concern with developing their sense of responsibility to their professional development and self-sufficiency.

The following incident illustrates yet another dilemma in the staff's relationship to the coordinator:

Originally three teachers in one elementary school got together to explore alternatives to the traditional reading approach they had been using. They felt strongly that primary students needed more reinforcement experiences in decoding, spelling, in using words in context. After exploring alternatives, they decided to invite a consultant from a nationally validated project to their school to work with them in developing a new approach to teaching reading. As news of the workshop spread, other teachers asked to be included in the workshops. Eventually the original group of three became a group of 20 in a proposal submitted to the staff development review committee for funding.

Our experience suggests that the larger groups like this became, the less inclined the original planners of the workshop are to see the experience as something they have control of, as something that was set up to serve their particular needs. In other words, the original client group loses whatever sense of responsibility for the success or failure of the venture that they might have had. In the long run, this inhibits the refinement of their skills in planning, implementing, and evaluating their own development programs.

At each of these junctures the coordinator is faced with assessing the relative advantages of making the client follow the steps of the model as outlined, believing that the long-term effects of following the steps will be powerful, and the advantages of the alternative course of action, which allows the client to gain easier access and possibly more confidence in the process. Inasmuch as these dilemmas were encountered in the implementation of the project in the original three school districts, we feel that they are bound to occur in settings that adopt the model. At least the problems need to be anticipated, at best resolved, if successful implementation of the model is to occur.

SUMMARY AND CONCLUSIONS

We have attempted to describe the four key components of an individualized staff development model designed to help staff members plan and evaluate their own professional development programs. We have focused on the role of the staff development coordinator and his/her interactions with staff members as a way of understanding the kind of support they need to participate in the process. To the extent that the coordinator can help staff members value and feel some ownership in the process, we believe the individualized staff development model will help teachers think more about how they learn and how their students learn and be more thoughtful in selecting and planning learning experiences for themselves and their students.

It may be that the way in which administrators approach teachers' learning is a powerful model for the way in which teachers approach students' learning. To the extent that administrators individualize staff development experiences for teachers, teachers may be more likely to individualize learning activities for students.

At the same time, districts that adopt the individualized staff development model may be able to break a set of bad habits that are all too characteristic of most staff development programs in schools: planning programs in response to problems that are too broadly defined, catching onto initial definitions of problems without further examination, not involving staff members in planning and therefore not encouraging them to take responsibility for what happens in or after the learning experience, requiring participation, not providing alternative formats and resources, and ignoring the critical need for follow-up support.

Helping Teacher: A Model for Staff Development

PAULINE S. RAUH

Stamford Public Schools, Stamford, Connecticut

I entered the field in March to assist teachers in planning, organizing, and implementing methods, materials and approaches to an integrated curriculum on levels K-6, by invitation only. I was ready to respond to any of the 142 teachers assigned to me, but apprehensive concerning the possibility of limited requests due to the already heavily scheduled classroom teacher. Although *I* knew that my role would be of great assistance to teachers, I feared that they may not have perceived it similarly. My unfounded fears dissolved with the first responses to an 8 a.m.-3:30 p.m. blank sign up sheet which I had left with a Media Specialist a few days before. Not only did I find each half-hour filled with a request for assistance, but extra notes were attached for the "overflow." My only error had been omitting a lunch break! When each visit at the 6 schools produced the same receptive response, with teachers willing to meet before school and stay after school (not to mention giving up their coffee breaks and/or lunches in their rooms, just to consult me about their programs), I realized how teachers valued the position of curriculum facilitator and how desperately teachers have needed professional and regular assistance from a non-administrative colleague, in providing meaningful instruction for today's students.[1]

A basic question facing educators is how to give teachers the help they need in a way that, in fact, will be seen as helpful by the teachers. This article describes the genesis of a staff-development program, based on the model of the "Helping Teacher," which has been in use in an

---

1 Joan M. McGee, "As a Curriculum Facilitator" (Unpublished document, 1974).

urban/suburban school district for some time. In the pages that follow, I describe the Helping Teacher model and its application to the social, political, and economic realities of the school district where the author presently directs staff-development activities.

OVERVIEW OF THE HELPING-TEACHER MODEL

The Helping Teacher model is based on the notion of the "helping relationship." This relationship, as described by Carl Rogers,[2] is one in which at least one of the parties has the intent of promoting the growth, development, maturity, improved functioning, improved coping with life, of the other.

The verb *help* is defined as:

> to give or provide what is necessary to accomplish a task or satisfy a need; contribute strength or means to; render assistance to; cooperate effectively with; aid; assist.
>
> . . . to give aid; be of service or advantage.
>
> . . . furnishing another with something needed, especially when the need comes at a particular time.[3]

A helping teacher is a professional staff member whose primary function is to assist other teachers in a peer-support role with the emphasis on improving their performance in actual classrooms.

The term *helping teacher* has its roots in "Jeanes[4] teachers," who served for sixty-two years (1908-1970) in Georgia schools, working on a county-wide basis in the employ of county school officials "to help" improve the work of the schools and community life of the Negroes. While their specific functions and positions changed as did the status of Negro education in the South, the role remained one of support and supervision.

More recently, the helping-teacher concept has taken hold in a variety of districts. For example, in New Jersey, the helping teacher is a state employee, a member of the field staff assigned to particular school districts in which there are no local superintendents. The role has been defined thus: "to help the teacher help the children." To accomplish this, the helping teacher works in a variety of ways.

2   Carl R. Rogers, *On Becoming a Person* (Boston: Houghton Mifflin, 1961), pp. 39-58.

3   *Random House Dictionary of the English Language*, unabridged ed. (1976), s.v. "help."

4   Georgia Association of Jeanes Curriculum Directors, *Jeanes Supervision in Georgia Schools: A Guiding Light in Education* (Athens, Ga.: Southern Education Foundation, 1975), p. 304.

She visits the classroom observing the children and the teacher at work; she brings new materials, resources, methods, and ideas to the attention of the teachers; she confers with the teacher and helps her plan effective ways to improve the educational program; she becomes a trusted co-worker and friend to whom the teacher can go with any problem. All her efforts are aimed at providing conditions which encourage teachers to develop their best potentialities and increase their competency.

The "helping teacher" works with teachers in groups as well as individually. She helps to sponsor, plan, and carry on workshops, conferences, and meetings of all kinds and through these group activities seeks to develop increasing understanding, insight, and skill. Over time, the role changed to become to a great degree a curriculum consultant on the staff of the county superintendent of schools.[5]

In Texas, the helping teacher is supported by a Department of Health, Education, and Welfare (HEW) School Based Educator project. "A school based teacher educator (SBTE) is a professional who has responsibilities for either preservice, in-service, or continuing teacher education and whose primary base of operations is in the elementary or secondary school."[6] And in Ann Arbor, Michigan, the "crisis teacher" fulfills a similar role as the school resource person who works in a school rescue operation with "problem students" and their teachers.[7]

While titles, roles, and functions vary according to time and place, the notion of the helping teacher is consistently characterized as the local district use of experienced teachers as resource people and problem solvers for local district staff-development efforts. The helping-teacher notion grows from the belief that if teachers are to experience success in reaching higher horizons and effectiveness, it is the obligation and responsibility of the school district to provide staff with time, assistance, and support in their professional growth, and to recognize that there is a need to help teachers in their own settings. This differs from most traditional staff-development approaches, such as after-school in-service classes, "outside expert" lectures, workshops, and university courses.

5   Eric Groesinger, "What Is a Helping Teacher?" *New Jersey Educational Review* 29 (March 1956).

6   Robert W. Houston et al., "Developing the Role of the School Based Teacher Educator," part 1, *Staff Development Newsletter* 3, no. 1 (August 1976): 1.

7   William C. Morse, *The "Crisis" or "Helping Teacher" in the Public Schools: Theory and Practice* (Ann Arbor, Mich.: University of Michigan Press, 1966).

LOCAL DEVELOPMENT OF THE MODEL:
THE INSTRUCTIONAL ASSOCIATE PROGRAM

In 1972, the school district in which I am employed completed the final phase of racial integration, K–12, through a total redistricting of the elementary schools. A new board of education policy calling for individualized instruction was to be implemented at the elementary level at the same time. Along with these events came numerous new curricula, materials, and instructional programs. Under these circumstances, the fact that individualized instruction was implemented to any degree was to the credit of a dedicated, overburdened staff.

The makeup of classes and school populations was now heterogeneous across the district. A wider range of student needs, experiences, and achievement levels within each classroom created new and/or different problems for teachers to solve. All students on the same page of the same book with the same assignment just didn't work! Consequently, some instructional alternative was urgently needed to better meet the range of abilities within the classroom.

One year later, a new elementary social studies curriculum became the "spearhead" and common denominator for opening new paths for student learning. Based on an inquiry, process approach, it required a wide departure from past instructional practices. A high discomfort level was created as teachers realized that some of their "favored" units — content, materials, activities, and lessons — were inappropriate. It became evident that a variety of approaches for individualizing and involving students were needed; small-group and individual activities frequently would be more appropriate than total class recitation. The basal textbook vanished, replaced by multimedia materials and multi-texts with a wider range of reading levels. No longer was there a full class set of books. Emphasis was on the development of concepts and the learning process, not acquisition of content alone.

Principals and district personnel recognized that the acceptance of the desired changes and implementation of this curriculum would be more immediate and encompassing if accompanied by planned training and staff support. Three curriculum-facilitator positions were created on a temporary (six-month), experimental basis to provide full-time assistance to elementary staff. Every elementary classroom teacher was involved in "hands on," all-day workshops focusing on this new curriculum.

Following the workshops, the facilitators were available to plan with teachers and to go into the classrooms to assist them with new strategies and management as well as, in some instances, different content. It was recognized that although the initial emphasis was social studies, many of the strategies, activities, and resources would be transferable to most subject areas of an individualized instructional program. It was clearly established at the outset that the facilitators were to serve and assist in curriculum implementation and not to evaluate staff—in no way were they to "usurp" the principal's role and responsibilities or to be a reporter or "snoopervisor" of teachers.

What actually did occur? Teachers were periodically brought out of their classrooms for meetings and workshops that pursued specified curricular goals and content as well as areas of concern that teachers themselves helped identify. Sitting down in small groups with outside experts and the local facilitators, teachers worked on specific content and problem solving or simply strove for improved, practical methodology.

These work days were frequently followed up in the classrooms by specific help and suggestions from the facilitators. Occurring only at the teacher's invitation and without the involvement of evaluation, this support system proved to be a great help to many teachers who needed new strategies and know-how or wanted other forms of assistance.

As the six months passed, the positive feedback on this experimental implementation model indicated an interest in maintaining a support system to assist teachers in their efforts to individualize (personalize, humanize, etc.) instruction. Teachers and administrators, individually and in small groups, spoke to the continuing needs for assistance and support in the general area of instructional development involving classroom methods and procedures necessary to *all* learning experiences.

A proposal by curriculum and building administrative staffs to establish a program that would continue the support program was accepted by the board of education, but not without "costs." In a personnel trade-off, ten reading-consultant positions were replaced by nine local facilitators. These were people to whom staff could turn for support, ideas, suggestions, and often "that extra pair of hands" when trying out something new in the classroom setting.

The facilitators were to work with teachers who requested their assistance, responding to the expressed needs of the teachers in terms of curricular implementation, the development of teaching strategies, and the improvement of teaching skills. The elementary helpers originally served as general curriculum specialists concerned with teaching strategies. The following goals were accepted in the establishment of the program:

1. To provide assistance to elementary school personnel as new instructional methods and materials are being introduced and/or developed.

2. To strengthen the overall support system within each school with the cooperation of the district's resources.

Formally called The Instructional Associate Program, this variation on the helping-teacher model has been in operation for four years. The facilitators are titled "Instructional Associates" or IAs and have grown to ten in number. Service now reaches K–8 staff. High school personnel have kept their distance, but with a watchful eye to events and consequences. Faced with the need to provide an alternative instructional program for low achievers, a small group of high school teachers, in strong command of their subject matter, have begun to work with IAs in terms of learning styles, motivational techniques, and instructional strategies appropriate to their students' needs.

At present, the local model has two distinct aspects: (a) peer support to individual teachers and small groups at teacher request, and (b) mandated program priorities of district or school-building scope. The model is being changed to meet both areas of responsibility and provide flexible utilization of staff—in view of identified goals and priorities. In order to accomplish desired change, things must be done in a systematic, purposeful manner. We recognize the need to refocus staff-development efforts in order to provide planned, sequential, intensive experiences that will increase the capacity of staff members to perform functions to their satisfaction and/or to the satisfaction of the organization. A problem-solving model of change with its components of user centeredness, user diagnosis of problems, and emphasis on building user capacity to solve problems will generally be employed.

This new model will allow concentration of staff-development resources—personnel, time, and funds—in a limited number of *TARGET schools/programs*[8] at a given time, focusing on certain schools and specific programs, and will employ a systematic approach to change. The people to be affected by and involved in the change must be allowed active participation and a sense of ownership in the planning and the conduct of the change. Stress will be placed on relating planning and evaluation to program implementation. Staff-development services will be a key component in operationalizing the TARGET's plan.

TARGET PARTICIPANTS

Prior to being designated TARGET participants, the staff (administration and teachers), in collaboration with the department of instruction,

---

8   Hereafter referred to as TARGETS.

will determine their own proposed general plan for change and renewal indicating the areas in which staff-development assistance, human and material resources, should be focused to achieve the identified end.

TARGETS for which intensive assistance will be provided to implement the action plan will be selected collaboratively by the curriculum/instruction and staff-development offices with the final approval of the superintendent. The specific criteria for identification of the TARGETS will be established/reviewed on a regular basis to ensure that the efforts and commitment are meeting the board of education goals, identified district priorities, and the TARGET's own stated objectives. The TARGET staff then will establish a systematic action plan working with the staff-development department.

The composition of the particular TARGET thrust will be representative of various needs and developmental levels (renewal, innovation, implementation, new roles/responsibilities) at any given time. The length of time a staff and/or school unit is involved in the in-depth TARGET program will depend on the scope of the task to be accomplished, with ongoing, joint assessment by building and district staffs. All staff in the TARGET will be required to participate as delineated in the specific plan for this TARGET.

DEVELOPMENTAL PHASES OF THE MODEL IN PRACTICE

The three phases of the helping relationship have been identified as: entry level, implementation, and self-renewal. In the section that follows, these three phases are used as a way to describe and analyze the developmental sequence of the model.

ENTRY LEVEL

First and primary to the model is the need to build trust between teacher and IA on a one-to-one basis. The way can be cleared by those at the top, district or building, but it is the relationship that actually develops between individuals that is crucial.

At the outset of our program, the district superintendent's support and expectations for the staff-support program were declared in a memo to the elementary principals:

> I am asking you to assume the responsibility to support and encourage the optimum utilization of this assistance program. There must be a team effort for this program to be most effective. You, as the instructional leader of your building, must set the pace to encourage and utilize wisely a most valuable opportunity for improving the educational program.

The Superintendent is totally commited to this program and feels certain that its value and potential are apparent to you in attempting to best meet the challenge of "individualization."[9]

Yet, a great deal more had to occur before most teachers (and principals) would venture to request IA assistance.

The initial plan provided a framework that would ensure a fair distribution of "contact" time for every school, yet be flexible in order to permit spontaneous response to requests as they were generated by teachers. The sixteen elementary schools were clustered into three geographically related groups, with teams of three associates assigned to a cluster. Definite service days each week were established for each school. Each IA had several school-assigned days, with the remainder of the week open for responding to individual teacher requests. The main determinant of time distribution was to be need and staff requests.

When they first started out in the schools, the IAs set up appointment charts in the school offices. It did not take them long to realize that this was not an effective way of communicating with the teachers. Many teachers held back, perhaps not wanting the principal and other teachers to think they needed help. The IAs then became what they like to refer to as "corridor walkers" — they literally walked the corridors making themselves very visible and available to the teachers. This approach proved more successful, with teachers making appointments with them as they walked by. IAs found that once teachers asked for help in one area, they inevitably sought advice or assistance in other areas.

The IAs found that a combination of conditions was necessary to get "business rolling" in a school. Establishing credibility was the most essential condition for an effective working relationship to develop. IAs who were experienced, practicing teachers within the district seemed to enjoy the greatest degree of early acceptance. Having recognized at the outset that they had no positional power, they worked from their own personal bases.

Basic to all initial endeavors was the understanding that the essential ingredient in the helping relationship is trust built on a one-to-one basis: the working out of mutual respect for each other. It was likewise essential to accept each teacher's and school staff's belief that their particular situation, problem, or need was unique.

The IAs had to be highly visible to the teachers — visible where they were actually working and producing with others. It was essential to have one teacher give the IA a chance to get a foothold. Knowing the school

9   Reigh W. Carpenter, memo, September 18, 1974.

social system was important so that there could be initial involvement with a teacher who was secure, commanded the staff's respect, was considered a strong teacher, yet willing to take a chance. The IAs found that when they worked with a key teacher, other teachers would watch, assess, and eventually follow suit.

A positive IA image was found to be low-keyed; energetic but not aggressive; self-confident, secure, but not egocentric; competent in his/her field but not flashy or "know-it-all" in style. Being a good listener and accepting whatever the teacher identified as the starting point exemplified the same "good teaching" methods used with students. The teacher's level and "felt" need must be accepted and valued. Without both respect and the proper entry-level behaviors, the assistance would be frustrating and fruitless if not detrimental.

The IA must be seen as a "helper" who not only gives ideas and directions but one who "rolls up his/her sleeves and works." Use of a new content or program target where the need focused on the "newness" and not on teacher inadequacy proved the best starting point. "Aim low, score high" served as a valuable beginning sight. Building on success, teachers were willing to stretch and chance.

In a voluntary milieu, growth can be haphazard because the teacher is in the "driver's seat." IAs cannot address needs they diagnose unless the teacher is receptive. A danger existed (and still exists to a limited degree) that IAs would be perceived as working only with the "poor teachers," those having problems, or those who want merely to impress and "polish the veneer" but not really change.

IMPLEMENTATION

Requests have been varied and often involve many facets of methodology. Typically, a first meeting with a teacher is based upon a discussion of curriculum, often focusing on the new Social Studies, since it was introduced at the workshops. The meetings move rapidly to a variety of subject areas, and while I often assist in suggesting key activities in a given situation, it frequently happens that the teacher has a marvelously creative idea for presenting or carrying out a particular unit of study, but perhaps has not quite had the courage, know-how, or the support to follow it through. The encouragement, support and suggestions that I offer are often just the needed incentive to launch many teachers into new areas that they otherwise may have taken much longer (if ever) to implement.[10]

10   McGee, "As a Curriculum Facilitator."

Crucial to any effort is the IA's ability to actively listen, to be able to sit down with a teacher, and, in a few minutes of "airing time," turn him or her around from focusing on personal feelings and roadblocks to moving forward on the task at hand. IAs employ a systematic action plan for teacher assistance and change, modeled on a problem-solving approach. The four basic components, used singly, in various combinations, or in total, are known by the anagram PIER: Planning, Implementation, Evaluation, and Resources. Evaluation is the component most frequently bypassed but actually is most important to ensure that teachers reflect on their learnings and experiences in order to improve, integrate, or delete strategies for future implementation.

Early requests usually focus in the resource or planning components. It is easy to secure new materials and assistance in planning; it is a whole different ballgame to have another professional observing, working, and assessing alongside you in your classroom! That step across the threshold of the classroom comes only when a good trust level has been established, and sometimes it never comes.

The IA starts with the teacher's initial requests, but if, after reasonable time and effort, the level and type of service sought remains static (e.g., materials drop-offs, demonstration lessons, brainstorming), the IA must prod, stretch, suggest, and cajole. If no movement in new directions is observed, there comes the point in time when the IA must confront this fact with the teacher. That "extra pair of hands" or "sounding board" is valid in the support-strategy model only when there is teacher commitment, energy, and effort for growth. Otherwise an amicable but firm closure to the relationship must be made by the IA, but always with care to leave the door ajar should the teacher be ready to make the move in the future.

After a track record of four years, staff has a greater understanding of what is within limits; there are fewer attempts made to use the IA for a "runner," and more in-depth, joint involvement in the total instructional cycle is occurring. For some needs, one or several components are valid, but usually, for true impact, a total approach (all pieces) is necessary to assure that the puzzle is completed.

Teachers and IA map out, at the first sessions, the objectives of their work together and specify the actions, activities, resources, and strategies necessary to accomplish them. The Action Plan, jointly developed by teacher and IA, provides a comprehensive approach in which work sequence, responsible agent(s), time frame, and formative assessment techniques are spelled out.

This plan serves as a working document that is continually updated and altered as needs arise. All parties know what is expected. The exit point is clear if the IA and the teacher have initially established where they are headed and how they will know if and when they get there—that is, continual, informal assessment.

The teacher must match the IA's involvement—resources, time, and effort expended—to ensure shared responsibility, ownership, and commitment. Unwritten, but understood, is the policy "to do with, not for the teacher." Only through shared efforts will professional growth occur.

There is an ever-present need to ensure that IA assistance be of the highest possible quality and purpose. The thrust in the early years of this model was in helping teachers organize and manage a multi-materials approach, maintain a record-keeping system, and use a variety of techniques. Only limited attention was given to student characteristics and learning patterns in terms of matching them with the most appropriate instructional approaches.

There are teachers who are ready, able, and willing to refine this process by diagnosing students' learning styles and subsequently modifying their teaching strategies. The IAs need to assist teachers in becoming more analytical about these issues.

The IAs strive to cluster as many resources—people, materials, and approaches—as appropriate. They work toward the integration of subject matter and skills development for meaning and application.

Rather than spending inordinate amounts of time and energy on specific content or strategies, IAs need a more transferable approach to assisting staff in the implementation phase. The approach should be to encourage the teacher to focus on underlying learning psychology and assumptions of instructional strategies, all of which can give the teacher a "handle" on the curriculum. In this way, teachers might be better able to pick and choose in order to develop their own handles.

Teachers need to see demonstration lessons, packaged programs, or specific plans not as rigid models to be replicated but rather as approaches to be internalized in a transferable way. This can be accomplished only when the teacher has achieved security and competence in everyday instructional performance. The first stage of assistance must be to respond to the teacher's immediate felt need with something of meaning and success, even if the requested action level seems extremely low.

There are no pat successful modes of operation; rather, the IA's work can best be described as "baptism by fire." Trial and error are necessary in first efforts with a particular teacher, a particular situation; what works in one place or with one teacher may not be the answer for another. IAs have been successful in identifying and developing what they can be by honestly assessing what they cannot be. Each individual support person brings certain strengths, experiences, and expertise to the position. The model will reach its fullest potential only when the IAs "match" and "trade" clients according to need, among themselves. In order to do this, the support staff needs time to share among themselves. Cross-pollination of ideas and experiences requires time and nurturing.

The IAs are not in competition with teachers. They are willing to work hard with teachers, and then "stand in the wings," giving all the credit to the teachers. Nothing breeds success like success!

The "Information Retrieval" approach to introducing a new model has been a method with which teachers have frequently requested assistance — often in areas other than Social Studies. In some instances, an integration of subject areas occurs as a result of discussions and planning. In other cases, teachers request assistance in a specific area, and then I can point up the similarity of this method to other instructional areas. I have been asked to assist in setting up an individualized reading program in one classroom; this led to the teacher's further understanding of a skills continuum check-list, a method of record keeping, applicable to any area of study. This also called for a gradual rearrangement of the classroom to accommodate small group and individual work arrangement as well as the usage of multi-media materials.

I have assisted in the planning of a look at American History that included a study of local, centuries-old grave yards; a study of the school structure itself, tracing its community's history back to the days of the Indians; and a simulated Archaeologist's procedure in which students collected wastebaskets throughout the school while others reconstructed the events of the day by examining and categorizing wastebasket remains. While there is never a dull moment, I drew the line at the written request that I just received: "I am beginning a unit on dairy products — can you bring a *cow?*"[11]

SELF-RENEWAL

The principal is the key to change. IAs have been most effective where building administrators acknowledge, support, and value — but do not "legislate" — IA use.

Prior to the TARGET model, efforts on a volunteer-teacher basis had not been concentrated enough; IA's were not involved enough in a school's

11   Ibid.

social system to effect long-term change. A critical mass of teachers is needed for change; scattered, voluntary involvement serves only to reinforce good teachers and allows less competent teachers to perpetuate their inadequate performance.

If the peer-support strategy is going to be effective, IAs must work toward whole school or subgroup involvement in order to help sharing and internal support occur. It is necessary to break down the normal school ethos (school vs. school concept) and to replace it with the tenet of help. Assisting a teacher on a one-to-one basis does leave that teacher better informed, yet still isolated.

IMPLICATIONS OF THE IA ROLE

There are few school districts that will be financially able to employ sufficient numbers of support staff to meet all needs and demands. Therefore, the reward system needs to include a vehicle by which teachers' experiences and expertise are recognized; expectations should be set that teachers have the extended responsibility, in turn, to share and/or promote whatever they developed with IA assistance. A supportive peer reference group can, under these conditions, become a responsive, dynamic entity in the process of renewal.

The IA position is not for everyone; it requires a mix of skills, personality traits, and competencies. IAs need to be "together" individuals— self-confident and skillful, realistic about others, yet not shirking from the responsibility of having opinions. The importance of matching people to the requirements of the job is every bit as crucial to the success of any effort as is the need to match the specific professional development endeavors to the client's needs and situation.

The selection of IAs is not a minor issue. "It is not inconceivable that well over half the battle is won or lost at the point of the initial selection decision."[12] A careful assessment of potential capabilities is essential. The successful IA must be a very special person—one who, as Lippitt suggests, needs to possess an "increased awareness of self, others, and the larger environment," allowing "for a more conscious use of self . . . as a professional tool."[13]

Concern, time, and effort must be expended to provide for the IAs' growth and support. They must have varied and continual opportunities

12   David P. Crandall, "Training and Supporting Linking Agents," in *Linking Processes in Educational Improvement*, ed. Nicholas Nash and Jack Culbertson (Columbus, Ohio: University Council for Educational Administration, 1977).

13   Ronald Lippitt and Gordon Lippitt, *Consulting Process in Action* (Washington, D.C.: Development, 1975), p. 217.

to develop professionally if they are to be effective with the teachers they serve. Initially, the primary selection criterion was evidence that the candidate was a "master teacher." Experience, however, has shown that as the model and teachers have moved from the initial level of requests for a specific activity or content to PIER, the diagnostic-perscriptive-evaluative loop, the IA must have the ability to use the skills of clinical supervision. This may require an in-depth training program for the support staff. Though the skills of clinical supervision are necessary, this does not mean that the IAs assume a superordinate position.

Indeed, in reality, the people who grow the most in this staff-support program are the IAs themselves—from formal experiences, but even more so from the contact with the many teachers with whom they work, interact, and share. IAs returning to the classroom frequently have experienced a feeling of isolation, frustration, and confinement.

Other implications of the IA role include several political issues:

1. The IA has the opportunity to meet and interact with many staff members in a variety of positions and levels in the district. Such exposure can be viewed as a "plus"—as the IA is seen as a master teacher and "mover." Some individual teachers, however, aspiring to secure administrative positions, seek the IA position as a stepping-stone for personal exposure and gain rather than as an opportunity to improve education for the students of the district. The motives of a few might dilute—even damage—the program for the many.

2. Confusion seems to perpetuate itself when IAs are pulled in several directions by the various "actors." Each actor has his/her own set of priorities. The IA clearly owes allegiance both to the system and to the individual teacher, and neither can develop without the support of the other. But when the demand for services exceeds the ability to deliver, it becomes necessary to establish priorities. In the pinch, who receives the services—those teachers trying to implement the district's endorsed curricular approach or those trying to have their own unique (yet equally valid) approaches?

3. To what extent should IAs use their firsthand knowledge of difficulties in implementing mandated policies and programs to give feedback to the responsible agents so as to change these policies (rather than changing the teachers)?

EPILOGUE

Instructional Associates have a legitimacy with classroom teachers. They have been staff members in the same schools, taught the same students, shared the same problems and pressures. They were members of the same "team" and will be returning to the same environment. As peers, IAs tend to be seen as credible sources of information, sharing the same values and trust.

Throughout this article, the concept of the need for internal change agents has been developed. The Instructional Associate model can help either to sustain and reinforce an existing program or to serve as a catalyst in innovation. Only when this dichotomy is addressed will the model be most effective.

Herb Shepherd, in his delightful article "Rules of Thumb for Change Agents," offers the following advice to support and change agents:

Staying alive means staying in touch with your purpose. It means using your skills, your emotions, your labels and positions, rather than being used by them. It means not being trapped in other people's games. It means turning yourself on and off rather than being dependent on the situation. It means choosing with a view to the consequences as well as the impulse. It means going with the flow even while swimming against it. It means living in several worlds without being swallowed up in any. It means seeing dilemmas as opportunities for creativity. It means greeting absurdity with laughter while trying to unscramble it. It means capturing the moment in the light of the future. It means seeing the environment through the eyes of your purpose.[14]

---

14   Herbert Shepherd, *Rules of Thumb for Change Agents: The Staff Specialist as an Internal Consultant* (Washington, D.C.: Organization Renewal, Inc., 1973).

Teacher Centers: A Model for Teacher-Initiated Staff Development

PATRICIA ZIGARMI

University of Texas, Austin

Teacher centers are not only creative, stimulating places where a rich exchange of materials and ideas can occur; they also represent an approach to staff development that is based on a different conceptualization of the kinds of assistance teachers[1] need in learning more about themselves and their practice. The overall purpose of this article is to look at the nature of the instruction and support teacher centers provide teachers as one model of staff development.

This article will begin with a description of what a teacher center is. An effort will be made to distinguish between different types of teacher centers and to describe how these centers differ in their origins and development, purposes and goals, uses and resources. Short descriptions of the various activities teacher centers sponsor will be included to illustrate the roles a center can play in the staff development of teachers.

The second part of the article will focus on the assumptions about teaching and staff development implicit in teacher centers that set them apart from other kinds of staff development. The discussion will focus primarily on three issues: (1) the question of who and what are seen as resources; (2) the nature of assistance centers provide teachers; and (3) the issue of teacher responsibility and control.

The article concludes with a description of how teacher centers might be established to complement and fit with other kinds of university and district-based staff-development programs already available to teachers.

---

1 Although the word "teachers" is used to represent the clients of a teacher center, teacher centers, in many parts of the country, serve administrators, other educators, parents, and community people.

DIFFERENT TYPES OF TEACHER CENTERS

Yarger and Schmieder, in *The Commissioner's Report on the Education Professions 1975–76: Teacher Centers,*[2] identify seven organizational types of teacher centers and four functional types. The seven organizational types of centers include:

1. the independent teacher center
2. the "almost" independent teacher center
3. the professional-organization teacher center
4. the single-unit teacher center
5. the free-partnership teacher center
6. the free-consortium teacher center
7. the legislative/political-consortium teacher center

The four functional types of teacher centers include:

1. the facilitating-type teacher center
2. the advocacy-type teacher center
3. the responsive-type teacher center
4. the functionally unique-type teacher center

Without Yarger and Schmieder's paragraph descriptions, it is almost impossible to distinguish among types of centers by the labels they give them, although the labels do imply different origins and goals. What we can observe is that there is no single model of a teacher center in American education. As Schmieder points out, the term "might just as well refer to three teachers opening a store front in Harlem as to a state-controlled network designed to serve literally thousands of teachers and other educational personnel."[3]

Feiman identifies three types of teacher centers—behavioral, humanistic, and developmental—on the basis of ideological differences.[4] She believes that "what basically differentiates teacher centers is not so much the organizational forms they take but the assumptions on which those forms

2 Sam Yarger and Allen Schmieder, "Understanding Existing Teacher Centers," in *The Commissioner's Report on the Education Professions 1975–76: Teacher Centers* (Washington, D.C.: U.S. Department of Health, Education, and Welfare, 1977), pp. 41–56.

3 Ibid., p. 41.

4 Sharon Feiman, "Evaluating Teacher Centers," in *Essays on Teachers' Centers*, ed. Kathleen Devaney (San Francisco: Teachers' Centers Exchange, Far West Laboratory for Educational Research and Development, 1855 Folsom Street, San Francisco, Calif. 94103, 1977), pp. 85–100.

are built. In other words, associated with different kinds of centers are certain beliefs about what teachers are like, who should control their education and training, and how they can best be helped to improve their work. Ultimately these perspectives stem from different views of the teaching/learning process."[5]

The "behavioral" type of teacher center is designed to improve specific teaching behaviors. Performance of these behaviors is considered the most valid measure of teacher competence. Two assumptions are embedded in a behavioral type of teacher center, according to Feiman: (1) teaching can be improved through multi-institutional collaboration, and (2) educational problems can be solved by technology, and, more specifically, teaching will improve when school personnel learn about the latest products of educational research and development. In other words, behavioral type teacher centers are designed to promote collaboration and to disseminate research products.

The second type of teacher center Feiman identifies in her typology is the "humanistic" center. The humanistic center rests on several assumptions: "(1) innovation and reappraisal of work in the classroom will come mainly through the efforts and activities of practicing teachers; (2) there exists among teachers a vast reservoir of untapped expertise and experience; (3) centers can provide a neutral arena in which teachers can work relatively free of constraints and the hierarchical assumptions often present in other training institutions; (4) centers should be organized and controlled as far as possible by teachers themselves."[6] Humanistic centers focus on creating a learning environment where teachers feel psychologically supported, places where they can benefit from each other's expertise.

The third type of center, the "developmental" center, encourages teachers to develop new understandings of their classrooms by reflecting on their teaching and studying children's learning. Most developmentally oriented centers, Feiman writes, emphasize curriculum development and provide teachers with in-classroom advisors. "The advisor becomes a listener to the teacher, creating an opening wedge to break down the teacher's isolation by providing a supportive and non-judgmental atmosphere in which the teacher can struggle with problems. This opening is widened when the advisor promotes exchange and sharing between teachers and arranges visits to other classrooms . . . . It is

---

5   Ibid., p. 86.
6   Dowd Burrell, "The Teachers Centre: A Critical Analysis," *Educational Leadership* 33 (March 1976): 422-27.

furthered as the advisor works with the teacher toward understanding and acceptance of parents' perspectives and participation . . . ."[7]

While the humanistic center provides short-term practical advice and support through workshops and consultations at the center, the developmental center is more concerned with long-term involvement with teachers in their classrooms. However, unlike the program development consultant in a behavioral-type center, the developmental advisor does not try to disseminate or sell ready-made programs, packages, or methods. Rather, the advisor's goal is to help the teacher become more sensitive to what is happening in his/her classroom and identify ways in which his/her teaching can be improved.

Since the purpose of this article is to explore how teacher centers might be established to complement other approaches to staff development, the remainder focuses on humanistic- and developmental-type teacher centers. I recognize that all teacher centers — including the behavioral-type teacher centers — vary in some way from existing staff-development opportunities or they would not be created. However, it is important to look at teacher centers that are most unlike traditional staff development programs — centers that take a different view of learning and provide different sorts of learning opportunities and support to the teacher as learner.

WHAT IS A TEACHER CENTER?
A DESCRIPTION OF THE ACTIVITIES OF A
TEACHER CENTER

A teacher center is both a place and a concept. It is a place where teachers exchange ideas, talk over problems, acquire skills, and have access to resources they can use and adapt to their own classroom situations. A teacher center is a responsive, supportive, non-threatening environment that promotes sharing and a sense of community, models new possibilities, promotes the active exploration of materials, and emphasizes the study of children's learning as the basis for teachers' professional development. No one who has ever been in a teacher center could deny the fact that centers bring excitement and creativity to what is often a lonely and routinized task.

A teacher center is also a concept that demonstrates the value of teachers' taking more responsibility for their own staff development and fosters teachers' understanding more about how children learn. A center that is working well is concerned as much with what a teacher

7 Beth Alberty and Ruth Dropkin, *The Open Education Advisor* (New York: Center for Open Education, 1975), p. 25.

is thinking and doing in his/her classroom as it is with the teacher's activities in the center.

Various metaphors have been used for teacher centers. A parent at the Teacher Curriculum Work Center in Chicago called the center a "workshop with very skilled craftsmen in residence."[8] Thomas C. O'Brien, the director of the Teacher's Center Project at Southern Illinois University, describes centers as "cottage industries"[9] with everything that the term connotes about intimacy, family, size, and scale. Finally, Matt Miles offers his definition of a teacher center as "an informal information-sharing network that permits low-energy access to trusted competence."[10]

ACTIVITIES IN TEACHER CENTERS

Whether considered as a place or a concept, teacher centers sponsor activities that can be grouped into five categories:

1. providing teachers with access to resources;

2. helping teachers get together to work on common problems;

3. helping teachers learn more about how children learn;

4. helping teachers acquire skills in curriculum development and implementation;

5. involving other groups — administrators, university faculty members, parents, and community members — in the program of the center.

PROVIDING ACCESS TO RESOURCES

It is believed teachers will be more effective in meeting students' learning needs if resource materials of many kinds are made available and if teachers are encouraged to think about how resource materials that are available can be used most effectively. In a teacher center, teachers can discuss ways of using new materials with teachers who have already introduced them in their classrooms. At a center, they can also actively explore new materials, and, in some cases, try them out with students in a practice situation before taking them back to their classrooms. Through a center, resource materials like learning games, professional books,

8   Kathleen Devaney and Lorraine Thorn (Keeney), *Exploring Teachers' Centers* (San Francisco: Far West Laboratory for Educational Research and Development, 1975).

9   Thomas C. O'Brien, "Pig Iron, Education, and Teachers' Centers," in Devaney, ed., *Essay on Teachers' Centers*, pp. 37-47.

10   Matthew Miles, "The Teacher Centre: Educational Change through Teacher Development" and "Reflections and Commentary on the Syracuse Conference on The Teacher Centre," in *In-Service Education and Teacher Centres*, ed. Elizabeth Adams (Oxford: Pergamon Press, 1975).

children's books, art supplies, audiovisual equipment, tools, duplicators and copiers, and recycled materials are made available to teachers. More importantly, resource people — staff members and other teachers — who can help a teacher make and use materials, develop curriculum, or solve a particular problem are available.

HELPING TEACHERS WORK ON COMMON PROBLEMS

A number of activities in teacher centers provide opportunities for teachers to get together to work collaboratively on a common need or interest. These activities include workshops, child-study groups, and curriculum-development groups. These activities are planned around teachers' expressed interests and their perceptions of their own staff-development needs. They provide opportunities for dialogue. Because leaders for workshops and study groups in teacher centers are often teachers, these activities give teacher-participants a role model, along with a sense of security and confidence to work through the problems they have identified. In many ways, the skills or knowledge participants acquire in a workshop at a teacher center may be less important than the new attitudes they develop about their own resourcefulness and expertise through this joint problem-solving process.

HELPING TEACHERS LEARN MORE ABOUT
HOW CHILDREN LEARN

Several activities at teacher centers are designed to extend teachers' understandings of how children learn. These activities include teacher-center staff interviews with teachers, workshops on documenting children's learning, child-study groups, in-classroom advising, curriculum development projects, and staff efforts to help teachers do research. All these activities help teachers focus on students' learning styles and problems and support the teachers' attempts to develop learning options. Many of these activities can cause teachers to think about how students learn in relation to the learning environments they provide and to think about the extent to which learning environments motivate and stimulate inquiry and the active use of materials. Furthermore, study groups in teacher centers help teachers focus on individual differences in students. With increased understanding of children's growth and development and sharper diagnostic skills, teachers can become more effective in meeting the special educational needs of their students.

A frequent activity in developmental-type centers is regular team meetings, or "staffings," that are designed to bring teachers together to talk about specific problems and ways of dealing with them. In these meetings, "a whole group of teachers often analyzes one teacher's particular learning or behavior problem and plans collectively how to deal with it. The meetings provide opportunities for sharing among teachers and collective reinforcement for teachers trying out new ideas."[11] These meetings also encourage patterns of mutual problem solving and resource sharing that will sustain themselves independent of the teacher center.

The activities in teacher centers that help a teacher explore his/ her ways of working with children and help that individual systematically reflect on classroom problems may shake a teacher's self-confidence at first, Elliott points out. "But the more access a teacher has to other teachers' classroom problems, the greater his/her ability to tolerate losses in self-esteem. . . . The more a teacher is able to tolerate losses in self-esteem, the more open he/she will be to feedback. . . . The more a teacher is open to feedback, the greater his/her ability is to self-monitor his/her classroom practice. . . . The more able a teacher is at self-monitoring his/her classroom practice, the more likely he/she is to bring about fundamental changes in it."[12]

HELPING TEACHERS ACQUIRE SKILLS IN CURRICULUM DEVELOPMENT AND IMPLEMENTATION

Many activities in teacher centers are designed to help teachers invent or adapt curriculum materials for use in classrooms. There is a sense in many teacher centers that new curriculum packages are not what teachers need. What they need is supportive, critical help in evaluating new materials and using them in their classrooms. As one teacher in an existing teacher center wrote, "If I am, in fact, going to select appropriate pieces of curriculum to fit my students, my basic need is to have a variety of resource people around whose practical experience I can respect and the ability to use these people—not in a one-shot workshop, but over time, in as much depth as I am ready for. It takes more than two days or a weekend or three months of classes once a week to put together a curriculum. You have to use resources, reflect on what happens to kids, and then revamp what you are doing."[13]

11 Robert P. Mai, "Inservice in the Classroom: The Advisory Approach," in Devaney, ed., *Essays on Teachers' Centers*, pp. 123-30.

12 John Elliott, *Developing Hypotheses about Classrooms from Teachers' Practical Constructs* (Grand Forks, N.D.: The North Dakota Study Group on Evaluation, Center for Teaching and Learning, The University of North Dakota, 1970), pp. 45-47.

13 Devaney, *Essays on Teachers' Centers*, p. 20.

In addition to helping teachers select and evaluate curriculum materials, teacher centers often help teachers and administrators to identify new resources for curriculum development. Through curriculum development projects like the Kansas City Learning Exchange's Unseen City Project and through recycling activities in a number of teacher centers around the country, teachers come to see the community and community resources, such as recycled materials, as vehicles for curriculum development and implementation.

INVOLVING OTHER GROUPS IN THE PROGRAM OF THE TEACHER CENTER

Activities like workshops for parents and recreational group leaders, recycling projects, and community educational fairs provide opportunities for teachers, administrators, parents, and community people to get together to share concerns, ideas, and expectations related to the education of their children. Interaction like this is important in arriving at an agreement as to what the learning needs of students actually are and as to each group's role in the process. This interaction also serves to break down teachers' isolation from other professions in the community and from other parts of a student's world.

SUMMARY

The effect of teacher center activities like those described in this article can be important in stimulating teachers to think about how they can improve. The activities can result in increased self-esteem and confidence, increased resourcefulness, and increased willingness to seek and share advice. I recognize that in many cases this is the potential and not the reality of teacher centers; and that although they promise to take a new approach to staff development, the approach, in fact, may not be very different. Sharon Feiman's descriptive study of a teacher center in Chicago revealed that "at least during open hours, . . . [the center functioned] as a make-and-take operation. The most frequent type of activity involved teachers replicating materials on display and the most frequent type of talk focused on how something was made. Only a small percentage of the observed interactions concerned broad curricular issues or specific classroom problems. While many of the materials teachers make at the center imply new approaches to teaching and learning, there was little talk about their uses, extensions, or implications. Obviously, observations alone cannot reveal whether teachers are seeing relationships or drawing connections between experiences in the center and activities in their classrooms. It seems, however, that this kind of thinking is not directly encouraged during open hours."[14]

When workshops and the construction of materials in teacher centers are seen as ends and not as steps in a developmental process, then these activities may not be very different from traditional university or district-based staff-development programs. However, when second-order questions like "How will you use what you have learned in your classroom?" or "What do you know about the students you work with, so that you can best apply what you have learned in your interactions with them?" are asked, then teacher centers offer a new and different kind of assistance to teachers in their professional development. In the next section we will look at the assumptions implicit in teacher centers about teaching and staff development and the implications these assumptions have for the program of a teacher center.

ASSUMPTIONS AND IMPLICATIONS

ASSUMPTIONS UNDERLYING TEACHER CENTERS

Leaders of teacher centers make a number of different assumptions about teaching and staff development that set centers apart from other kinds of staff development. In the first place, there is the assumption that teachers, not organizational plans or curriculum packages, are the most important part of the instructional program and that the classroom is the focus and vehicle for aiding teachers to move in directions that are appropriate, both personally and professionally.

Second, that teachers, like students, have different needs at different times and that teachers, if given time and support, are in the best position to know those needs. Essentially, a teacher center is a support system for teachers, who will lean on the elements of the system that are of most benefit at a given time as needs arise. Similarly, we see by the variety of activities offered by most teacher centers that teachers may need different kinds of support and different resources at different stages of their development, which is something that traditional in-service programs generally do not offer.

Third, there is the assumption that growth is a slow process and that development, although continuous, is not even-paced. Leaders of teacher centers are aware that periods of high activity on the part of teachers alternate with periods of assimilation in which little apparent movement takes place. Because centers take this developmental stance toward staff

14 Sharon Feiman, "Patterns of Teacher Behavior in a Teacher Center," *Interchange* 6, no. 2 (1975).

development, they may have a better view of the amount of energy required for change and of how that energy can best be sustained over time.

The fourth assumption underlying teacher centers relates to the whole notion of how much time is required for change. Providing teachers with new knowledge and skills may not be sufficient for change to occur. Programs in teacher centers are structured with the recognition that it may take time for teachers to understand why they need certain skills or information—this understanding develops as problems arise in their classrooms. As Kathleen Devaney writes in an essay entitled "Mapping New Territory," teacher center leaders are confident that the homemade, helpful atmosphere of a teacher center can release the ingenuity and increase the self-confidence of teachers whose problem-solving talent has not been nourished in conventional teacher education programs.[15] In turn, they recognize that long-term growth takes time and so they structure activities in teacher centers that give teachers time to develop understanding of their needs and the needs of the students with whom they work.

These four assumptions, related to the importance of the teacher, the developmental nature of change, the need for different kinds of support, and the time change takes, have a number of implications for program development in a teacher center. The implications can be grouped in issues related to resources in teacher centers, the nature of assistance that centers provide teachers, and the question of teacher responsibility and control. These issues are discussed in the sections that follow.

IMPLICATIONS OF THE ASSUMPTIONS UNDERLYING TEACHER CENTERS

Who and What Are Seen as Resources in a Teacher Center The aim of a teacher center is to increase teachers' sense of their own resourcefulness. For the most part, teacher centers accept teachers' perceptions of their own needs as starting points for staff development. That is not to say that staff members in a teacher center might not try to get a teacher to think more about his/her needs or to shape a teacher's understandings of his/her needs, but in general they would not try to substitute a need they perceive for what the teacher experiences. Lillian Katz observed that the "task of a teacher is to help the learner improve, refine, develop, or, in some way modify his or her understanding of the concept, task, idea, or skill to be learned."[16] Similarly,

---

15 Kathleen Devaney, "Mapping New Territory," in *Essays on Teachers' Centers*, p. 162.
16 Lillian Katz, "Some Generic Principles of Teaching," in ibid., p. 30.

the most important task of a teacher center may be to help teachers uncover their own understandings of teaching/learning so that they can change their approach or attitude or skill. Teacher centers also accept teachers as resources and encourage the exchange of resources among teachers as a way of enhancing personal and professional growth. As was mentioned earlier, many leaders for workshops in teacher centers are teachers.

The Nature of Assistance Provided by Teacher Centers What sorts of assistance do teacher centers provide for teachers that help them to learn about themselves and their practice? And how is that assistance different from what teachers receive in other kinds of staff-development experiences?

O'Brien commented that "the issue is one of purpose. If the goal is to entertain one's clients or to provide an afternoon of change of pace or just plain fun, there is no question that isolated workshops fill the bill. If the goal, however, is to cause growth or to improve education, something else is needed. What is needed, at least, is time for the teacher to reflect and organize and try out and extend. . . . What is needed as well is the chance to try out one's own ideas on others, to entertain alternatives, to elaborate one's ideas and to build toward coherence, stability, and generalizability. What is needed, in short, is a continuing framework—a support system in which teachers can work."[17]

Teacher centers are rooted in a different conceptualization of how change occurs and what kinds of support are needed during the change process. In the way things are organized and in the kinds of services they provide, centers involve teachers as collaborators, provide teachers with support in a way that lowers their resistance to change, and encourage local leadership rather than reliance on outside consultants— all characteristics of successful change efforts that the Rand Corporation identified in its study *Federal Programs Supporting Educational Change.*[18] Leaders of teacher centers tend to recognize that change is more than just getting started and that support must be extended to the teacher throughout the change process. They also recognize that useful peer interaction, informal peer evaluation, and the mutual exchange of ideas and resources—all the activities that occur in a teacher center—may be more important than formal staff-development activities designed to help teachers acquire skills in curriculum or instruction. Lillian Weber,

17 O'Brien, "Pig Iron, Education, and Teachers' Centers," p. 41.
18 Paul Berman and Milbrey Wallin McLaughlin, *Federal Programs Supporting Educational Change, Vol. IV: The Findings in Review* (Santa Monica, Calif.: The Rand Corporation [R-1589-4 HEW], April 1975).

who directs the Workshop Center for Open Education in New York City, writes:

> That change in schools depends on the teacher to us is self-evident; for this reason, we have shaped our support structure so as to focus on the teacher as the agent of change. We concentrated on change in teacher education, on advisor support for teachers, on easing the constraints in institutional settings, on teacher efforts to change. We emphasized that the teacher as agent of change had to be a volunteer; only voluntary and reflective commitment would produce the energy necessary for the painful and difficult process of change . . . .
>
> For all these changes the teacher needed help, and the advisor's task was spelled out: help in observing and understanding children; workshops in curriculum; help in organizing the setting to support changes—all with the commitment to respect each teacher's unique way of changing. In addition . . . there existed the community of teachers . . . that would support, politically and psychologically, the change each teacher was making. The exchange of experience among the teachers in the community would broaden the base of any one teacher's perspective. The communal assessment and reassessment process would help maintain the direction of change.[19]

One of the ways in which teacher centers provide assistance to teachers who are changing is to model possibilities for change. Often the creative use of space in a teacher center or the ways in which materials are organized and stored give teachers ideas about how to manage these tasks in their classrooms. In the same way, by bringing teachers together to share and work on problems in team meetings or curriculum development groups, centers are used to intentionally model the use and value of the strategy of small-group problem solving for students. The provision of in-classroom advisors to teachers who are changing is recognition of the fact that routines are comfortable and predictable and not easily broken, and that for change to occur, ongoing support is required. In many ways, it appears that traditional in-service programs are not designed with these understandings in mind. More often than not, little support is provided to a teacher who is interested in applying what he/she has learned in a staff-development workshop after the initial experience is completed. It is as if the planners of the workshop are unaware of the resistance, discouragement, and conservatism the teacher

---

19 Lillian Weber, "Letter from the Director," *Notes from Workshop Center for Open Education* 3, no. 1 (Spring 1974): 1.

will encounter in trying to do something different both within himself/ herself and within the school. In many ways, especially by extending into classrooms, teacher centers provide an invaluable connection between what is learned in a workshop and the reality of the classroom. Finally, because much of the content of what is learned in activities in teacher centers relates to learning, teachers who participate in a teacher center may be better prepared to anticipate and cope with the reactions and resistance of students to new ideas and new ways of doing things. In these ways, teacher centers provide both concrete, immediate help and ongoing assistance to teachers who are interested in changing.

The Issue of Teacher Responsibility and Control   The third factor characterizing teacher centers that is not usually characteristic of other staff-development programs relates to the whole issue of teacher responsibility and control. In a teacher center, teachers have responsibility for identifying a need and seeking assistance, for initiating contact with the center, and for decision making in relation to the program of the center. Unlike many other staff-development programs, teachers—not curriculum coordinators, administrators, or university professors—take the lead in deciding what they want from a center and how its program is developed. Although immediate help and ongoing support are provided at a teacher center, staff members in teacher centers assume that the teacher is ultimately responsible for taking the next step in his/ her learning and development. In this spirit, use of teacher centers, in contrast with many staff-development programs, can minimize a teacher's dependence on and use of a predetermined curriculum or a single set of instructional materials and, rather, encourage critical judgment, independence, and professional responsibility.

Teacher centers also tend to rely on new incentives for encouraging teacher participation in the program of the center. It is assumed that teachers want to improve and are willing to participate in staff-development programs if they feel they are not alone, if they feel they can make a difference in their classrooms as a result of their participation, and if they feel their participation and efforts will be recognized. As Kathleen Devaney of the Teachers' Centers Exchange pointed out, teachers' intrinsic aspirations (motivations) for collegiality and professionalism are hidden resources that as yet have not been tapped in traditional in-service programs.[20] These motivations are at the heart of a functioning teacher center program.

---

20 Kathleen Devaney, "Warmth, Concreteness, Time, and Thought in Teachers' Learning," in *Essays on Teachers' Centers*, p. 23.

SUMMARY

Although it is not possible to generalize about teacher centers any more than it is possible to generalize about other kinds of staff-development programs, the assumptions made in a teacher center about teaching and staff development and the implications of these assumptions for the kind of program teacher centers provide, do, in fact, constitute a new approach to staff development. At this point in time, as the federal government provides new funding for teacher centers in the United States, it is important that we figure out how this new approach can complement, not displace, other kinds of staff development, which, in my opinion, are still needed. In order to prevent teacher centers from becoming another federal program that did not work primarily because it was not implemented, we may also need to limit our expectations about what teacher centers can do so that we set realistic and achievable goals that can be implemented. These ideas are explored more fully in the final section.

THE RELATIONSHIP OF TEACHER CENTERS TO OTHER KINDS OF STAFF-DEVELOPMENT PROGRAMS

In order to be responsive to and supportive of teachers' perceptions of their own needs and to allow responsibility to remain with the teacher, a teacher center can have no agenda of its own, which is in sharp contrast to many staff-development programs that incorporate district, building-level, or curriculum objectives as their own. With no agenda of their own (except perhaps a focus on children's learning), teacher centers can effectively respond to teachers' individualized staff-development needs that are not easily accommodated in university or district-based staff-development programs. In fact, a teacher center is likely to be better at working with these needs because it provides a variety of resources, assistance, and formats for staff development and recognizes that different kinds of help may be needed at different stages in a teacher's development.

For example, when a teacher initially contacts a teacher center, he/she may want help in needs assessment or more information about a new program. A teacher center can provide a teacher with needs-assessment instruments, information, or strategies for documenting children's learning, or an advisor who can observe the teacher in his/her classroom. To stimulate interest or provide the teacher with firsthand information about a particular instructional approach or program, a center can provide a short introductory workshop within a short amount of time of the request or arrange for the teacher to talk with or visit another experienced teacher's classroom. Samples of materials in the center can be copied or adapted to support use of the new program in the classroom. It is possible that, through a workshop in a teacher center, teachers can have the opportunity to practice a new skill or approach before implementing it in their classrooms. Furthermore, teacher center advisors can help teachers prepare to use new ideas or programs in their classrooms by offering advice on the use of space and time, the arrangement of the room, grouping patterns for students, etc. As teachers implement new ideas in their classrooms, workshops or discussion groups at the center can help them solve problems related to implementation. Staff members in the center, advisors in classrooms, and other teachers who are using the particular program can provide emotional support and logistical help as needs arise. As teachers attain a level of routine use and become more interested in assessing the impact of what they are doing on students, a teacher center can flexibly provide assistance in documenting childrens' learning through workshops, peer consultation, and in-classroom observation. The informal exchange among teachers that has supported an individual teacher's efforts to acquire information, build confidence, work out implementation problems, and assess the impact of the program on students, at this point in the change process, then becomes a natural stepping-stone to formal collaboration and teaming in the use of the new programs. Traditional in-service programs can rarely provide this range of help to the individual teacher at different stages of his/her development.

In essence, what a teacher center does well that traditional staff-development programs cannot do as well, because they are designed differently and have different goals, is to respond better to the needs of individual teachers. They provide teachers with individualized assistance, a variety of resource materials and learning options, and different kinds of assistance at various stages in the process of development.

What I am afraid might happen with the availability of federal funding and a new interest in teacher centers nationally is that teacher centers will be asked to take on too much responsibility for staff development; that, in fact, they will become the only staff-development program in some school districts. If that happens, a teacher center's ability to provide for individualized staff-development needs will be compromised. Teacher centers cannot be expected to do everything—to orchestrate district-wide curriculum implementation efforts; to provide training in response to external or district-wide mandates in basic skills or bilingual education and other areas, for example; to help building staffs plan and implement building-level staff-development programs; to provide developmental experiences for parents, administrators, and others concerned with childrens' development; *and* to respond individually to teachers. Centers can only be reasonably expected to do what they do well and that is to provide personalized assistance to teachers who request assistance on the basis of self-diagnosed needs.

I am not saying that teacher centers should not take on different responsibilities in different schools as needs arise (in fact, teacher center programs should vary from school district to school district depending on local needs and priorities), but centers cannot be expected to take on everything or they will fall into the trap the Rand Corporation so articulately identified of being discarded because they don't work before they've actually been implemented.[21] In that teacher centers offer school districts, teachers, and administrators a rich opportunity to rethink conventional formats for staff development, program substance, needs assessment, incentives, and the administration of the program, I hope that those of us in schools who are interested in teacher centers will rethink our expectations for centers and recognize the value of the resources and assistance they provide teachers. I hope that we will thoughtfully plan how to get them to fit with other in-service opportunities already available and that we will make room for an individualized approach to teacher staff development in our planning.

21 Berman and McLaughlin, *Federal Programs Supporting Educational Change, Vol. IV.*

Faculty Development in Higher Education

JOHN A. CENTRA

Educational Testing Service, Princeton, New Jersey

Most colleges and universities for many years have had some practices to aid in the professional development of their staffs. Sabbaticals and financial assistance to attend professional meetings would be the best examples. But it has been mainly in the 1970s that faculty development has expanded to include a variety of practices and special programs. The majority of programs and practices that have been devised attempt to help faculty members grow in teaching effectiveness by sharpening their teaching skills and knowledge. Other practices try to help faculty better understand themselves and their institutions, or try to foster better environments for teaching and learning.

Several reasons might be cited for the recent upsurge in faculty development. First, there has been a decrease in faculty mobility due to a declining rate of growth in postsecondary education. With less turnover and less new blood, colleges can no longer depend on new staff to help keep them vital; nor can teachers broaden perspectives simply by changing jobs. Teaching-improvement programs and faculty-renewal efforts of various kinds have become a partial remedy for this steady-state condition.

Another reason for the recent emphasis on faculty development and instructional improvement is the general disenchantment — expressed by students, parents, and legislators — with the quality of college instruction. Students seem less timid about expressing their dissatisfaction than they once were, and many parents are not at all sure that instruction is as effective as the high costs of a college education suggest it should be.

This article is based on a study supported by the Exxon Educational Foundation, titled Faculty Development Practices in U.S. Colleges and Universities, *Educational Testing Service, Princeton, N.J., 1976.*

Legislators have pressured public institutions to become more accountable and in some states have earmarked funds specifically for instructional improvement. At the national level, a 1972 report submitted to the president and Congress by the National Advisory Council on Education Professions Development singled out the need for more effective training of community college teachers.

It is unlikely that the recent expansion in faculty development would have been nearly as spectacular without the support provided by various funding agencies. In addition to money allocated by states to upgrade teaching, federal funding has emerged through such agencies as the Fund for the Improvement of Postsecondary Education (FIPSE) and the National Institute of Education (NIE). A number of private foundations also have focused on faculty development by funding programs at individual colleges or through consortia arrangements.

The lack of emphasis on faculty development in college prior to the 1970s is documented by several studies. A 1960 survey of 214 southern colleges by Miller and Wilson[1] identified a few widely used practices designed to orient new faculty to an institution or to help update faculty members, such as precollege workshops, financial assistance for attendance at professional meetings, and occasional department conferences on teaching. But the authors concluded that there was "a dearth of well-articulated, comprehensively designed *programs* for faculty development." A briefer survey, conducted in the late 1960s with a broader sample of institutions, reached a similar conclusion.[2] Still further evidence for this finding emerged from the results of a questionnaire study done as part of the AAUP Project to Improve College Teaching: Eble[3] reported that faculty members at some 150 schools stated almost unanimously that their institutions did not have *effective* faculty-development programs. Eble further noted that few institutions set aside specific percentages of their budgets for faculty development.

Nevertheless, a handful of universities did begin instructional improvement programs in the middle to late 1960s. Alexander and Yelon[4]

1 W.S. Miller and K.W. Wilson, *Faculty Development Procedures in Small Colleges* (Atlanta: Southern Regional Board, 1963).

2 W.A. Many, J.R. Ellis, and P. Abrams, *In-service Education in American Senior Colleges and Universities: A Status Report* (DeKalb, Ill.: College of Education, Northern Illinois University, 1969).

3 K. Eble, *Career Development of the Effective College Teacher* (Washington, D.C.: American Association of University Professors, November 1971).

4 A.T. Alexander and S.L. Yelon, *Instructional Development Agencies in Higher Education* (East Lansing, Mich.: Continuing Education Service, 1972).

collected information on about fourteen so-called instructional-development (or educational-development) programs. More recently, Crow et al.[5] compiled descriptions of eleven development centers in southern universities. Other discussions of development programs and issues have been published by Freedman,[6] the Group for Human Development in Higher Education,[7] and O'Banion.[8] O'Banion's work has focused on instructional-improvement and staff-development programs in selected community colleges.

Useful models of development programs have been provided by Bergquist and Phillips[9] and by Gaff.[10] The former describe three components of faculty development: instructional development, personal development, and organizational development. Under the first category they include such practices as curriculum development, teaching diagnosis, and training. Personal development generally involves activities to promote faculty growth, such as interpersonal-skills training and career counseling. Organizational development seeks to improve the institutional environment for teaching and decision making and includes activities for both faculty and administrators. Team building and managerial development would be part of organizational development.

Gaff's framework also includes instructional and organizational development, but he substitutes "faculty" development for "personal" development. Thus, he includes not only activities related to the affective development of faculty members but also those directed toward improved teaching behavior. Gaff views instructional development as focusing on course design and learning materials. His work and that of Bergquist and Phillips provide a departure point for the study described here.

To find out specifically what colleges are currently doing in faculty development, I recently undertook a national survey. The survey results shed light on current practices and how effective they appear to be, the types of faculty most involved in development activities, and how programs

5   M.L. Crow et al., *Faculty Development Centers in Southern Universities* (Atlanta: Southern Regional Education Board, 1976).

6   M. Freedman, *Facilitating Faculty Development* (San Francisco: Jossey-Bass, 1973).

7   Group for Human Development in Higher Education, *Faculty Development in a Time of Retrenchment* (*Change* publication, 1974).

8   T. O'Banion, "Staff Development: A New Priority for the Seventies," *The College Board Review*, no. 99 (Spring 1976).

9   W.H. Bergquist and S.R. Phillips, "Components of an Effective Faculty Development Program," *Journal of Higher Education* 46, no. 2 (1975): 197-211. (Also in W.H. Berquist and S.R. Phillips, *A Handbook for Faculty Development* [Washington, D.C.: The Council for the Advancement of Small Colleges, 1975]).

10   J.G. Gaff, *Toward Faculty Renewal* (San Francisco: Jossey-Bass, 1975).

are funded and organized. The study began late in 1975 with a letter sent to the presidents of every college and university in the United States asking whether their institutions, or any part of their institutions, "had an organized program or set of practices for faculty development and improving instruction." Of the approximately 2,600 accredited degree-granting institutions in the country (two-year colleges, four-year colleges, and universities), we heard from just under 1,800. About 60 percent (1,044) said that they had a program or set of practices and identified the person on campus who coordinated or was most knowledgeable about it. Another 3 to 4 percent said that they were planning such programs. Assuming that the nonrespondents would be less likely to have programs, we could estimate that perhaps half, or slightly over half, of the post-secondary institutions in the United States now provide some sort of program or set of staff-development activities. Of course, the estimate depends on how the institutions surveyed chose to interpret what constitutes an organized program or set of practices.

Each of the 1,044 college coordinators was sent a four-page questionnaire in the spring of 1976; and 756, or 72 percent of the group, responded. Generally, the respondent was a director of instructional development or faculty development, a dean or associate dean, or a faculty member spending part time as coordinator.

HOW VARIOUS DEVELOPMENT PRACTICES ARE SEEN

To learn about specific development activities, respondents were asked to estimate the proportion of faculty at their institutions that used each of forty-five practices and how effective they thought the practices were. The list included activities directly related to instructional improvement as well as those dealing with personal-development efforts such as improving self-awareness, interpersonal skills, and the like. The practices fell into five general categories: (1) a category of institution-wide practices such as sabbaticals and annual teaching awards; (2) analysis or assessment by students, by colleagues, by use of videotape, or by other means; (3) workshops, seminars, or similar presentations; (4) activities that involved media, technology, or course development; and (5) miscellaneous practices.

INSTITUTION-WIDE POLICIES OR PRACTICES

Thirteen institution-wide policies or practices are listed in Table 1 along with the percentage of each type of institution at which each practice existed and the percentage of respondents indicating the practice was effective. Annual awards to faculty for teaching excellence are a common practice at universities, but they were not viewed as especially effective in improving teaching: 79 percent of the universities used the awards, but only 27 percent rated them as either effective or very effective. The circulation of a development newsletter or other teaching-related material also appears to be fairly ineffective at each type of institution although this was common at about two-thirds of the sample. Both practices have considerable visibility and signal an institution's intent to reward or publicize teaching. According to most coordinators, however, they were not seen as being effective at their institutions.

Among the institution-wide practices seen as effective by close to two-thirds of the respondents were summer grants for projects to improve instruction, sabbatical leaves, and travel grants or funds. Interestingly enough, the latter two practices have been curtailed at many institutions in recent years because of restricted budgets. The remaining practices were viewed as effective or very effective by close to half of the schools that used them, though one practice—enabling first-year faculty to have a lighter than average teaching load—existed at only one in five of the institutions. For about half of the practices, respondents at universities gave lower effectiveness ratings than did respondents at two- or four-year colleges.

ANALYSIS OR ASSESSMENT PRACTICES

An analysis or assessment of teaching performance ideally provides the teacher and possibly a development specialist with diagnostic information. This information may result in some dissonance or dissatisfaction in the teacher and, theoretically, this helps open him or her to change.[11] The analysis or assessment may come from students, from colleagues, from experts, by use of videotape, or by other means. Estimates of the use and effectiveness of ten analysis and assessment practices were obtained in the survey.

Systematic ratings by students to help faculty improve instruction were widely used and perceived as moderately effective. At least a fifth of the faculty at over 80 percent of the 756 institutions used them. About half of the respondents estimated the ratings to be effective, although fewer university than two- or four-year college respondents saw them as effective.

Respondents rated formal or informal assessments by colleagues as less effective than either consulting with faculty who had expertise or working with master teachers. The analysis of in-class videotapes to improve

11 L. Festinger, *A Theory of Cognitive Dissonance* (Evanston, Ill.: Row, Peterson, 1957); and F. Heider, *The Psychology of Interpersonal Relationships* (New York: John Wiley, 1958).

TABLE 1

Use and Estimated Effectiveness of Institution-Wide Policies or Practices in Development (N = 756)

	Percentage of institutions at which the practice existed				Percentage indicating practice was effective or very effective[a]			
	All (N = 756)	2-yr. (326)	4-yr. (315)	Univ. (93)	All	2-yr.	4-yr.	Univ.
1. Annual awards to faculty for excellence in teaching	38	20	44	79	28	37	24	27
2. Circulation of newsletter, articles, etc. that are pertinent to teaching improvement or faculty development	68	71	65	67	27	32	22	25
3. A specific calendar period is set aside for professional development	44	62	33	14	52	52	55	38
4. There is a periodic review of the performance of all faculty members, whether tenured or not	78	87	71	77	59	63	56	49
5. Sabbatical leaves with at least half salary	67	60	72	82	66	60	73	61
6. A policy of unpaid leaves that covers educational or development purposes	72	70	73	80	51	47	55	49
7. Lighter than normal teaching load for first-year faculty	21	15	23	25	53	64	51	45
8. Temporary teaching load reductions to work on a new course, major course revision, or research area	61	58	59	81	64	68	63	59
9. Travel grants to refresh or update knowledge in a particular field	52	46	56	61	64	67	64	57
10. Travel funds available to attend professional conferences	93	95	92	95	62	69	59	51
11. Visiting scholars program that brings people to the campus for short or long periods	55	37	65	86	57	60	57	54
12. Summer grants for projects to improve instruction or courses	58	61	56	62	70	72	66	74
13. There is a campus committee on faculty development	61	63	60	62	50	55	48	46

[a]Percentages based only on institutions at which practice existed.

instruction was thought to be one of the more effective practices, though it was used frequently by only a very small proportion of the faculty on campuses where it was available (about 60 percent of the institutions). Another practice rated effective but little used was the professional- and personal-development plan for individual faculty members: Just under 40 percent of the institutions used this practice with at least 5 percent of their faculty, and almost two-thirds of the respondents from these colleges rated it effective. These individual-development plans, known also as growth contracts, usually call for a self-development program drawn up by a faculty member in conjunction with a development specialist or administrator. They were most common among the two-year colleges in the sample, though a number of four-year colleges also use this approach.

Generally speaking, the analysis or assessment practices were rated as more effective by respondents from the two-year colleges than by respondents from either four-year colleges or universities. For example, 55 percent of the two-year college respondents rated formal assessments by colleagues as effective, compared with 42 percent of the respondents from four-year colleges and 33 percent of those from the universities.

WORKSHOPS, SEMINARS, AND SIMILAR PRESENTATIONS

From a list of ten topics that might be the focus of workshops, seminars, or similar presentations, respondents indicated that those dealing with specific techniques of instruction and with new knowledge in a field were among the best attended and most effective. Workshops to help faculty improve their research and scholarship skills were generally least used, except at universities.

Workshops to acquaint faculty with institutional goals and characteristics of enrolled students were much more common at two- or four-year colleges than at universities, where, ironically, there is typically a broader range of goals. In fact, on the whole, workshops and similar presentations were less often rated as effective by university respondents than by other respondents. The size of most universities, along with an emphasis on research as well as on teaching, probably contributes to this difference.

Perhaps the critical point regarding workshops and seminar programs, as pointed out by some development people, is that they be planned in response to the needs of faculty members, with participants knowing pretty much what to expect.[12] With that in mind, most of the ten topics listed (and several others added by the respondents) might serve the needs

12   J.R. Wergin, E.J. Mason, and P.J. Munson, "The Practice of Faculty Development," *The Journal of Higher Education* 47, no. 3 (1976): 289–308.

of a significant portion of faculty. One rule of thumb might be that a workshop deal not with generalities, but with topics that have the potential of providing concrete help to faculty members. For example, workshops that explore general issues or trends in education were estimated by respondents to be less effective than those dealing with more specific topics.

MEDIA, TECHNOLOGY, AND COURSE-DEVELOPMENT PRACTICES

Most of the seven practices in this category listed in the questionnaire involved specialists providing teaching assistance to faculty members. One of the more widely used is assistance in employing audiovisual aids. Media or audiovisual specialists are not as new as most of the other instructional specialists and this may, in part, account for their greater use. A newer service, the instructional- or course-development specialist, existed at about a third of the institutions and was viewed as effective by 63 percent of these. Special professional libraries devoted to teaching improvement are very common but are used on most campuses by only a small proportion of the teachers. This may be why they are not perceived to be as effective as many other practices.

Though the responses suggest greater use of media, technology, and course-development specialists among two-year colleges and universities, analyses by institutional size indicated that larger institutions, including four-year colleges, were most likely to have these services for faculty.

MISCELLANEOUS PRACTICES

Five practices did not fit neatly into any of the previous categories. One of the practices was used extensively and rated high in effectiveness: grants to faculty members for developing new or different approaches to courses or teaching. These grants varied from small amounts of money for minor alterations in a course to released time for faculty members, with financial support. About 90 percent of the universities and slightly fewer of the two- and four-year colleges had faculty grant programs.

Three of the miscellaneous practices are low- or no-cost items and were judged by the respondents to be reasonably effective. One such practice involves faculty visitations to other institutions or to other parts of their own institutions to review innovative projects, a practice that two-year colleges in particular use extensively. Much less common are faculty exchange programs with other institutions, used by about a third of all institutions (slightly more by the universities). One advantage of interinstitutional or consortium arrangements among colleges involved in faculty development is that they make such practices as faculty exchanges easier to accomplish.

And exchange programs are probably one of the less expensive ways of helping to renew faculty in their middle and later years.

The third inexpensive practice is that of encouraging faculty to take courses offered by colleagues. Three-fourths of the institutions had some faculty who did so. While most faculty probably monitor courses in their own or related disciplines, there are potential benefits from faculty members' learning more about unrelated fields as well—for example, a physical scientist taking a course in the humanities.

TYPES OF FACULTY-DEVELOPMENT PROGRAMS

A major purpose of this study was to determine what patterns of development practices predominate among colleges and universities. That is, given the forty-five practices listed in the questionnaire, is it possible to identify reasonable categories of activities based on the extent of faculty use among the institutions? To explore this question, responses from each institution to the forty-five practices were factor analyzed, enabling a grouping of the practices according to the extent to which they were used at the 756 institutions. The resulting factors or groups of practices were then related to the additional information collected about the institutions and their programs. This included the proportions of the various groups of faculty involved in development practices on each campus, how activities were funded and organized, and institutional characteristics, such as size, type, and source of control.

Four factors or groups of development practices seemed to define patterns of estimated use of the practices among the institutions. These were high faculty involvement, instructional-assistance practices, traditional practices, and emphasis on assessment. The four factors and the practices that have significant loadings on each factor are listed in Table 2. A brief discussion of the four factors follows.

1. *High faculty involvement.* The development practices in this first group tend to involve a high proportion of the faculty at the colleges that use them. Many of the practices are run not only for the faculty but *by* the faculty as well: Experienced teachers work with inexperienced teachers, and those with special skills offer assistance to others. Good teachers, older teachers, and those needing improvement all tend to be involved.

Several of the practices in this group were more likely to be used by the smaller colleges in the sample and seem appropriate for small-college settings. Workshops on institutional purposes or on academic advisement are examples. In the wake of declining enrollments and

214

TABLE 2

Factor Analysis of the Approximate Use of the Faculty-Development Practices

Group 1 (Factor 1): High Faculty Involvement	Factor Loading
Workshops, seminars, or program to acquaint faculty with goals of the institution and types of students enrolled.	.65
"Master teachers" or senior faculty work closely with new or apprentice teachers.	.61
Faculty with expertise consult with other faculty on teaching or course improvement.	.60
Workshops or program to help faculty improve their academic advising and counseling skills.	.57
Personal counseling provided individual faculty members on career goals, and other personal development areas.	.53
Workshops or presentations that explore general issues or trends in education.	.51
Informal assessments by colleagues for teaching or course improvement.	.48
System for faculty to assess their own strengths and areas needing improvement.	.46

Group 2 (Factor 2): Instructional-Assistance Practices	
Specialists to assist individual faculty in instructional or course development by consulting on course objectives and course design.	.75
Specialists to help faculty develop teaching skills such as lecturing or leading discussions, or to encourage use of different teaching-learning strategies such as individualized instruction.	.70
Specialists to assist faculty in constructing tests or evaluating student performance.	.69
Assistance to faculty in use of instructional technology as a teaching aid (e.g., programmed learning or computer-assisted instruction).	.65
Specialists on campus to assist faculty in use of audiovisual aids in instruction, including closed-circuit television.	.56
Workshops or presentations that explore various methods or techniques of instruction.	.42

Group 3 (Factor 3): Traditional Practices	
Visiting-scholars program that brings people to the campus for short or long periods.	.58
Annual awards for excellence in teaching.	.52
Sabbatical leaves with at least half salary.	.43
Workshops or seminars to help faculty improve their research and scholarship skills.	.43
Summer grants for projects to improve instruction or courses.	.43
Temporary teaching load reductions to work on a new course, major course revision, or research area.	.39
Use of grants by faculty members for developing new or different approaches to courses or teaching.	.37
Travel grants to refresh or update knowledge in a particular field.	.33

Group 4 (Factor 4): Emphasis on Assessment	
There is a periodic review of the performance of all faculty members, whether tenured or not.	.55
Travel funds available to attend professional conferences.	.47
Systematic ratings of instruction by students used to help faculty improve.	.41
Formal assessments by colleagues for teaching or course improvement (i.e., visitations or use of assessment form).	.40
A policy of unpaid leaves that covers educational or development purposes.	.40
Systematic teaching or course evaluations by an administrator for improvement purposes.	.40

higher costs, many smaller colleges have begun to examine their goals more closely. These colleges also see good academic guidance and attention to individual students as special strengths. Small institutions would also be less likely to afford full-time specialists in teaching or instructional development—thus the reliance on "master teachers" or faculty with expertise. Because of the emphasis on close personal relationships in most small colleges, these colleges could be expected to provide counseling and other personal-development practices for faculty. Smallness, finally, also apparently encourages more informal assessments by colleagues, or more self-assessment, rather than formal systems of teaching evaluation.

2. *Instructional-assistance practices.* Instructional development is an important aspect of this second group of practices, as evidenced by the high factor loading for "specialists to assist individual faculty in instructional or course development." The second practice, specialist assistance to the faculty in improving teaching skills or strategies, is part of both instructional-development programs and broader teaching improvement or faculty-development programs. Three of the additional practices also deal with providing assistance in the instructional process: (1) in teaching and evaluating student performance, (2) in applications of instructional technology to teaching, and (3) in the use of audiovisual aids. Workshops or presentations exploring methods of instruction, the last practice with a significant loading, would logically fit in with the other practices in this group.

These instructional-assistance practices were found in many of the two-year colleges and in some of the universities in the sample. Few of the four-year colleges included them. Public rather than private institutions were also somewhat more likely to have these practices. Not surprisingly, most of the institutions had development units or offices on campus. Finally, in comparison with other practices, the practices that comprise this group were more likely to be evaluated in some way.

3. *Traditional practices.* As Table 2 indicates, the practices in this group included visiting-scholars programs, annual awards in teaching, sabbatical leaves, grants for instructional improvement or travel, and temporary teaching-load reductions. The only workshop or seminar included was one designed to help faculty improve their research and scholarship skills. Thus, with the exception of the use of small faculty grants to improve instruction, these practices have been used by many institutions for a number of years and are, therefore, fairly traditional.

By themselves, the activities involve a relatively small number of faculty at any one time. The practices in this group, as the further analysis indicated, were most likely to be used at universities and larger four-year colleges.

4. *Emphasis on assessment.* Four of the six practices with significant loadings in this group emphasize various assessment techniques as means of improving instruction. Formal ratings by students, by colleagues, and by administrators are among those listed in Table 2. A periodic review of all faculty members is also a common practice. It is interesting to note that the less-formal assessment or analysis practices, such as the use of in-class videotapes or informal assessments by colleagues, are not part of the group.

Travel funds to attend professional conferences and unpaid leaves for educational or development purposes also had significant loadings on this factor.

Among the types of institutions, two-year colleges (particularly public two-year colleges) tended to emphasize the practices in this group.

These four descriptions provide a somewhat different view of development programs than do the heuristic models discussed by Bergquist and Phillips[13] and by Gaff,[14] though the "instructional-assistance" category does overlap with their shared concept of instructional development.

Judging by the further information provided by the institutions in the sample, programs in faculty development varied in other ways as well as those described above. Some colleges had a few uncoordinated practices with minimal budgets. Limited faculty-development programs, if they can be referred to as programs, were most likely to be found in the sample among the small colleges with under one thousand students enrolled. It should be added, however, that several larger institutions — including some of the most prestigious — reported (in response to the initial letter) that they did not have programs in faculty development.

Some development programs appeared to operate on the fringes of the schools they served: Coordinators reported generally minimal faculty participation and, in some instances, that a significant part of their support came from foundations or the government.

Over 40 percent of the institutions (two-thirds of the universities) had some kind of development unit. Some had decentralized offices. A few units included several specialists in such areas as instructional development, evaluation, technology, and media. The majority, however, had

13 Bergquist and Phillips, "Components of an Effective Faculty Development Program."
14 Gaff, *Toward Faculty Renewal.*

more modest staffs—often only a director or coordinator. Found frequently at medium-sized two- and four-year colleges, most of these units had existed only two or three years and had not yet been evaluated adequately. In fact, less than a fifth of all institutions had completely evaluated their programs or activities.

Certainly an evaluation of an institution's program would include a close look at the characteristics of faculty members who participate. Ideally, one would hope that faculty who really need to improve would be among those most involved in development activities. Yet, so far, this does not generally appear to be the case. The survey questionnaire included six general descriptions of faculty members and asked the respondents to estimate the extent to which each group was involved. Among the six types of faculty, the most actively involved in development activities were "good teachers who want to get better"; at about 70 percent of the institutions, half or more of this faculty group were involved. The least actively involved were "faculty who really need to improve," followed by older faculty—those with over fifteen or twenty years of teaching experience—and younger faculty in their first years of teaching. Nontenured and tenured staff participated about equally.

Given the fact that participation in most development activities is usually voluntary, perhaps it is not especially surprising that good teachers who want to get better comprise the major clientele. After all, they are frequently the most interested in teaching. They may also be the best group to involve in development activities in the initial stages of a program so that it does not get a reputation as being largely a clinic for deficient teachers.

But eventually it would seem that faculty who need to improve should become active in development practices if the programs are to be deemed effective. Yet how does one draw faculty needing improvement into development activities? One possibility is that every faculty member should be expected to spend roughly 10 percent of his or her time in improvement activities.[15] The four-to-six hours per week might be spent on any number of activities, depending on the faculty member's needs, and, for some, it might largely involve helping other teachers rather than being recipients of help. Another possibility for involving more faculty in development activities—particularly those most in need of improvement— is to tie participation into the reward structure. Currently, it seldom is.

15 Group for Human Development in Higher Education, *Faculty Development in a Time of Retrenchment.*

CONCLUSION

A variety of practices and programs currently exist under the banner of faculty development, many of which have emerged in the last few years. How effective they are is not yet entirely known. The views of people who direct or are knowledgeable about development activities at 756 colleges and universities were the basis of this report. Their perceptions of the practices and programs on their campuses, while probably not free of bias, help illuminate this burgeoning area.

CONTRIBUTORS

JEFFERY AMORY was director of the individualized staff development program described in chapter 10 for the first two years the program was in operation. Since then he has worked as a free lance consultant with Nova University and several social service agencies in southern Florida.

JOHN A. CENTRA is a Senior Research Psychologist at Educational Testing Service in Princeton, New Jersey. He has been conducting studies of college teaching for many years and recently edited the book *Renewing and Evaluating Teaching* (Jossey-Bass, 1977).

MYRNA COOPER, Director of Special Projects for the United Federation of Teachers, is currently responsible for the extensive in-service program sponsored by the local. She represents the union on various city, state, and federal bodies interested in teachers and teaching. Mrs. Cooper is a classroom teacher and a specialist in teacher training.

MAXINE GREENE is the William F. Russell Professor in the Foundations of Education at Teachers College, Columbia University. Professor Greene comes to the problem of staff development from the vantage points of educational philosophy and the humanities. Her latest book is *Landscapes of Learning* (Teachers College Press, 1978).

GARY A. GRIFFIN is Associate Professor of Education at Teachers College, Columbia University. His principal professional interests are curriculum planning, school change, and professional development of educators. The article in this issue of the *Record* was written during his sabbatical year when he was Visiting Scholar at the Far West Laboratory for Educational Research and Development.

GENE E. HALL is Director of the Procedures for Adopting Educational Innovations Project at the Research and Development Center for Teacher Education, The University of Texas at Austin. His research and development activities focus on change in schools and colleges, teacher education program development, and evaluation of innovative practices.

ANN LIEBERMAN is Associate Professor in the Department of Curriculum and Teaching and Associate Director of the Horace Mann–Lincoln Institute at Teachers College, Columbia University. She is on leave during 1978–79 to be Project Coordinator of a statewide dissemination effort of the Beginning Teacher Evaluation Study in California, a study that has important implications for both the pre- and in-service education of teachers.

MAURICE LEITER is an executive board member of the United Federation of Teachers. As a District Representative for that organization, he deals, on a daily basis, with teacher concerns related to educational policy practice. Mr. Leiter has taught English for nearly two decades.

SUSAN F. LOUCKS is Assistant Director of the Procedures for Adopting Educational Innovations Project at the Research and Development Center for Teacher Education, The University of Texas at Austin. Her professional interests include implementation of innovations, program evaluation, and staff development.

MILBREY WALLIN McLAUGHLIN is a member of the staff of The Rand Corporation and project leader of various studies conducted under the auspices of the National Institute of Education, the Office of the Assistant Secretary for Education (HEW), and the Office of Planning and Evaluation (USOE). Her interests in research and research management are centered on educational innovation and development, organizational change in the public sector, and evaluation of planned change efforts.

DAVID D. MARSH is Assistant Professor in the Department of Teacher Education at the University of Southern California. He is currently directing a study of the school-site planning process of in-service teacher education at four places across the nation and teaching graduate courses including a course on innovative approaches to preservice teacher education and a leadership course in in-service education.

LYNNE MILLER is most recently of the University of Massachusetts where she was Assistant Professor of Education and Director of the National Alternative Schools Program as well as affiliated with a regional Teacher Corps Project as a field-based instructor. She is currently involved in research and writing about staff development and school improvement efforts and serves as an advisor to several staff development projects nationally.

PAULINE S. RAUH is Coordinator of Staff Development, Stamford Public Schools, Stamford, Connecticut, and has served as classroom teacher, media specialist, and curriculum developer.

JUDITH SCHIFFER is Assistant Professor in the Department of Early Childhood Education at William Paterson College, and has served as adjunct Assistant Professor in the Department of Curriculum and Teaching at Teachers College and on the faculty in the

Department of Education at Stony Brook University. She is author of *School Renewal through Staff Development,* which will be published by Teachers College Press in 1979.

RICHARD C. WILLIAMS is Associate Professor and Chairman of the Administrative and Policy Studies in Education Specialization in the UCLA Graduate School of Education. He is the coauthor of *Effecting Organizational Renewal in the Schools.*

THOMAS E. WOLF has just finished services as the director of the ninth and eleventh cycle University of Massachusetts/Worcester Teacher Corps Project. His interest in inservice and school change grows out of his experience as a high school and alternative high school teacher, a teacher trainer, and an evaluator of and consultant to school change efforts in a number of different settings.

DREA ZIGARMI is an Assistant Professor, Assistant Department Chairman of Teacher Education, and Director of the McGuffey Laboratory School at Miami University, Oxford, Ohio. He was formerly Director of Title IV-C for the State Department of Education in South Dakota.

PATRICIA ZIGARMI is a researcher with the Concerns Based Adoption Model Project at the Research and Development Center for Teacher Education at the University of Texas of Austin. She also works as a free-lance consultant in staff development. She was formerly Director of Staff Development for the State Department of Education in South Dakota.

Index